The Sounds of People and Places

The Sounds of People and Places

A *Geography of American Folk and Popular Music*

THIRD EDITION

Edited by
George O. Carney

Rowman & Littlefield Publishers, Inc.

ROWMAN & LITTLEFIELD PUBLISHERS, INC.

Published in the United States of America
by Rowman & Littlefield Publishers, Inc.
4720 Boston Way, Lanham, Maryland 20706

3 Henrietta Street
London WC2E 8LU, England

British Cataloging in Publication Information Available

Library of Congress Cataloging-in-Publication Data

The Sounds of people and places : a geography of American folk and
popular music / edited by George O. Carney. — 3rd ed.
    p.   cm.
Includes bibliographical references and index.
1. Music—United States—History and criticism.   I. Carney,
George O.
ML3551.S603   1993   781.64′0973—dc20   93-9930   CIP   MN

ISBN 0-8476-7787-7 (cloth: alk. paper)
ISBN 0-8476-7788-5 (paper: alk. paper)

Printed in the United States of America

 ᵀᴹ The paper used in this publication meets the minimum requirements of
American National Standard for Information Sciences—Permanence of Paper
for Printed Library Materials, ANSI Z39.48—1984.

To Mom and Dad Carney—
Who Made It All Possible.

Contents

List of Figures and Graphs

Figures

Graphs

List of Tables

Preface

This anthology had its genesis while I was a child growing up in the Ozarks of Missouri. In our family farmhouse, I sat by the old Philco radio and listened to the "Hillbilly Hit Parade" on KCMO (Kansas City) and the "Ozark Jubilee" from KWTO (Springfield). My parents paid for a series of piano lessons from a local teacher and I learned to play enough hymns to become our one-room country church's "official" pianist. From these two early experiences I developed a lifelong admiration for country and religious music.

As a teenager in the 1950s, I began listening to rock and roll on WHB (Kansas City) when it initiated one of the first Top 40 formats in the nation. I will always remember watching Elvis Presley's first appearance on the Ed Sullivan show and attending an Ike and Tina Turner and the Ikettes concert. Thus, rock and roll and rhythm and blues were added to my listening habits.

During my freshman year in college, my adviser enrolled me in a music appreciation course where I studied and listened to Haydn, Mozart, Rimsky-Korsakov, and Beethoven. It was an "eye-and-ear opening" experience, and to my amazement, I did learn to "appreciate" classical music—a radical outcome for an Ozarks farm boy who had "cut his teeth" on hillbilly music. While in graduate school, I roomed with a musician (tenor saxophonist in a local stage band) who had a penchant for Big Band jazz. We listened and studied to the music of Les and Larry Elgart, Stan Kenton, and Woody Herman. During my first teaching stint at a junior college, my roommate taught me the finer points of jazz, especially the more recent sounds of bebop and "cool" jazz. Every evening we would prepare lectures to the sounds of Dizzy Gillespie, Dave Brubeck, and Miles Davis. Thus, one can see my involvement in music came by progressive stages to embrace a wide spectrum of America's varied musics. Paralleling this evolutionary process was a growing conviction that no aspect of our music should or could be excluded in order to understand and appreciate the whole panorama of American music.

By the time I completed my Ph.D. in American social and cultural history, I had developed an awareness that place-to-place variations existed in American music styles and tastes and that music played a vital role in helping to shape the character of places. This idea was supported by reading several works in ethnomusicology, most notably Bruno Nettl's 1964 book in which he stated that music must be studied in its "spatial" context. He added that

> studying the geographical distribution of musical phenomena and the ways in which music changes, and participates in culture change, is important to an understanding of the role of music in culture change. (p. 225)

Having become an instructor in the Department of Geography at Oklahoma State University, my notion of a geography of music manifested itself modestly with the inclusion of a few lectures in my introductory cultural geography course in the late 1960s. With the encouragement of John Rooney, my department head, an entire course had evolved by 1973—the first such course in an American geography department. It came at a fortuitous time because a few other geographers had broken the publishing barrier with articles on music geography (Nash, 1968; Ford, 1973).

Looking back over my academic career, it is interesting to note some of the landmarks along the path of my twenty-year association with geography and music. For numerous reasons (none of them good) cultural geographers had largely eliminated music from their research agendas. Any misgivings that I may have had were quickly eliminated by the strong encouragement I received from a host of professional colleagues, some of whom I never met, while others I communicated with on a regular basis. There were times when my research was criticized for being "frivolous" and "nonscientific"; however, I always turned to the words of Carl Sauer, that eminent cultural geographer, who declared in "The Education of a Geographer" (1956)

> that we (geographers) have not really prescribed limitations of inquiry, method, or thought upon our associates . . . from time to time there are attempts to the contrary, but we shake them off after a while and go about doing what we most want to do.

Although I was never acquainted with Sauer, his writing provided inspiration to forge ahead with the task at hand.

There were other prominent geographers who unknowingly through their printed words influenced my decision to pursue music geography as a teaching/research avenue. Peter Nash, the "father of music geography," had published in 1968 the ground-breaking article on the topic. I realized that if someone of Nash's stature saw potential in a geography of music, I should not despair. For the past twenty years Peter and I have corresponded regularly, and in 1992 he created the second geography of music course at the University of Waterloo. Then there was Wilbur Zelinsky, the venerable "Dean" of American cultural geographers, who wrote in his 1973 *Cultural Geography of the United States* that many untapped research topics existed for cultural geographers, including folk music. Thereafter, Wilbur became a "sounding board" in testing my ideas concerning music geography, especially at the North American Culture Society meetings in the 1970s and 1980s.

The incentive derived from Nash's article and Zelinsky's book energized my research. I collected data on the origin and diffusion of bluegrass music festivals, prepared maps, wrote a paper, and delivered it at the Oklahoma Academy of Science conference in 1973. My peers accepted the idea and positive reactions to it resulted in an expanded version being placed in the publication "pipeline." Harm de Blij, then editor of *The Journal of Geography*, was so excited about and receptive to the manuscript that he published it without editorial review. Once again, a well-known geographer had helped pave the way for music geography as well as putting into print my first manuscript—a milestone for a lowly assistant professor. It must have pleased other colleagues as well because I was presented with *The Journal of Geography* award that year (1974) for "Best Content Article," an achievement that provided further motivation to pursue music research.

Armed with several positive signs from the profession and that a small nucleus within the discipline was also interested in music (Nash, Larry Ford, Charles Gritzner, and James Curtis), I continued to seek new sources for music data. The Country Music Association had just conducted a survey of country music radio stations. These data resulted in a manuscript on diffusion processes related to country music radio. Larry Brown, the noted diffusion theorist, published it in his Diffusion of Innovation Series at Ohio State. This monograph was recognized by my dean and provost for its "scientific" value and resulted in my promotion to associate professor. Once more, a distinguished geographer had acknowledged the value of geography and music and, at the same time, had given me a boost up the academic hierarchy.

In 1978 Joseph E. Spencer, a noted UCLA cultural geographer, authored an article entitled "The Growth of Cultural Geography" that appeared in the *American Behavioral Scientist*. He stated that

> the nature and distribution of systems of language, religion, art, *music*, architecture . . . have long been recognized as among the important differentials distinguishing human culture systems and their respective landscapes.

Support for a geography of music had again been called for by a widely acclaimed cultural geographer. Spencer's statement provided additional stimulus for a project I had contemplated for some time—an anthology on music geography. By this time, a number of journal articles and theses had been completed by geographers. My proposal to University Press of America was accepted and the first edition of *The Sounds of People and Places* became a reality in 1978.

As we approach the "silver" anniversary of music geography (1968–1993) and the third edition of *The Sounds of People and Places*, I am deeply indebted to the likes of Rooney, Sauer, Nash, Zelinsky, de Blij, and Spencer (a cultural geographer's Hall of Fame) for their printed words of support and professional advice to "keep the faith." Music geography during the past twenty-five years has become a legitimate and respected subfield of cultural geography. Geographers have produced considerable research on the topic with more than 100 journal articles, theses/dissertations, monographs, and books. Morever, special sessions on the geography of music have been organized for the National Council for Geographic Education (NCGE) and Association of American Geographers (AAG) meetings, culminating in a 1993 special session at the Atlanta convention organized by David Lee and Peter Nash. Furthermore, music geography has been recognized as a growing subfield by its inclusion in the leading textbooks in cultural/human geography as well as regional texts on North America, and a myriad of academic books and journal articles have cited research on the topic.

I am proud to report that by 1993 a network of more than fifty colleagues interested in music geography has been established. The list includes geography professors and applied geographers, folklorists, ethnomusicologists, and music historians located in Canada, Great Britain, Japan, Italy, Australia, New Zealand, and the United States. Additionally, music maps crafted by geographers have been printed and analyzed in various media outlets ranging from PBS and the *Washington Post* to the Oklahoma *Bluegrass Times* and the Stillwater (Okla.) *News-Press*.

Call it "geography of music," "music geography," "geomusicology," "soundscapes," or whatever nomenclature one would like to apply to the ongoing research of the past twenty-five years, it gives me tremendous pride to serve as editor for the third edition of *The Sounds of People and Places*.

Acknowledgments

To many people an edited book may seem a relatively simple undertaking. To one who has experienced three editions of this volume, it is a time-consuming and demanding task; yet, at the same time, an extremely challenging and rewarding experience. It is acknowledged, however, that without the interest and cooperation of many individuals, *The Sounds of People and Places* would not have been possible. My debts to these people are many.

I wish to express my gratitude, first of all, to those authors who contributed articles to this volume. To the new participants (Butler, Lehr, Arkell, Sexton, and Kuhlken) a sincere note of appreciation for their efforts. Dick Butler and John Lehr, our Canadian authors, graciously proofed their manuscripts and furnished map originals. Tom Arkell made a number of international calls from his office in Italy and faxed materials concerning his essay. Rocky Sexton and Bob Kuhlken quickly responded to editorial inquiries and cooperated throughout the editorial process. To the "old" authors (Gritzner, Ford, Henderson, Horsley, Curtis, Rose, Lornell, and Glasgow), I am indebted to each for their long-standing support, encouragement, and thoughtfulness. Many of us have toiled in geography of music research for more than twenty years without much recognition for the fruits of our labor. And much credit for this book goes to John F. Rooney, Jr., who opened avenues for me as a teacher and researcher.

Second, acknowledgment is in order to Jon Sisk, editor in chief of Rowman and Littlefield, who gave me the opportunity to put in print the best anthology on this topic for which I hold such great admiration. Moreover, Jon's staff has lent constructive support throughout completion of the book.

Third, the secretarial and cartographic staff in my department are among the best anywhere. I would like to thank Susan Shaull, our office supervisor, who located the discs from the 1987 book and converted them to a different format. She also makes working in our department a distinct pleasure because of her kind and delightful personality. Kimberly Cundiff, our chief word processor, typed most of the articles from the second edition and always had a smile and kind word for the weary professor. Brian Schulz, my graduate assistant, invested countless hours in word processing the new articles as well as helped with the final stages of organization. A note of appreciation is extended to Tom Wikle, my knowledgeable colleague on cartographic matters, and Jennifer Sartorius, geography major, who helped with map preparation and proofreading.

And last, but not least, a big hug goes to Janie, my wife of twenty years; Brian, my oldest son who is now a freshman in college; and Mark, my youngest, now a delightful sixteen-year-old. If it were not for their patience, support, and loving attitude, this third edition would not have become a reality.

Introduction

The ubiquitous presence of music in America ranging from the "elevator music" that pervades our office buildings to the chanting sounds of "rap" blaring from the boom boxes of the inner city strongly attests to the fact that modern society is deeply engrossed in music as either an active participant (performing as amateur or professional) or passive spectator (attending concerts, listening to recorded music, or watching MTV). Moreover, the constant inclusion of music in various sectors of our culture such as economics, politics, religion, and sports demonstrates that music permeates and affects many facets of our daily lives. Sir Kenneth Clark, British cultural historian, observed: Today, we immerse ourselves in sound. We've become acoustic skindivers. Music is no longer for listening to, but for merging with.

American music, folk and popular, has emerged as a field of study beginning slowly around the turn of the twentieth century and growing in its momentum over the past generation. Locally, regionally, and nationally, American folk and popular music is being performed and noticed in concerts and on recordings. Academic courses and special instructional programs on American folk and popular music topics are flourishing. New organizations and societies promoting American folk and popular music have been founded; government agencies (federal and state) have been established by legislative action to sponsor the study, preservation, and performance of American folk and popular music; special conventions and conferences have been held; journals begun and books have been published—all devoted to different aspects of the folk and popular music of America. The pervasive presence of music in American culture coupled with the increased attention by academicians and lay public demands explanation and interpretation from a geographer's viewpoint.

Geography as a discipline is concerned with the character of place as well as the spatial arrangement and organization of the myriad phenomena on the

1

earth's surface, both natural and human made. It is primarily an exercise in locational analysis seeking to understand why various phenomena are where they are. Human geography research has focused on virtually every segment of human spatial behavior ranging from industrialization to settlement patterns. It has concentrated on the material (tangible/visible) and nonmaterial (oral/spiritual) elements of human spatial behavior including the distributions and effects of value systems, languages, religions, architecture, politics, sports, and foodways. But for years, cultural geographers largely ignored the spatial and environment components of one of the most significant traits in American folk and popular culture—music.

Wilbur Zelinsky, in his updated version of *The Cultural Geography of the United States* (1992), had this to say:

> the recent accomplishments of the cultural-geographic community have been substantial. . . . We have begun flashing light into hitherto shadowy corners of the cultural cosmos. . . . A few of the new paths along which promising starts are visible include the geography of sport, foodways, and music. . . . (p. 144)

With the above quote in mind, the third edition of *The Sounds of People and Places* continues to explore the "new path" and fulfill the "promising start" of geography of music. In collecting, organizing, and editing material for this updated volume, thirteen articles from the 1987 second edition are retained and three deleted. Seven new articles, five of which have been published since 1987, are added, giving this volume a total of twenty readings. The new articles give a more balanced treatment of American folk and popular music from a geographic perspective than the 1987 edition, especially from a regional viewpoint and types of music presented in a geographic context. The 1984 article by Dick Butler on rock and roll develops the relationship between American and British rock music forms from a chronological and spatial point of view, serving as a complement to the 1973 rock and roll article by Larry Ford. The 1983 essay by John Lehr on Canadian country music broadcasts covers the connections between American and Canadian country music lyrics as well as investigates the efforts by the Canadian broadcasting system to promote a "sense of place" in Canadian country music.

The three new articles on blues by geographer Thomas Arkell, zydeco authored by anthropologist Rocky Sexton and geographer Bob Kuhlken, and Ozark ballads by George Carney give the anthology more breadth in terms of regional and ethnic-oriented music. Finally, the new introductory articles in Part I present a stronger and more detailed overview of music geography than the 1987 version. The four new authors give the list of contributors more regional coverage—two from Canada (Lehr and Butler), one from Great Britain (Arkell) and two from the American South (Sexton and Kuhlken).

Although this edition is much improved in coverage of American folk and popular music, I am ever mindful of the imbalances in the contents of the anthology, primarily because cultural geographers have failed to deal with many American folk and popular music forms. Still neglected are Tex-Mex, Cajun, and Native American in terms of ethnic music as well as the vast array of other music genres such as black gospel, martial music, polka, music of the theater and film, and the most recent music phenomenon, rap. More than one-third of the readings (seven) deal with country music and its various substyles and broadcast systems, three with folk, two with rock and roll, and one each with white gospel, jazz, blues, zydeco, popular, and Latin American. The two introductory articles cover a wide spectrum of American folk and popular music, helping to bring attention to the geographical neglect by the discipline. Should there be a fourth edition, perhaps these deficiencies will be ameliorated. In the meantime, I hope that music geographers will undertake studies on these ignored genres of American music.

Over the years, my experiences in the classroom, conducting research, and conversing with music geography colleagues has resulted in a number of major conceptual subdivisions of a geography of music, which are reflected in the organization of this book:

1. The spatial variation of music (i.e., the place-to-place differences in the music tastes and preferences of Americans). For example, the country-music southerner as opposed to the classical-music devotee of New England.

2. The evolution of a music style with place (i.e., place-specific music such as New Orleans and jazz, Nashville and country, and Detroit and Motown rock and roll).

3. The origin (cultural hearth) and diffusion of music phenomena (e.g., styles, instruments, songs, and musicians).

4. The psychological and symbolic elements of music pertinent to shaping the character of a place (e.g., perception of places via music lyrics such as the "surfin' rock" depiction of southern California).

5. The effect of music on the cultural landscape (e.g., concert halls, polka ballrooms, and rock festivals).

6. The spatial organization of music phenomena (e.g., marketing divisions of recording companies).

7. The relationship of music to the natural environment (e.g., an outdoor concert at Wolf Trap or the use of wood in the construction of a Native American courting flute).

8. The interrelationships of music with other culture traits in a spatial

sense (e.g., religion, dialect, politics, foodways, and sports in the American South).

Based on this conceptual framework, the twenty readings are divided into four parts: (1) The Geography of Music: An Emerging Field of Cultural Geography, (2) Regional and Ethnic Studies of American Folk and Popular Music, (3) Cultural Hearths and Cultural Diffusion of American Folk and Popular Music, and (4) The Role of Place in American Folk and Popular Music.

Part I includes two articles authored by Carney. The first traces the evolution of American music from the colonial era to the present in a geographic/historic context. The second is an examination of the music geography literature published during the last twenty-five years as well as a discussion of the origin and development of the geography of music as a subfield of human/cultural geography.

Part II contains six articles, four of which focus on various folk and ethnic musics of America ranging from Ozark and Appalachian mountain music of the Upland South to the blues and zydeco styles of the Deep South. The other two articles investigate the origin of country music personalities, one at the state level (Oklahoma) and the second at the regional level (the South). Although this section emphasizes the regional nature of American music, additional geographic concepts are introduced, including location factors (distance and connectivity) and spatial organization, distribution, and diffusion.

Part III consists of seven articles that deal with culture hearths (origins) and trace diffusion paths of four types of American folk and popular music: country, gospel, jazz, and rock. Three articles on country music outline the vocal and instrumental components of country music and delineate seven country music substyle regions, examine the types of diffusion processes associated with country music radio programming, and treat bluegrass (a substyle of country music) in the context of William Pattison's four traditions of geography (regional, man/land, physical, and spatial). The gospel music reading delimits gospel music regions, charts the diffusion of gospel music from its origins in the South, and details significant agents of diffusion (gospel radio stations, touring groups, and gospel albums). The jazz essay traces the diffusion of this music genre from its origins in New Orleans (c. 1900) up the urban hierarchy to Chicago (1920s) and to New York City (1930s). The two articles on rock music identify numerous geographic centers of early rock, trace various diffusion paths, and examine the relationships between American and British rock music forms.

Part IV includes five articles on the role of place and perception of places as expressed in American folk and popular music. The Woody Guthrie study focuses on his compositions (Dust Bowl Ballads) that illustrate myriad geographic themes including physical and cultural landscapes, migration, images of place (California), and realities of place. The Miami Sound essay analyzes a type of popular music associated with a particular place (i.e., place-specific music) as well as the influence of ethnicity on American music. The Canadian country music article examines the significance of place in Canadian and American country music lyrics. The fourth essay on popular music from 1890 to 1970 evaluates place images portrayed in songs dealing with cities, states, and regions. Positive and negative perceptions of places as expressed via popular music are summarized. The last article suggests that country music is the true folk music of America and is an avenue for studying such basic geographic concepts as location, sense of place, and environmental perception.

I would like to call special attention to the chapter endnotes, perhaps an unusual practice for the editor of an anthology. I have reasons, however, for most earnestly advising readers that the notes are in this case far from perfunctory. Beyond the normal and obligatory documentation of sources, they serve two further and even more important functions. First, they provide a number of recorded examples that are indispensable illustrations of the points being made in the text. Second, the notes often cite additional background, references, and relevant "asides," beyond what could be incorporated into the text itself, thus opening up avenues of further exploration for the interested reader. I especially recommend the Chapter 2 notes for a thorough review of the geography of music literature not included in this volume.

The "Reading and Listening" chapters at the end of each part are quite selective and geared to the individual essays. The bibliographies include only those works that are apt to be readily available, eminently readable, and important to any further investigation of the music geography topics discussed in each article.

Listening to the music associated with each reading is of course mandatory if one is to better understand the objectives of the authors as well as the anthology's potential use for the classroom or your interests as a researcher. Certain genres of American folk and popular music are represented by excellent anthologies that have become "classics," such as the Smithsonian series on jazz and country. I have based my selections on their availability in the likelihood that most are to be found in institutional libraries. The listening lists focus on the LP record, which still is the basic medium for most libraries, despite the fact that 1990s discographies now reflect the rapid displacement of the LP by the compact disc and the cassette. As a reminder to readers, discography dates rapidly, especially that recorded music related to popular culture.

An introduction is perhaps not the place for an extended commentary on music resources; however, I would like to present a mere sampling of those which are invaluable to students of American folk and popular music. We now have at our disposal a comprehensive four-volume reference work in *The New Grove Dictionary of American Music* (1986); this may well be regarded as supplementary material for every subject in this anthology. A unique inventory of source materials for future researchers has been compiled in the *Resources of American Music History* (1981), while an outstanding guide to the literature on American music has been assembled in the *Bibliographical Handbook of American Music* (1987), both published by the University of Illinois Press. The latter continues to add volumes to its already impressive list of more than thirty titles in the Music in American Life series covering music from cowboy ballads to coal mining songs. Taking the lead from the Illinois press series, the University of Michigan Press has inaugurated an American Music Series. And, of course, the *Harvard Dictionary of Music* has become a standard reference work and occupies an important place on my library shelf.

In the field of recording, the comprehensive *Recorded Anthology of American Music* produced by New World Records is approaching the 200 mark in LP selections. With the death of Moses Asch, veteran producer and folk music enthusiast, the vast and seminal Folkways library of recordings has taken a new lease on life, safe in the archives of the Smithsonian Institution, which also continues its own series of important issues on country, jazz, and popular music.

The Archive of American Folk Song, now the Archive of Folk Culture, in the Library of Congress retains its significant collection of field recordings made in the first half of the twentieth century. Also located in the Library of Congress, the relativly new American Folklife Center has published since 1983 its annual *American Folk Music and Folklore Recordings: A Selected List* to help promote the best recordings of American folk music issued each year.

Scholarly organizations, publications, and conferences are valuable forums for sharing the fruits of research across the whole spectrum of American folk and popular music. Among the best are the annual meetings of the Popular Culture Association, American Folklore Society, and our own North American Culture Society (founded by geographers and folklorists in 1974). With the burgeoning interest in American folk and popular music, a number of research centers have been established. The Institute for Studies in American Music at Brooklyn College of the City University of New York publishes an impressive list of monographs and a semiannual newsletter covering a wide range of American music topics. The Center for the Study of Southern Culture at the University of Mississippi, headed by Bill Ferris, focuses on the collection, preservation, and production of the vast array of southern music including blues, gospel, and country. The Center for Popular Culture (Bowling Green State University), under the leadership of Ray and Pat Browne, publishes several journals and books devoted to popular music forms. Charles K. Wolfe has created the Center for Popular Music at Middle Tennessee State University (Murfreesboro), which has become the focal point for a number of journal publications such as the *J.E.M.F. Quarterly* back issues.

For specialized music research, the best centers for jazz are the William Hogan Jazz Archive at Tulane University (New Orleans) and the Institute for Jazz Studies at Rutgers University; the Country Music Foundation in Nashville is the main archive for country music researchers; and the Center for Black Music Research at Columbia College in Chicago holds great potential for all types of African-American music. Finally, the folk and popular music community is served by a variety of periodicals; several of which are pertinent to the types of music represented in this volume. The aforementioned Center for the Study of Southern Culture publishes *Rejoice!* (a nonsectarian quarterly on all aspects of gospel music, black and white); *Old-Time Country* (a quarterly featuring book and record reviews, bibliographies, discographies, and filmographies); and *Living Blues* (a bimonthly publication that reports on blues people and activities around the world). The *Journal of Country Music* is published by the Country Music Foundation in Nashville. *Sing Out!: The Folk Song Magazine* maintains its long-standing position as a voice of both traditional and contemporary folk music. For other types of American folk and popular music, the best publications are *Cadence* and *Downbeat* (jazz); *Bluegrass Unlimited* (bluegrass); and *Rolling Stone* (rock). *Come-All-Ye*, a quarterly newsletter out of Hatboro, Pennsylvania, reviews books covering a wide spectrum of American music.

In conclusion, when the original version of this anthology appeared in 1978, I had no idea what sort of reception it would have. My doubts were generated by one basic consideration: I had directed it at a readership consisting of only one audience—my geography of music class. There was then no other book-length treatment of music geography, nor is there any now other than the present volume. The fact that other geographers seemed to like it, that critical reaction was on the whole positive, that it was inflicted on so many students, and that it somehow stayed in print year after year has driven me to edit a third edition. In closing, I would like to offer a quote from Act 3 of William Shakespeare's *The Taming of the Shrew*:

> *Preposterous ass, that never read so far*
> *To know the cause why music was ordain'd!*
> *Was it not to refresh the mind of man,*
> *After his studies or his usual pain?*

Part I

The Geography of Music:
An Emerging Field of Cultural Geography

1

North American Music: A Historic-Geographic Overview

George O. Carney

North Americans enjoy numerous styles of music for a variety of reasons. For many, there appears to be an identification with a certain lyrical content, whereas others listen to a particular instrumental sound that pleases their ear. Music has become a cultural trait that can best be described as a summing up of many of the familiar patterns of life including family, love, conflict, and work. These lifestyle experiences, expressed in music, help give a place its special character. Folklorist Alan Lomax has stated: "The map sings." From early settlement to the present, the map of North America has sung to us and the rest of the world.

Myriad Indian tribes distributed throughout the continent provided the first of many music traditions. Singing styles ranged from the deep bass unison of the Pueblos located on the plains of Canada and the United States to the piercing falsetto employed by the Navajos and Apaches of the American Southwest. From the British Isles came the sea chanteys heard along the Atlantic Coast and interior Great Lakes, and from France came the paddling songs from the French Canadians traveling along the St. Lawrence. European ballads transplanted in Newfoundland, Nova Scotia, and New England migrated West. Pilgrims and Puritans brought church music via the Bay Psalm Book, and the New England church singing-school concept diffused

Adapted from "Music and Dance" in John F. Rooney, Jr., Wilbur Zelinsky, and Dean R. Louder (eds.), *This Remarkable Continent: An Atlas of United States and Canadian Society and Cultures* (College Station: Texas A&M University Press, 1982), 234–53.

Native American dance music still plays an important role in pan-Indian celebrations in Oklahoma known as "pow-wows." Note the turtle-shell rattles, or "shackles," worn only by the women. These are used to accompany ceremonial music and dance (photo by George Carney).

southward to other colonies. With increased urbanization and secularization, operas were performed in Charles Town, South Carolina, and New York City prior to the American Revolution.

From West Africa through the Sea Islands, slave melodies spread across the Deep South from the Carolinas to Texas. As settlement moved westward into the Appalachians, new ballads and love songs were created and eventually were carried across the Upland South to the Ozarks of Missouri, Arkansas, and Oklahoma. Black workers chanted songs while building the South's railroads and levees, and from the cotton plantations of the Mississippi Delta came the field hollers that, combined with the work chants, were the foundation for country blues, one of the many indigenous North American music forms. The country blues migrated up and down the Mississippi River. At the mouth of the "Big Muddy," New Orleans became a musical crossroads for African, Spanish, and French sounds. The cultural mixture resulted in jazz, another North American musical innovation. To the northern end of the Mississippi, blacks took the blues into the cities of the Midwest to produce ragtime in St. Louis and urban blues in Chicago. Around New Orleans in the bayous of southern Louisiana, Cajun rhythms could be heard on the fiddle and concertina.

New immigrant groups such as the Germans brought chamber music to the colonies and later polkas to the Upper Midwest. As people spilled onto the Great Plains and Far West, songs and ballads depicted the culture of the miner, cowboy, and farmer. And from the Southwest came the *alabado* and *mariachi* music of the Mexican American. The sounds of people and places have indeed become an important segment of North American culture.

One tries in vain to view the development of North American music or any single phase of it as a simple organic process of growth. Rather, it developed, like the continent itself, from a number of different origins and in a number of different directions. North American music, like our peoples, is a mixed bag. Old World forms and Old World peoples have produced sometimes collaboratively, sometimes anonymously, and more often spontaneously the formulas that have become the motley concoction of the music of North America. Some broad trends and patterns, however, may be delineated in order to better understand our musical mosaic.

Sacred and Secular Period

During the colonial era, North American music can be divided into sacred and secular forms. New England worship music, specifically the psalmody, sung in religious meetings and at home, had originated in mid-sixteenth-century Protestant sects of Western Europe. Agitation among Puritan ministers for better singing in their churches resulted in the singing-school concept, which diffused to the southern colonies by the mid-eighteenth century. The singing-school movement diminished in New England, but it was to have a profound effect on later southern music types including early country music, white and black spirituals, and modern gospel.

Secular music of the colonial period has greatly influenced North American music. The English, Scottish, Irish, and French ballads were the popular music of the day. Very few of the colonial ballads were written down because the press was controlled by the clergy who were not interested in propagating secular music. Rather, these ballads were transmitted orally from performer to performer and from one generation to the next to become a major portion of our folk music tradition.

Balladry in the American colonies tended to be selective. None of the bawdy and few of the happy British ballads survived because the influence of religion extended itself over secular music. Early Americans preferred the sad, lonesome ballads dealing with tragedies in people's lives or disastrous events. As colonists began to set their new experiences to music, an extensive body of American ballads emerged.

In Canada, the French *habitants*, who tilled farms along the St. Lawrence, and the *voyageurs*, who pushed their way inland, sang hundreds of ballads from medieval France, often adapting them to new purposes. Of the native Canadian ballads, the largest number were composed by men who worked on the sea or in the woods. The coasts of Newfoundland and Nova Scotia produced hundreds of songs describing whaling, sealing, and cod-fishing trips and about ships and men who were lost at sea. In the lumber woods of New Brunswick and Ontario, the "shanty boys" composed songs narrating their work in the camps.

As was the case for ballads, early American dance music was seldom published. Despite Puritan influence, Samuel Sewall's diary in 1685 stated that colonial dancing did exist. French dance music was introduced during early settlement of Canada and the United States. Formal dances such as the minuet, gavotte, and allemande were inherited from seventeenth-century France. Less stately were the French folk dances. The music of a line dance like the *contredanse* (country dance) was often the same as for a square dance like the cotillion or the quadrille. From the British Isles came a legacy of dance music: hornpipes (England); schottisches, reels, and strathspeys (Scotland); and jigs (Ireland). The music of early North America provided the basis for many of our modern folk dances.

The fiddle, despite being frowned upon by many religious denominations as the devil's instrument, provided the chief source of instrumentation at colonial and later frontier dances. The fiddle dance tunes are among the most genuine folk melodies preserved in North America. The fiddle was the music instrument of westward migration from the expedition of Lewis and Clark to the era of "barn-warmins" on the agricultural Great Plains. In the United States, the fiddle was to become the backbone of early rural string bands whose music eventually evolved into bluegrass, a particular style of country music. As the fiddle spread across the country, it served an important role in the *fais dodos* (all-night dances) of Cajun Louisiana, and "house parties" and "kitchen sweats" in Texas and Oklahoma. The latter served as the foundation for the modern western swing and Texas fiddling styles, both still widely practiced in Oklahoma and Texas today. The fiddle tradition also remains strong in Canada, where it is used as instrumentation for the Celtic-derived clog dancing (predecessor of modern-day tap dancing) and the French quadrille.

The increasing diversity and dispersion of the population along with growing commerce and prosperity furthered the secularization of eighteenth-century American society. Another form of secular music migrated across the Atlantic with the signing of the Treaty of Utrecht of 1713—the English ballad opera. Although several centers of music activity existed in early North America, the focal point of formal music was Charles Town (Charleston after the Revolution), South Carolina. The ballad opera *Flora* was performed there in 1735, and in 1762 Charles Town music devotees founded the St. Cecilia Society, the first organization of its kind to achieve any sort of permanence in North America.

The ballad opera was made to order for the colonial American situation as compared with the more "pretentious" Italian opera because it was easily staged, used everyday language, and was performed with familiar music. Ballad opera was both fashionable and popular in the United States, and in 1750, *The Beggar's Opera*, an English production, was performed in New York City.

Italian, German, and French opera did not gain a foothold in North America until 1825, when the first foreign-language opera was presented in New York City. By far the most lively operatic center was New Orleans, where a cultivated French contingent of the cosmopolitan population had maintained support for French opera since the late 1700s. Northern cities heard their first grand opera when the New Orleans company toured Boston, Philadelphia, and Baltimore from 1827 to 1833. After the demise of the popular ballad opera in the late nineteeth century, the opera tradition became the least widely heard of all the kinds of North American secular music, especially in the hinterlands.

Cultivated, Vernacular, and Folk Traditions (Nineteenth Century)

With the beginning of the nineteenth century and through the present, North American music may be categorized into three major traditions: cultivated, vernacular, and folk. Cultivated music is a body of music that North America had to cultivate consciously, approach with some effort, and appreciate for its edification (moral, spiritual, or aesthetic values). We colloquially speak of this category as classical. The vernacular tradition is defined as a body of music more plebeian, not approached self-consciously but simply grown into as one grows into one's vernacular tongue; music understood and appreciated simply for its utilitarian or entertainment value. We commonly call this tradition popular music. The folk music category includes two forms: a legacy of older musical traditions still to be found in isolated areas and the traditional communal music found among various immigrant or ethnic minorities.

Whether one speaks of a certain music as folk or vernacular often depends on the point in time being considered. The British ballads of the colonial era, which functioned as some of the vernacular music of early America, eventually lost their popularity; and yet many of them still survive, but now as folk music. Conversely, some folk music occasionally becomes vernacular; for example, today's commercial folksingers and the music they have popularized to the point where it is now vernacular. The rapidity with which such shifts in social functions and status of various musics have occurred in North America is one of the most striking aspects about our dynamic musical culture, a reflection of our culture at large.

Orchestra music was the dominant cultivated music form in the nineteenth century. The Romantics of this era were convinced that instrumental music in general was the purest, most sublime music. One of the most characteristic trends in American music since the mid-nineteenth century has been the proliferation of independent symphony orchestras. In Europe such orchestras were associated with opera houses; however, the symphony orchestra in North America has tended to develop as an independent entity, reflecting our penchant for concerts rather than operas. Two decades before the Civil War, the first permanent orchestra still in existence today, the New York Philharmonic, was founded.

In the vernacular tradition, religious music became prominent in the 1900s. New England composers rejected the singing-school idea in favor of a more "scientific" church music. Crowded out of the northern and eastern cities, shape-note singing schools flourished in the Upland and Lowland South as well as on the western frontier. Shape-note singing formed the basis for two types of religious music that are still alive today—spiritual folk songs and gospel hymns.

Spiritual folk songs are religious songs set to folk melodies, commonly called spirituals. The complex relationships between white spirituals and black spirituals are not yet wholly clear. What is known is that both types of spirituals arose out of the evangelical songs of the great revivals in the American South and West in the period after 1800. The Great Revival movement began in Cane Ridge, Kentucky, in 1801, an event that set off a wave of emotional religious revivalism led by the Methodists, Baptists, and Presbyterians that swept across the Upper and Lower South.

The gospel hymn was also a product of the revival movement. However, unlike the earlier nineteenth-century spiritual, which arose mainly in rural areas, the gospel hymn of the last half of the century was urban, receiving its impetus from the "City of Revival" of the 1870s. Growing out of the gospel hymn was the organization of gospel quartet music, which took the gospel hymn pattern of repeated refrain-choruses sung in four-part harmony. A century after the gospel hymn movement began, some three thousand traveling professional and semiprofessional white gospel quartets are based throughout the United States.

The general styles of folk music emerged in the nineteenth centry: hillbilly, the Anglo-influenced music of the poor white southerner; and blues, the Afro-influenced music of the poor black southerner. Despite the richness of their vocal and instrumental repertory, and despite the diversity of their heritage, these two types of southern rural music remained unnoticed by the outside world until the 1920s when the first field recordings were made. Folklorists generally agree that the country blues originated the last decades of the nineteenth century in the Mississippi Delta region. The Yazoo Basin and the areas in and around Memphis and Jackson have proved to be the most prolific sources for blues performers. The blues is related to two earlier forms: the field holler, an unaccompanied monody of irregular length and structure; and the work song, which preserves the "call-and-response" pattern of African choral singing. In the blues format the call is represented by the vocal line, and the response by the instrument, usually a guitar. The most common blues was the "twelve-bar" form. The twelve-bar stanzas were three lines each wherein the first line was repeated, giving the vocalist an opportunity to extemporize a third line.

Hillbilly music, the genesis of modern country music, derived its basic ingredients from Anglo influences. Lyrics were inherited from the older British ballads, but with the passage of time the rural white southerners developed a body of songs that sang of landscapes and events of their own American experience. The British ballads underwent, in terms of subject matter, a degree of Americanization as local names and places replaced those of British origin.

A major force affecting hillbilly music in the late nineteenth century was the creation of string bands. The fiddle, already a permanent fixture in southern rural music, was joined by the banjo. Originally a four-stringed instrument, the banjo was changed in the nineteenth century by the addition of a fifth, or drone, string. Although the banjo was a favorite instrument among the "Forty-Niners," it did not gain wide currency in the rural South until the late nineteenth century. Information concerning other hillbilly instruments such as the guitar and mandolin, which ventured into rural areas later than the fiddle and banjo, is scarce. Folklorists believe, however, that these instruments of European origin (mandolin from Italy and guitar from Spain) entered the rural South through the mail-order catalog route. These four instruments, along with an occasional autoharp or plucked dulcimer, supplied the necessary ingredients for a hillbilly ensemble.

Cultivated, Vernacular, and Folk Traditions (Twentieth Century)

With the advent of unprecedented prosperity following World War I, Americans witnessed a notable change in their music; especially affected were the vernacular and folk traditions. Significant technological developments occurred in the 1920s: the establishment of commercial radio stations, the development of the electrical recording process, the public address system, and the sound track for film. All tended to broaden the audience—in a sense to nationalize it—for vernacular (popular) music, but at the same time to make it a more passive listening audience rather than participants. This tended to heighten the importance of professionalism among both performers and arrangers; it also tended to increase commercialism in the transmission of popular music to its audience. Thus the era of the American popular-music industry was born.

An indigenous and unprecedented form of American music achieved national popularity beginning with the 1920s: jazz. Although jazz had existed long before the post–World War I period, it had been an exclusively black music unknown to the larger American community. What had been a music of and for southern blacks began to be diffused through several processes: the earliest phonograph recordings of blues and jazz; World War I, which found black soldiers, blues and jazz performers among them, spread over both North America and Europe; commercial radio stations began to program more jazz; and the increased mobility of southern blacks, particularly in the direction of northern cities like Chicago and New York. New Orleans dominated the jazz scene in the latter nineteenth century, but with the migration of blacks up the Mississippi, Chicago replaced New Orleans as the major center in the 1920s, to be replaced by New York in the 1930s.

The Great Depression of the 1930s wrought extensive changes in American music. By 1933 the phonograph companies were forced to curtail much of their operations. The contracts of many of the popular and folk performers, especially those who had exhibited little commercial appeal, were not renewed. On the other hand, the thirties was a period of expanding radio coverage for hillbilly and blues music. Radio stations in the South and Midwest, recognizing the popularity of rural music in the 1920s, programmed more during the 1930s. Diffusion of hillbilly music was aided by the powerful Mexican border stations that operated on wattage as much as two or three times in excess of the 50,000 watt limit in the United States. The X-stations (so-called because of their call letters) boomed the sounds of country music throughout the United States and Canada.

The period following World War II, like that after World War I, was one of rapid development in American music. Rising prosperity in the 1950s resulted in an increased audience for music. Folk music flourished in the postwar decades, especially in the cities where young people and transplanted hill people yearned to hear the traditional sounds of country music. A traditional substyle of country music that reached national prominence during the so-called "folk music renaissance" of the fifties and sixties was bluegrass. Evolving out of the rural string-band music of the 1920s, bluegrass used five basic instruments: five-string banjo (picked in the three-finger style), fiddle, mandolin, flat-top guitar, and stand-up string bass. The most distinguishing elements of the bluegrass ensemble were the five-string banjo featured as a lead instrument and that all instruments were unamplified or nonelectric.

Bill Monroe, the acknowledged creator of bluegrass, named his band, The Bluegrass Boys, after his native state of Kentucky although the style did not originate in the Bluegrass Basin of Kentucky. Most of the professional bluegrass performers were born in the hill-country sections of North Carolina, Tennessee, Virginia, and Kentucky. Since 1965 bluegrass music has diffused through the southeast, south central, and western portions of the United States, primarily because of the growing popularity of the outdoor bluegrass fesivals. Bluegrass vocals are characterized by the "high, lonesome" lead tenor practiced by Monroe, and the three-and four-part harmony reminiscent of rural church singing of the South.

After the war, singing and listening to folk music became a form of sophisticated entertainment (sometimes seasoned with protest in the 1960s) in concert halls and cabarets. Folk festivals and "hootenannies" multiplied on university campuses and in coffee houses where hillbilly and blues singers swapped songs and traded "licks" with city musicians who had picked up their versions from books and a growing catalogue of records. The folk music revival also sparked the organization of folk music societies and clubs, which were established to preserve the older sounds of the country.

While folk music thrived, American popular music underwent a major transformation. As had happened before the vernacular tradition, the main source of change was the music of black Americans. The term "rhythm-and-blues" (introduced by the recording industry in 1946 to replace the outmoded term "race" music) covered several styles of music American blacks were making in the postwar years: the dance music of the big bands rooted in the Kansas City swing style; the urban blues of Memphis and Chicago derived from the self-accompanied singers of country blues; and the close harmony of singing groups, which originated in the gospel singing of rural evangelistic and urban storefront churches.

White adolescents of the 1950s wanted a music of their own. Rebelling against the "pop" music of their parents, who were listening to Frank Sinatra and Perry Como, the economically strong "youth culture" turned to black rhythm-and-blues because it was new to them and because it possessed danceable rhythms. In 1954 an old blues term, "rock 'n' roll," was introduced by Alan Freed, a Cleveland disc jockey, in order to popularize rhythm-and-blues.

Rock and roll music by the mid-1950s had become a synthesis of diluted hillbilly and blues music. The heavy, monotonous beat and electric-guitar instrumentation of rock and roll suggested the sounds that had sprung from the juke joints of the Delta, the bars of Chicago's southside, and the honky tonks of the Southwest. The wailing vocal styles and rolling piano chords, such as those of Little Richard and Jerry Lee Lewis, were inherited from rural black and white church services of the South. Lyrics tended to be urban-oriented, where the black and white teen-age purchasing power was located.

One of the principal agents in the diffusion of rock and roll was the small, independent record company that emerged during the period. The major recording studios viewed the new music with skepticism, which allowed the independent companies—for example, Sun in Memphis, Chess in Chicago, and Imperial in Los Angeles—to capitalize on the growing popularity of rock and roll.

The rock and roll revolution of the 1950s effected a decentralization of geographic centers (performance, recording, and publishing) of popular music: Memphis, Philadelphia, Nashville, Detroit, San Francisco, and Los Angeles were as important breeding grounds and distribution centers as New York. By the late 1960s and into the 1990s variants of rock and roll multiplied rapidly and the new popular music came to be called simply "rock." Offshoots of the fifties sound were folk rock, blues rock, hard rock, acid rock, glitter rock, punk rock, and heavy metal rock.

Rap, a new form of popular music, originated in Jamaica and diffused to the Bronx in the late 1960s in the person of Kingston-born Clive Campbell (a.k.a. DJ Kool Herc). Herc's pioneering methods (manipulating records on the turntable with his hands while vocalists spontaneously created lyrics) were appropriated by New York City deejays (e.g., Grandmaster Flash) in the late

1970s. To the Jamaican techniques, New York City rappers added "scratching" (repeated hands-on manipulation of a single passage or beat on a record) and "punch phrasing" (use of a memorable vocal drum beat or horn phrase as formal punctuation). The first album of Public Enemy in 1987 (*Yo, Bum Rush the Show*) was notable for its ethnocentric point of view and its technological experimentation with "sampling" (incorporation of prerecorded material in a new composition with the help of a computer). From its origins associated with inner-city African Americans, the latest generation of rappers are definitely diverse, ranging from the hard-core gangster style of N.W.A. to the socially conscious work of KRS-One to the macho braggadocio of LL Cool J to the feminist Salt-n-Pepa. Whether one considers rap "real" music or not, its cultural antecedents are substantial (some say its roots lie in the "talking" blues and James Brown's rap-like monologues). Rap's presence on the 1990s musical scene is significant, and it raises many important technological and social issues concerning the direction of American music.

The music of North America is as diverse as the people who are found in the various culture regions of the continent. Alan Lomax has stated that music is a viable indicator of the cultural milieu of our continent. It therefore provides one of the pieces of the cultural puzzle we as cultural geographers are attempting to put together.

Thus we must move ahead in completing the unfinished task of examining our rich and diverse music heritage. These music traditions have helped bridge the gap between our culture and other regions of the world. Where our way of live is unknown and where our government policies remain a mystery, our music can be heard from jazz in Moscow to bluegrass in Tokyo. The melodies of North America may not only be the most far-reaching but perhaps the most effective diplomats for our culture.

2

The Geography of Music:
Inventory and Prospect

George O. Carney

More than twenty years have elapsed since Peter Hugh Nash of the University of Waterloo published the first article by a geographer on music.[1] Presented at the twenty-first International Geographical Congress in New Delhi, India, Nash's "Music Regions and Regional Music" paper caused a great deal of comment. He recently described the proceedings:

> I was skeptical about the reception it might receive on the part of my colleagues because its contents were quite untraditional. However, it must have hit a responsive chord with my Oriental colleagues, who were quite surprised that an American geographer (especially one primarily concerned with city planning) should investigate a "humanistic" phenomenon such as music.[2]

The editor of *The Deccan Geographer* immediately offered Nash the opportunity to publish the manuscript as the lead article in the next issue. Thus a subfield (music) of a subfield (cultural) of geography was born.

Two years later Jeffrey Gordon, a graduate student at Pennsylvania State University, completed the first Master's thesis in geography on music. His "Rock-and-Roll Music: A Diffusion Study" investigated record chart data from the 1960s to determine diffusion patterns for selected American urban centers.[3]

The first full-length article on music geography in an American journal

Reprinted by permission from *Journal of Cultural Geography* 10 (1990): 35–48.

appeared in 1971.[4] While a teaching assistant at the University of Oregon in the late 1960s, Larry Ford developed a rock and roll music theme for an introductory cultural geography course. Later, to a packed house at the 1970 California Council for Geographic Education meeting, Ford presented an expanded version of his research on the origin and diffusion of rock and roll. Based on an overwhelmingly positive response, he sent the manuscript to Harm deBlij, then editor of the *Journal of Geography*, who, Ford stated, was excited about the research and published it with few revisions. The article created such a stir in the profession, Ford related, that henceforth at national meetings he was referred to as "Rock and Roll" Ford.[5]

In addition to these three pioneers in music geography, a dozen others deserve recognition—Charles Gritzner, Ben Marsh, Jim Curtis, Floyd Henderson, A. D. Horsley, Jon Glasgow, Richard Francaviglia, Lou Woods, John Lehr, George Carney, John Crowley, and Jean Tavernor. All were instrumental in the development of music geography during the past twenty years.

Reactions to research in the geography of music have been and continue to be mixed. Some colleagues have characterized it as "frivolous," "such nonsense," and simply "untraditional," while others just raised their eyebrows with skepticism whenever it was mentioned. A graduate student allegedly lost his teaching assistantship for dabbling in this "radical" topic. One faculty member feared denial of promotion if he published music geography research. Yet another assistant professor's promotion was rejected by an academic vice-president who viewed his music geography publications as "unscientific." Finally, a former editor of the *Annals* told one of the aforementioned pioneers in music geography that to be taken seriously in the profession he should avoid research on "gays and country music."

In general, however, reactions within and outside the discipline were largely positive. Nash's paper was widely acclaimed at the International Geographic Congress meeting, and Joe Spencer, then editor of the *Annals*, reprimanded Nash ("gave me hell" in Nash's words) for not giving him an opportunity to first consider the manuscript.[6] Marsh's graduate career at Pennsylvania State University was reportedly saved by a professor who encouraged him to develop a seminar paper on music geography into a thesis.[7] Subsequently, a condensed version of his thesis was published in *Harper's*, a popular national magazine.[8] In 1973, music geographers were given encouragement by the eminent cultural geographer, Wilbur Zelinsky, who called for studies on folk music to better understand the spatio-temporal phases of American culture.[9] A 1974 article, "Bluegrass Grows All Around: The Spatial Dimensions of a Country Music Style," was selected for a *Journal of Geography* award by the National Council for Geographic Education.[10] At the first Society for the North American Cultural Survey (SNACS) meeting in 1974, music was given a prominent role in the deliberations. It appeared as a separate chapter in the organization's *Scratch Atlas I* and *II*, and eventually in *This Remarkable Continent: An Atlas of United States and Canadian Society and Cultures.*[11] Those outside the discipline, especially historians and folklorists, have recently recognized the growing body of literature in music geography including B. Lee Cooper's popular music resource guide, D. W. Krummel's bibliographical handbook of American music, and the William Ferris and Charles Wilson encyclopedia of southern culture.[12] In addition, special sessions and individual papers on music geography have been well received at professional meetings. Most notable were the 1974 National Council for Geographic Education convention in Chicago (three papers), the first such session devoted to the use of music in the geography classroom; the 1982 Association of American Geographers special session on music in San Antonio (four papers); the special session on music at the 1985 Association of American Geographers meetings in Detroit (four papers); and three music papers at the 1986 Association of American Geographers meetings in Minneapolis. Regional and state geography conferences have also included music geography papers during the past twenty years.

Finally, Carney's two anthologies on music geography received favorable reviews in such outlets as *The Professional Geographer* (November 1988), *Journal of Geography* (March–April 1988), and *Journal of Cultural Geography* (Fall–Winter 1988) as well as being cited in the Association of American Geographers-National Geographic Society–sponsored A *Geographical Bibliography for American Libraries.*[13]

Productivity

Over the past two decades, a significant amount of research in the spatial dimensions of music has been conducted. Twenty-seven articles were published in ten international journals, seven national journals, one regional journal, and five state journals including several outside the field, whereas twenty-six papers were delivered at international, national, regional, and state meetings.

Based on total output, one might describe the 1970s as the "Golden Age of Music Geography." During that decade, music geography made fifty-two appearances in professional outlets. Ironically, while professional interest declined in the 1980s as measured by the number of theses, dissertations, and journal articles, the number of papers presented at professional meetings more than doubled from the previous decade. Moreover, acceptance of music geography as a cultural geography subfield was seemingly legitimized in the 1980s by an increase in human geography textbook citations (Table 2-1).

Research Categories

Most of the research has focused on American folk and popular music. Nash's work on world-music regions, Tavernor's essay on regional music of Latin America, and Sister Violita's essay on Indian music are among the few exceptions.[14] Lack of studies on music from a global perspective may be attributed to three factors: (1) an overwhelming majority of music geographers were Americans trained at American universities, (2) most geographers were concerned with the cultural geography of the United States, and (3) the subject matter of music was extremely complex at the global scale. John Bale, a University of Keele cultural geographer who closely observes popular culture in Great Britain, stated that music studies by geographers are "virtually nonexistent" there.[15] Even Lehr's work in Canada was a comparative study of country music in Canada and the United States.[16]

Music phenomena that geographers have studied can be divided into eight general categories: (1) styles, (2) structure, (3) lyrics, (4) performers and composers, (5) centers and events, (6) media, (7) ethnic, and (8) instrumentation. In terms of style, more than half of all music geography output has concentrated on American country music and its various substyles, lyrics, and instrumentation.[17] Rock music and its myriad spinoffs accounted for about 15 percent, with classical music generating nearly as much attention.[18] The remainder of the professional output has focused on a variety of music

Table 2-1. Productivity of Music Geographers

Professional Outlets	1960–69	1979–79	1980–89	Total
Journal articles	1	24	2	27
Books	0	1	1	2
Atlas maps	0	1	1	2
Theses/dissertations	0	8	2	10
Book chapters	0	1	3	4
Professional meeting papers	0	7	19	26
Human geography textbook citations	0	3	7	10
Miscellaneous (unpublished manuscripts, bibliographies, etc.)	0	7	1	8
Total	1	52	36	89

Source: Data compiled by author.

genres, including folk, gospel, jazz, ethnic, and popular.[19] Additionally, there is a smattering of unpublished research on the blues.[20]

The structural nature of music received little recognition from geographers despite the fact that folklorists have long studied this phenomenon, culminating in Alan Lomax's Cantometrics project, which mapped vocal music structural elements on a world scale.[21] The only contributions by a geographer in this class were Nash's maps of music scales, neumatic notation, and polyphony.[22]

In contrast, lyrics and the content analysis thereof drew considerable attention from geographers. Ford and Henderson, Curtis, and James Kracht studied the role of place and the perception of places in popular and folk music.[23] Research by Gritzner and Woods examined the multifaceted dimensions of country music lyrics including the rural/urban dichotomy as well as sacred and profane images.[24] Jeffrey Gordon's work investigated the lyrics of one particular song to convey geographic skills for classroom use.[25]

Research on composers and performers includes Carney's work on bluegrass performers and country music notables, Ford's research on rock and roll performers, Nash's study of classical music composers, and Butler's analysis on origins of rock and roll acts in the United States and United Kingdom.[26] The origins of selected performers or composers, tour routes, and performance locations have likewise been mapped and analyzed.

Music geographers have identified important geographic centers for music and investigated sites for a number of music events. Nash's maps of classical music centers, Ford's analysis of emerging rock and roll nodes, and Carney's bluegrass festival sites account for most of the research in this category.[27]

Significant research was devoted to the role of media in music, especially diffusion processes. Gordon's thesis on rock and roll, Carney's article on American country music, Lehr's work on Canadian country music, and Ann Kellogg's dissertation on popular music centered on the role of radio in the diffusion of these music styles.[28]

Although it has been studied by folklorists and ethnomusicologists for years, ethnic music has largely escaped the attention of music geographers. This is surprising inasmuch as cultural geographers have investigated other facets of ethnicity, and there is a wealth of material by other disciplines on the subject. James Curtis's and Richard Rose's article on "The Miami Sound," a chapter in the James Curtis/Thomas Boswell book on Cuban-Americans, Lauren Post's chapter on Cajun music, Jon Glasgow's research on black jazz, and the Rocky Sexton/Robert Kuhlken piece on zydeco music are noteworthy exceptions.[29]

Finally, published works by music geographers on patterns of instrumentation are also scarce. Yet, again, ethnomusicologists have mapped the distribution of instruments since the 1920s.[30] Music geographers have focused primarily on the fiddle, including the distribution and diffusion of fiddling styles, fiddle tunes, and membership in old-time fiddling organizations. Among the best of these studies are the James Renner and Margaret Schultz theses, Charles Gardner's unpublished manuscript, and John Crowley's recent article.[31] Carney examined nuclear hearths and diffusion paths of five basic country music instruments in a study on country music in the American South; Nash produced a map of church organs in western Europe in his early work on classical music; Malcolm Comeaux completed a study on the accordion in Cajun music; and Violita discussed the origins of a variety of wind, percussion, and stringed instruments in her music geography research.[32] Elliott Fout's recent thesis is an exhaustive study on the origin and diffusion of drum and bugle corps in the United States.[33]

Research Approaches

As with the diversity of music phenomena studied, a multiplicity of approaches and themes have been used by music geographers. Most research falls into five general categories: (1) perception (image of place, sense of place, place perception, place consciousness, and place-specific); (2) cultural hearth and cultural diffusion (diffusion agents, diffusion processes, diffusion paths, and diffusion barriers); (3) culture region (formal and functional, nodes and cores, and macro and micro); (4) spatial interaction (migration, connectivity, transportation routes, and communication networks); and (5) human/ environment relationships (cultural ecology).

Curiously, music geographers have completed little in the way of cultural landscape interpretation, although the topic lends itself to this approach. Cultural landscapes possess audible signatures as well as visual components, and the possibilities for landscape analysis using music seem endless. Furthermore, cultural integration appears to be a viable theme for music geographers. Although a few articles have implied that music is spatially interrelated with other culture traits, the function of music in such areas as religion, sports, occupations, and the military has been largely ignored.

Like much of cultural geography, music research can be characterized by several adjectives—empirical, descriptive, humanistic, atheoretical, nonanalytic, and subjective. Occasionally, music geographers have flirted with diffusion theory, but by and large research results have been more idiographic than nomothetic.[34]

Although music geography research has been criticized for its diverse approaches, unscientific methodologies, and scattered results, one could argue that the pluralism exhibited in this subfield reflects the discipline as a whole. Diversity, after all, remains one of geography's distinctive characteristics. Marvin Mikesell described this lack of consensus as one of the profession's unifying principles and a tradition that makes our discipline attractive.[35] Thus music geographers, like so many in our profession, do not necessarily "hear the same drummer" or "march under the same banner."

Retrospect

Assessing music geography over the past two decades raises a major question: Was the peak for music research reached in the 1970s an "episode," as Mikesell described research trends that come and go in the history of our discipline?[36] Some might suggest that it was a reaction to the quantitative revolution of the previous decade, but most would agree with Mikesell who stated that cultural geographers were never bothered much by it.[37]

Based on the interviews conducted for this study, the popularity of music geography research in the 1970s can be attributed to four major factors. First, music geographers were influenced by *zeitgeist* (spirit of the times). They were affected by what was "out there." The emergence of rock and roll in the 1950s, the folk music renaissance and recognition of black music traditions in the 1960s, and the resurgence of country music in the 1970s most likely had a bearing on their cumulative interests. Similarly, a majority of music geographers were "baby boomers" who matriculated in graduate school in the 1960s and 1970s when the social and ecological issues of those decades were principal concerns of that generation. And, importantly, music was a vital component of those movements. In short, subject matter was abundant, and there was plenty "out there" to see and hear.

Second, cultural geography was undergoing a transition that likewise mirrored the times. Studies on folk culture were the traditional avenues for research. Cultural geographers had shown a clear bias toward the study of rural areas in America and preindustrial societies abroad.[38] Little had been accomplished in the field of popular culture research. Music stood alongside foodways, sports, fashion, literature, and art—a few of the seemingly neglected segments of culture virtually ignored by cultural geographers. For many music geographers, music was a ready vehicle to help legitimize the spatial analysis of popular culture and thus broaden the base of cultural geography. Cultural geographers also had traditionally maintained a predilection toward material culture, particularly house types. Therefore, the study of music was a mechanism to augment the historically restrictive dimensions of cultural geography by including nonmaterial elements of culture.

A third reason for the emergence of music geography is one associated with converting an avocation into a vocation. Nash, a classical music devotee, attended symphony concerts during his graduate days at Harvard. Gordon, a long-time rock and roll fanatic, played drums in several rock and roll bands in college and graduate school. Gritzner's appreciation for country music was honed in high school when he listened to Marty Robbins's noontime radio program on KTYL in Mesa, Arizona. Francaviglia, a disc jockey during his undergraduate years, researched and wrote scripts on the history of rock and roll. Curtis began guitar lessons at UCLA under an instructor from Oklahoma. It was from her that he was introduced to the life and lyrics of native Oklahoman and Dust Bowl chronicler Woody Guthrie. Glasgow was a jazz aficionado during his undergraduate career at Miami University of Ohio. Ford was his high school's representative to *High School Hit Parade*, Columbus, Ohio's version of *American Bandstand*. Horsley had sung gospel music for fifteen years and was a member of four gospel quartets during that time.[39] Perhaps music geographers were first more interested in the music per se than the geography of music. But they all saw *what, where,* and *why* questions in music and made a common commitment to answer those questions by using music to enhance cultural geography.

Finally, one might argue that the rise of music geography in the 1970s was an attempt by a group of young geographers to stake a claim for themselves to be, or at least seem to be, different from their older-generation professors in cultural geography. Many were in search of a niche, or some sort of specialization, within the geography field. Moreover, they were living in an era of specialization when qualifying adjectives to precede "geography" and "geographer" became fashionable (i.e., "hyphenated geographers").

Prospect

While the literature on music geography is fairly impressive, a number of research questions remain. What specifically ought music geographers examine in the future? They need to be more aggressive in sharing their research with those outside the discipline. To the ethnomusicologists, folklorists, and music historians, notice should be given that cultural geographers offer a different perspective on music and that they have a contribution to make in understanding music as an element of culture. Bruno Nettl, a noted ethnomusicologist who devotes an entire chapter to "The Singing Map" in his *The Study of Ethnomusicology: Twenty-Nine Issues and Concepts*, discusses spatial distribution of music traits, culture areas based on music, and cultural diffusion of music.[40] Yet, he fails to cite any of the work by geographers, although he admits there is "a cultural geography of music." Alan Lomax, the eminent folklorist, delimits folk song style regions in North America. While proclaiming that "the map sings," he, too, totally ignores research by music geographers.[41] It remained for a nongeographer to make those outside the discipline aware of music geography. Kip Lornell, a brilliant young folklorist, introduced the geography of music literature to sister disciplines in his *Current Musicology* article.[42]

In addition to doing a better job of "tooting their own horns," music geographers need a revival. One might say the Young Turks of the 1970s have become the Old Pashas of the 1980s. As Ford recently proposed: "Music geography needs a theoretical breakthrough."[43] Perhaps cultural geographers are too tradition bound and conservative to develop the "new" music geography with model building and statistical manipulation. But the new wave of geographers would probably be more attracted to cultural geography in general and music geography in particular if there were some social-theory models to be tested. Much remains to be accomplished whether the research foci are nonanalytic or theoretical. Even after twenty years, geographers have not yet begun to tap the wide range of music data and ask geographical questions about them.

Little is known about the stylistic variations of music around the world or, for that matter, in the United States. One need only contrast ragas to reggae or blues to Bach to see that place-to-place differences exist. As with many facets of nonmaterial culture, styles are difficult to map because of the problem of establishing precise boundaries. This problem, however, has not prevented many cultural geographers from delineating religious, linguistic, and architectural cores, domains, and zones.

The geographic knowledge of ethnic music, as previously noted, is practically nil despite the fact that anthropologists, folklorists, and ethnomusicologists have studied variations in both rural and urban contexts. And it is not a failure of cultural geographers to study ethnicity, for a wealth of material in print covers blacks, Hispanics, and Cajuns. Yet almost nothing has been published on their music from a geographical point of view. Where are the geographical studies on the music contributions of Asian, African, European, and Latin American immigrants? What about the rich and variegated music traditions of the Hispanic Southwest, French of Upper New England, Germans and Scandinavians of the Upper Midwest, and black Americans of the Deep South?

Little is known about religious music ranging from Gregorian chants to gospel. Nor has much attention been given to martial music despite the fact that America abounds with marching bands in local communities, armed services, and university campuses. Stage and film music likewise has been geographically neglected. Music geographers need to produce monographs on the various forms of place-specific music; for example, New Orleans and jazz, Memphis and blues, Detroit and Motown, Nashville and country, and southern California and surf rock. Additionally, they ought to examine the geographic implications of music technology and the music industry, including the phonograph and radio industries as well as compact discs and even MTV (Music Television). Finally, a multitude of geographic data exists on music clubs and organizations, music festivals, and music-oriented magazines, all of which await the geographer's consideration.

Final Remarks

The output is sparse and the duration is short when one compares the study of music geography to the wealth of material and long tradition of music research in the sister disciplines of history, sociology, anthropology, and folklore. Why is the geographic contribution so little and so late?

In part, it is due to the overwhelming amounts of material and diversity of subject matter. The apparent "shotgun" nature of music geography research was a function of the small number of geographers who embarked on such a monumental topic. There was little, if any, concerted effort on the part of music geographers to coordinate their research or synthesize their findings. The literature on music geography was scattered. After being rejected by geography journals, many sought outlets outside the field in folklore or popular-culture journals. Therefore, keeping abreast of published works on music geography proved difficult. Little communication existed among the handful of geographers researching music, beyond the annual meetings where papers were delivered. Music geographers were widely dispersed from the SUNY (State University of New York) system to San Diego State and from Oklahoma State to South Dakota State. Neither did a department or center emerge specializing in music geography—a place where coordination of research ideas could occur as well as attract and train graduate students in this subfield. Furthermore, no precedents existed. Music geography virtually started from scratch. A few individuals were tackling a topic never before researched by geographers. Finally, there was the question of data. Although music geographers knew where to locate data customarily used in geography (e.g., census and climatic statistics), research methodology seminars provided no training on data sources for music or how to gain access to that information.

Although much remains to be done, music geographers have built a solid foundation for continued research. But it represents only the beginnings of a comprehensive process of music data collection, mapping, and analysis. The results to date are encouraging and suggest that they should persevere in examining more facets of the geography of music. The older generation of geographers in concert with some of the new generation hopefully will turn their attention to those questions, promote improved communication in regard to research results, and rejuvenate this subfield of cultural geography. The wedding of cultural geography with the study of music constitutes an important research frontier—a frontier complete with ready-made questions, a more-than-ample data base, and a seemingly endless future. In his conclusion to "The American Scene," David Lowenthal asks geographers to open their eyes to look around, to see, "just as long as we see something."[44] This plea needs to be extended to cover not only one's sense of vision, but the auditory sense as well. Geographers need to open their ears to the auditory components of culture—the sounds of people and places.

Notes

1. Peter Hugh Nash, "Music Regions and Regional Music," *The Deccan Geographer* 6 (July–December 1968), pp. 1–24.

2. Personal correspondence with Peter Hugh Nash, Waterloo, Ontario, Canada, January 1989.

3. Jeffrey J. Gordon, "Rock-and-Roll Music: A Diffusion Study" (unpublished Master's thesis, Pennsylvania State University, Department of Geography, 1970).

4. Larry Ford, "Geographic Factors in the Origin, Evolution, and Diffusion of Rock and Roll Music," *Journal of Geography* 70 (November 1971), pp. 455–64.

5. Telephone interview with Larry Ford, San Diego State University, San Diego, California, February 1989.

6. Personal correspondence with Nash, January 1989.

7. Ben Marsh, "Sing Me Back Home: A Grammar of Places in Country Music Song" (unpublished Master's thesis, Pennsylvania State University, Department of Geography, 1971).

8. Ben Marsh, "A Rose-Colored Map," *Harper's* 225 (July 1977), pp. 80–82.

9. Wilbur Zelinsky, *The Cultural Geography of the United States* (Englewood Cliffs, N.J.: Prentice-Hall, 1973), p. 107.

10. George O. Carney, "Bluegrass Grows All Around: The Spatial Dimensions of a Country Music Style," *Journal of Geography* 73 (April 1974), pp. 34–55.

11. John F. Rooney, Jr., Wilbur Zelinsky, and Dean R. Louder, eds., *This Remarkable Continent: An Atlas of United States and Canadian Society and Cultures* (College Station: Texas A and M University Press, 1982), pp. 234–53.

12. B. Lee Cooper, *The Popular Music Handbook: A Resource Guide for Teachers, Librarians, and Media Specialists* (Littleton, Colo.: Libraries Unlimited, 1984), pp. 50–51; D. W. Krummel, *Bibliographical Handbook of American Music* (Urbana:

University of Illinois Press, 1987), p. 57; and Charles R. Wilson and William Ferris, eds., *Encyclopedia of Southern Culture* (Chapel Hill: University of North Carolina Press, 1989), pp. 988–89, 955, and 1002.

13. George O. Carney, ed., *The Sounds of People and Places: Readings in the Geography of Music* (Washington, D.C.: University Press of America, 1978); George O. Carney, ed., *The Sounds of People and Places: Readings in the Geography of American Folk and Popular Music* (Lanham, Md.: University Press of America, 1987); and Chauncey D. Harris, ed., *A Geographical Bibliography for American Libraries* (Washington, D.C.: Association of American Geographers, 1985), p. 233.

14. Nash, *The Deccan Geographer*, pp. 1–24; Jean Tavernor, "Musical Themes in Latin American Culture: A Geographical Appraisal," *The Bloomsbury Geographer* 3 (1970), pp. 60–66; and Sister Violita, "The Geography of Music," in *Recent Trends and Concepts in Geography*, ed. by R. B. Mandal and V.N.P. Sinha (New Delhi: Concept Publishing, 1980), pp. 353–66.

15. Telephone interview with John Bale, University of Keele, Staffordshire, England, United Kingdom, January 1989.

16. John C. Lehr, "Texas (When I Die): National Identity and Images of Place in Canadian Country Music Broadcasts," *The Canadian Geographer*, 27 (Winter 1983), pp. 361–70.

17. George O. Carney, "Geography of Music: A Bibliography," *Journal of Cultural Geography* 1 (Fall–Winter 1980), pp. 185–86.

18. Gordon, "Rock-and-Roll Music: A Diffusion Study," 1970; Ford, *Journal of Geography*, 1971; R. W. Butler, "The Geography of Rock: 1954–1970," *Ontario Geography* 24 (1984), pp. 1–33; Nash, *The Deccan Geographer*, 1968; Peter Hugh Nash, "Music and Cultural Geography," *The Geographer* 22 (January 1975), pp. 1–14; and Peter Hugh Nash, "Music and Environment: An Investigation of Some of the Spatial Aspects of Production, Diffusion, and Consumption of Music," *Canadian Association of University Schools of Music Journal* 5 (Spring 1975), pp. 42–71.

19. James R. Curtis, "Woody Guthrie and the Dust Bowl," *Places* 3 (July 1976), pp. 12–18; A. D. Horsley, "The Spatial Impact of White Gospel Quartets in the United States," *John Edwards Memorial Foundation Quarterly* 15 (Fall 1979), pp. 91–98; Jon A. Glasgow, "An Example of Spatial Diffusion: Jazz Music," *Geographical Survey* 8 (January 1979), pp. 10–21; James R. Curtis and Richard F. Rose, "The Miami Sound: A Contemporary Latin Form of Place-Specific Music," *Journal of Cultural Geography* 4 (Fall–Winter 1983), pp. 110–18; and Larry Ford and Floyd Henderson, "The Image of Place in American Popular Music: 1890–1970," *Places* 1 (March 1974), pp. 31–37.

20. Douglas Langille, "The Spatial Dynamics and Diffusion of a Culture-Specific Artform: The Geography of Blues" (unpublished Bachelor's thesis, University of Guelph, Department of Geography, 1975), and Margaret Schultz, "Spatial Elements in the Development of Afro-American Fiddle Styles" (unpublished seminar paper, Eastern Washington College, Department of Geography, 1977).

21. Alan Lomax, *Cantometrics* (Berkeley: University of California Press, 1976).

22. Nash, *The Deccan Geographer*, pp. 1–24.

23. Ford and Henderson, *Places*, pp. 31–37; Curtis, *Places*, pp. 12–18; and James B. Kracht, "Perception of the Great Plains in Nineteenth Century Folk Songs: Teaching About Place," *Journal of Geography* 88 (November–December 1989), pp. 206–12.

24. Louis A. Woods and Charles F. Gritzner, "Expressions of Rural-Urban Dichotomy in Country Music," in *Program Abstracts of the* A.A.G., ed. by Phillip Kane and David Hornbeck (Washington, D.C.: Association of American Geographers, 1981), p. 194; Louis A. Woods and Charles F. Gritzner, "A Conceptual Model of the Pastoral Elements in Country-Western Music, in A.A.G. *Program Abstracts 1982*, ed. by Daniel R. Fesenmaier and Richard L. Nostrand (Washington, D.C.: Association of American Geographers, 1982); pp. 172–73, and Louis A. Woods and Charles F. Gritzner, "Sacred Time and Sacred Place in Country Music," in A.A.G. *1986 Abstracts*, ed. by Rose F. Roberts (Washington, D.C.: Association of American Geographers 1986), p. 272.

25. Jeffrey J. Gordon, "How to Teach Comprehensive Geography Skills: 'The Wreck of the Edmond Fitzgerald,' " *The Social Studies* 75 (September–October 1984), pp. 186–92.

26. Carney, *Journal of Geography*, 1974; George O. Carney, "T for Texas, T for Tennessee: The Origins of American Country Music Notables," *Journal of Geography* 78 (November 1979), pp. 218–225; Ford, *Journal of Geography*, 1971; Nash, *The Deccan Geographer*, 1968; and Butler, *Ontario Geography*, 1984.

27. Nash, *The Deccan Geographer*, 1968; Ford, *Journal of Geography*, 1971; and Carney, *Journal of Geography*, 1974.

28. Gordon, "Rock-and-Roll Music: A Diffusion Study," 1970; George O. Carney, "From Down Home to Uptown: The Diffusion of Country Music Radio Stations in the United States," *Journal of Geography* 76 (March 1977), pp. 104–10; Lehr, *The Canadian Geographer*, 1983; and Ann E. Kellogg, "Spatial Diffusion of Popular Music Via Radio in the United States" (unpublished Ph.D. dissertation, Michigan State University, Department of Geography, 1986).

29. Curtis and Rose, *Journal of Cultural Geography*, 1983; James R. Curtis and Thomas D. Boswell, *The Cuban-American Experience: Culture, Images and Perspectives* (Totawa, N.J.: Rowman and Allanheld, 1983), pp. 136–57; Lauren C. Post, *Cajun Sketches from the Prairies of Southwest Louisiana* (Baton Rouge: Louisiana State University Press, 1962), pp. 158–62; Glasgow, *Geographical Survey*, 1979; and Rocky Sexton and Robert Kuhlken, "Origin and Diffusion of Zydeco Music" (unpublished manuscript, Louisiana State University, Department of Geography, 1990).

30. Curt Sachs, *Geist und Werden der Musikinstruments* (Berlin: J. Bard, 1929).

31. James R. Renner, "Geographic Implications of the Fiddling Tradition in Oklahoma" (unpublished Master's thesis, Oklahoma State University, Department of Geography, 1979); Margaret Schultz, "An Analytical Methodology for Study of Regional Fiddle Styles Applied to Texas Style Fiddling" (unpublished Master's thesis, Oklahoma State University, Department of Geography, 1977); Charles Gardner, "Anglo-American Fiddling Styles: Core Regions and Diffusion" (unpublished manuscript, Stephen F. Austin State University, Department of Geography, 1979); John M.

Crowley, "Old-Time Fiddling in Big Sky Country," *Journal of Cultural Geography* 5 (Fall–Winter 1984), pp. 47–60.

32. George O. Carney, "Country Music and the South: A Cultural Geography Perspective," *Journal of Cultural Geography* 1 (Fall–Winter 1980), pp. 16–33; Nash, *The Deccan Geographer*, 1968; Malcolm L. Comeaux, "The Cajun Accordion," *Louisiana Review* 7 (1978), pp. 117–28; and Violita, "The Geography of Music," 1980.

33. Elliott Dean Fouts, "A Geographical Analysis of Competitive Drum and Bugle Corps in the United States: 1921–1988" (unpublished Master's thesis, Oklahoma State University, Department of Geography, 1990).

34. George O. Carney, *The Diffusion of the All-Country Music Radio Station in the United States, 1971–1974* (Columbus: Ohio State University, Department of Geography, Diffusion of Innovations Discussion Paper Series No. 38); and Glasgow, *Geographical Survey*, 1979.

35. Marvin W. Mikesell, "Continuity and Change," in *The Origins of Academic Geography in the United States*, ed. by Brian W. Blouet (Hamden, Conn.: Archon Books, 1981), pp. 1–2.

36. Ibid., pp. 9–10.

37. Marvin W. Mikesell, "Tradition and Innovation in Cultural Geography," *Annals Association of American Geographers* 68 (March 1978), p. 10.

38. Ibid., p. 4.

39. Peter Hugh Nash, personal correspondence, Waterloo, Ontario, Canada, January 1989; Jeffrey J. Gordon, personal correspondence, Bowling Green State University, Bowling Green, Ohio, January 1989; Charles F. Gritzner, personal correspondence, South Dakota State University, Brookings, South Dakota, March 1989; Richard V. Francaviglia, telephone interview, Ohio Historical Society, Columbus, Ohio, April 1989; James R. Curtis, personal interview, Oklahoma State University, Stillwater, Oklahoma, April 1989; Jon A. Glasgow, telephone interview, State University of New York, New Paltz, New York, May 1989; Larry Ford, telephone interview, San Diego State University, San Diego, California, May 1989; and A. D. Horsley, telephone interview, Southern Illinois University, Carbondale, Illinois, May 1989.

40. Bruno Nettl, *The Study of Ethnomusicology: Twenty-Nine Issues and Concepts* (Urbana: University of Illinois Press, 1983).

41. Alan Lomax, *Folk Songs of North America* (Garden City, N.Y.: Doubleday, 1960).

42. Kip Lornell, "The Geography of Folk and Popular Music in the United States: An Annotated Bibliography," *Current Musicology* 37–38 (1984), pp. 127–35.

43. Ford, telephone interview, May 1989.

44. David Lowenthal, "The American Scene," *Geographical Review* 58 (January 1968), pp. 61–88.

3

Selected Reading and Listening I

Chapters 1 and 2

Bohlman, Philip V. *The Study of Folk Music in the Modern World.* Bloomington: Indiana University Press, 1988.

Chase, Gilbert. *America's Music: From the Pilgrims to the Present.* Urbana: University of Illinois Press, 1987 (Rev. 3rd ed.).

Cooper, B. Lee. *The Popular Music Handbook.* Littleton, Colo.: Libraries Unlimited, 1984.

———. *Popular Music Perspectives : Ideas, Themes, and Patterns in Contemporary Lyrics.* Bowling Green, Ohio: Popular Press, 1991.

Gillett, Charlie. *The Sound of the City: The Rise of Rock 'n' Roll.* New York: Pantheon, 1984 (Rev. ed.).

Hitchcock, H. Wiley. *Music in the United States: A Historical Introduction.* Englewood Cliffs, N.J.: Prentice Hall, 1974 (2nd ed.).

Lomax, Alan. *The Folk Songs of North America.* Garden City, N.Y.: Doubleday, 1960.

Malone, Bill C. *Southern Music–American Music.* Lexington: University of Kentucky Press, 1979.

———. "Music." *Encyclopedia of Southern Culture.* Edited by Charles Reagan Wilson and William Ferris. Chapel Hill: University of North Carolina Press, 1989, pp. 981–1091.

Nettl, Bruno. *Theory and Method in Ethnomusicology.* New York: Free Press of Glencoe, 1964.

———. *Folk Music in the United States: An Introduction.* Detroit: Wayne State University Press, 1970 (3rd ed.).

————. *Folk and Traditional Music of the Western Continents.* Englewood Cliffs, N.J.: Prentice Hall, 1973 (2nd ed.).

————. *The Study of Ethnomusicology: Twenty-nine Issues and Concepts.* Urbana: University of Illinois Press, 1983.

Oliver, Paul. *The Story of the Blues.* New York: Chilton, 1969.

Sandberg, Larry, and Weissman, Dick. *The Folk Music Sourcebook.* New York: Da Capo Press, 1989 (Rev. ed.).

Shaw, Arnold. *Black Popular Music in America.* New York: Schirmer Books, 1986.

Tudor, Dean. *Popular Music: An Annotated Guide to Recordings.* Littleton, Colo.: Libraries Unilimited, 1983.

Archive of American Folk Song (Library of Congress)
   Afro-American Spirituals, Work Songs, and Ballads (L-3).
   Anglo-American Shanties, Lyric Songs, Dance Tunes, and Spirituals (L-2).
   Cowboy Songs, Ballads, and Cattle Calls (L-26/27).

Folkways/Smithsonian Institution
   Anthology of American Folk Music, Vol. 1, Ballads; Vol. 2, Social Music; Vol. 3, Songs (Folkways 2951/53).
   An Introduction to Gospel Song (Folkways RF-5).
   History of Jazz (Folkways 2801).
   North American Indian and Eskimo Music (Folkways 4541, 2-LP set).
   Smithsonian's Folk Song America (99 vintage recordings from 1919 to 1987, edited by Norm Cohen).

New World Anthology of Recordings
   I'm on My Journey Home: Vocal Styles and Resources in Folk Music (NW-223).
   Songs of Earth, Water, Fire, and Sky: Music of the American Indian (NW-246).

Southern Folk Heritage Series (Atlantic HS-1/complete set)
   Sounds of the South (Atlantic 1346).
   Blue Ridge Mountain Music (Atlantic 1347).
   Roots of the Blues (Atlantic 1348).
   White Spirituals (Atlantic 1349).
   Negro Church Music (Atlantic 1351).
   The Blues Roll On (Atlantic 1352).

Folk Music in America (Library of Congress—A Special Bicentennial Set of 15 LPs—LBC 1-15, 1976).

Part II

Regional and Ethnic Studies of American Folk and Popular Music

The Ozarks: A Reinterpretation Based on Folk Song Materials

George O. Carney

A voluminous body of literature exists on the Ozarks, ranging from poetry and fiction to more scientific studies by economists, sociologists, and geologists. Surprisingly, cultural geographers have not investigated the Ozarks as much as one might expect given the variety of elements that have forged its culture complex. On the occasion of the fortieth anniversary of the publication of *Ozark Folksongs*, this paper focuses on one of the many traits woven into the cultural fabric of the Ozarks—folk music. From a native Ozarkian perspective, it represents a long acquaintance with the region as well as a deep affection for its folk music and how the music has helped shape the character of the area. As for Carl Sauer, this essay is for me a study in "home geography."

Some Previous Studies

A number of studies have outlined the physical boundaries of the Ozarks.[1] Most scholars agree that it is an area of approximately 50,000 square miles that lies in four states. The bulk of the region, or roughly 33,000 square miles, is found in southern Missouri; with an additional 13,000 in northwest Arkansas; 3,000 in northeast Oklahoma; and the remainder in southeast

Reprinted by permission from *North American Culture* 6 (1990): 40–55.

Kansas. In terms of physical geography, it is distinguished by the "hill and holler" topography, karst features (caves, springs, and sinkholes), and an abundance of dolomite and chert (Fig. 4-1).

The first major treatise on the Ozarks by a human geographer was Carl O. Sauer's Ph.D. dissertation completed at the University of Chicago.[2] His study, however, covered only the Missouri portion of the Ozarks in which sixty-four counties were identified as part of the region. More recent analyses of the Ozarks by human geographers include Russel Gerlach's research on ethnic groups and Milton E. Rafferty's overview.[3] Gerlach's study, like Sauer's, covered only the Missouri Ozarks. Gerlach also used sixty-four counties in examining the ethnic composition of the region. On the other hand, Rafferty recognized all or parts of ninety-three counties in the four states of Missouri (sixty-two counties), Arkansas (twenty-two counties), Oklahoma (eight counties), and Kansas (one county).

In 1968 E. Joan Wilson Miller, a cultural geographer, produced a different interpretation of the Ozarks in which folk materials were used as a data base rather than physical, economic, or population statistics.[4] Based on Vance Randolph's four volumes of folk tales, Miller identified an Ozark folk culture region consisting of eight counties in southwestern Missouri and three counties in northwestern Arkansas[5] (Fig. 4-2).

The Folk Song Map

Using the Miller study as a model, this paper focuses on a reinterpretation of the Ozarks based on folk song materials compiled by Vance Randolph.[6] Of

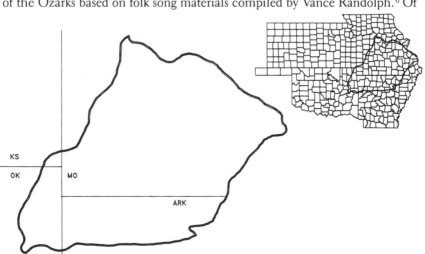

Fig. 4.1. Ozark physical region.

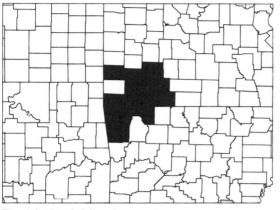
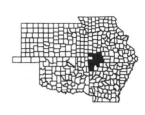

Fig. 4-2. Ozark folk culture region.

the 1,644 texts found in the four volumes of folk songs, 1,566 were located in Missouri, Arkansas, Oklahoma, and Kansas. The remainder were sent to Randolph by informants located outside the four states. Each text included the home town of the informant, which was mapped to determine a distribution pattern in the Ozark states. A minimum of ten folk song locations per county was used as the threshold for inclusion in the folk song map. Located within the four states were twenty-five counties that met the criteria (seventeen in Missouri and eight in Arkansas). Pike, Boone, Jackson, and Henry in Missouri as well as Polk, Garland, and Pulaski in Arkansas were excluded because they fell outside the Ozark physical boundaries.

The most significant cluster is a group of thirteen contiguous counties in southwest Missouri and northwest Arkansas. The folk song map reveals a second cluster of four contiguous counties in south central Missouri (Texas, Wright, Howell, and Oregon) and one outlier in central Missouri (Camden) (Fig. 4-3). In comparing the folk song map with Miller's folk tale region, a nine-county overlap exists in southwest Missouri and northwest Arkansas (seven in Missouri and two in Arkansas). The folk song map, however, adds nine counties not covered by the folk tale region (three in Arkansas and six in Missouri). On the other hand, Miller's region contains two counties not included in this study (Christian in Missouri and Carroll in Arkansas). When both groups of counties are combined, a total of twenty counties fall within the Ozark physical boundary (fourteen in Missouri and six in Arkansas). With the addition of nine counties based on folk song materials, a more complete picture of Ozark folk culture as outlined by Miller is presented (Fig. 4-4).

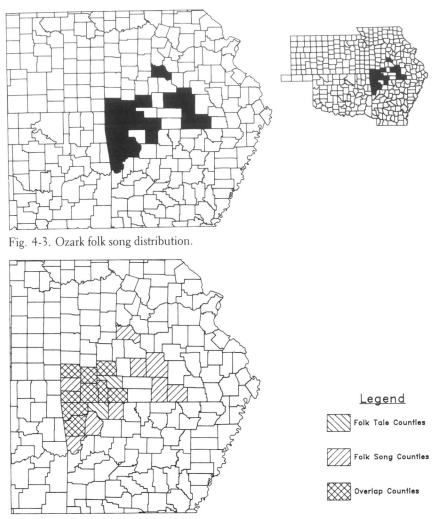

Fig. 4-3. Ozark folk song distribution.

Legend

Folk Tale Counties

Folk Song Counties

Overlap Counties

Fig. 4-4. Combined Ozark folk tale and folk song distribution.

Analysis of the Folk Song Map

To help explain the causes for a plethora of folk songs in some Ozark counties while others yielded few, if any, several observations from a geographical perspective are offered. Items to be considered are: (1) places where Randolph resided during his folk song collection period (c. 1920–40), (2) location of key informants in counties where he did not live, (3) sites of Ozark folk festivals which Randolph helped organize, (4) retreat of Ozark folk culture by the 1920s, and (5) settlement patterns of Ozark ethnic groups.

Randolph purchased a home in 1920 in Pineville, Missouri, where he spent roughly twelve years. It was here in this tiny southwestern Missouri hamlet that he began his serious collection of folk songs. The Pineville period was influenced by two circumstances. First, Randolph married Marie Wilbur, the daughter of one of Pineville's leading citizens, who became one of his most valuable informants. Being the daughter of the local physician, she also helped Randolph establish contacts with people in and around the community.[7] Second, he began editing a monthly column in the Pineville *Democrat* titled "The Songs Grandfather Sang." Readers were invited to contribute texts of old songs to the paper in exchange for a dollar if the words were printed.[8] Through these two avenues as well as other contacts, Randolph gathered 380 folk song texts in McDonald County.

In 1933 Randolph moved to Galena, Missouri, where he lived for approximately the next four years. He resided in the home of the Short "clan," a prominent family in the area. While in Galena he was appointed deputy sheriff, a position he used to make valuable contacts.[9] With Galena serving as home base, Randolph garnered an additional ninety-four songs in Stone County. Following the death of his wife in 1937, Randolph returned to Pittsburg, Kansas (his birthplace), about twenty miles northwest of Joplin, Missouri. For the next three years he cared for his elderly mother, who died in 1938, and spent the rest of his time in Joplin, the county seat of Jasper County.

According to Randolph, who developed a penchant for drink, Joplin was the site of the "nearest good bar" in the area.[10] This three-year period resulted in the collection of another seventy-seven songs from Jasper County. Finally, he spent about a year in Day, Missouri, helping Rosie O'Neill work on her memoirs. O'Neill, a magazine writer/illustrator, was best known as creator of the "Kewpie" doll. According to Randolph's biographer, there was a "genuine intimacy" between the two that many took for romance.[11] From O'Neill and her many friends in Taney County, Randolph collected sixty-nine more texts.

The late 1920s and early 1930s were Randolph's busiest years. In Pineville, Galena, Joplin, and Day, he made contacts with locals at various places of public congregation including Elks' clubs, American Legion dances, and bars.[12] The twenty-some years he spent in or near the four southwestern Missouri counties of McDonald, Jasper, Stone, and Taney yielded 420 of the 1,566 texts, or almost 27 percent of the total (Fig. 4-5).

The locations of Randolph's friends and acquaintances, other than those where he lived from 1920 to 1940, also played a significant role in his field work. One of his favorite informants was May Kennedy McCord of Spring-

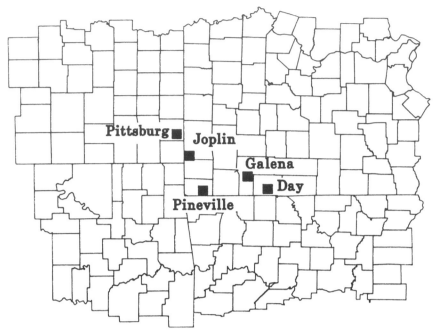

Fig. 4-5. Randolph's places of residence (1920–1940).

field, Missouri, who contributed seventy-two texts and helped collect another eighty-seven songs in Greene County. McCord, known as "Queen of the Hillbillies," was widely known in southern Missouri both as a folk song performer and contributor to the Springfield *Leader-News* and Springfield *Daily News*. Through her "Hillbilly Heartbeats" column in these local newspapers from 1932 to 1942, she was able to contact folk song informants and compile lists of them for Randolph.[13]

In addition to McCord, four other women were principal informants in the four-county cluster in south central Missouri. Two of these females were greatly admired by Randolph. Lillian Short, whom Randolph "loved very much" and wanted to marry, contributed all seventy-four texts from Texas County.[14] Rose Wilder Lane of Mansfield, another of Randolph's female companions, provided all nineteen songs from Wright County. Sylvia Hill of Thayer was the only source for the eleven folk songs from Oregon County, and Cinderella Kinnaird of Willow Springs supplied all but two of the fifteen texts from Howell County. According to Cochran, Randolph's adoration of women resulted in proposals of marriage to no less than seven during his lifetime. His lack of driving ability (Randolph never owned an automobile) may have also been a contributing factor in making acquaintances with

women who owned automobiles, a situation upon which Randolph capitalized in transporting him to remote sections of the Ozarks.[15]

Randolph's main informant in northwest Arkansas was Dr. George Hastings, head of the English department at the University of Arkansas in
Fayetteville. Dr. Hastings, also a collector of folk songs, contributed fifty texts
and introduced Randolph to the legendary Booth Campbell of nearby Cane
Hill, Arkansas, and others who served as informants for the 335 texts from
Washington County.[16] Another collector of folk songs who became a prime
informant for Randolph was Otto Ernest Rayburn, a "hack" journalist who
edited several Ozark-oriented magazines in the 1920s and 1930s. From 1925
to 1930 he published *Ozark Life* in the tiny community of Kingston,
Arkansas; followed by a two-year stint in Eminence, Missouri, where he
produced *Arcadian Magazine*.[17] Rayburn proved to be a valuable resource in
the northwest Arkansas counties as well as the south central counties in
Missouri, where his magazines were published during Randolph's folk song
collection period. He not only contributed folk songs but also compiled a list
of informants in these locations for Randolph.

Additional individuals included in Randolph's list of favorite informants
were Jewell Lamberson of Bentonville, Arkansas, who submitted the majority
of texts from Benton County; Arlie Freeman from Natural Dam and Isabel
Spradley from Van Buren who supplied all but one of the thirty-two songs
from Crawford County, Arkansas; and Myrtle Lain of Linn Creek, who
furnished twelve of the thirteen songs from Camden County, Missouri.

Thus it appears that Randolph's network of contacts was created with the
help of a select group of key acquaintances including female companions,
college professors, and journalists (Fig. 4-6). These prime contacts and their
acquaintances accounted for an additional 680 texts or roughly 43 percent of
the total. Therefore, 1,100 texts, or about 70 percent of the total, were drawn
from in or near places where Randolph resided and from his favorite
informants.

A third factor behind Randolph's folk song materials centers around the
folk festival movement, which began in the 1930s. Plans for a National Folk
Festival emerged in 1933. Preliminary festivals were to be held in fourteen
states with the national event to take place in St. Louis in 1934. May Kennedy
McCord of Springfield was on the National Advisory Committee, and quickly
enlisted her friend Randolph to help with the planning. The first series of
local festivals to screen artists for the St. Louis happening were scheduled in
the Ozarks. Four sites were selected—three in Missouri (Rolla, West Plains,
and Aurora) and one in Arkansas (Eureka Springs). These were to be followed
by an All-Ozark Festival in Springfield (Fig. 4-7).

Randolph was a vital member of the planning committee for each of these

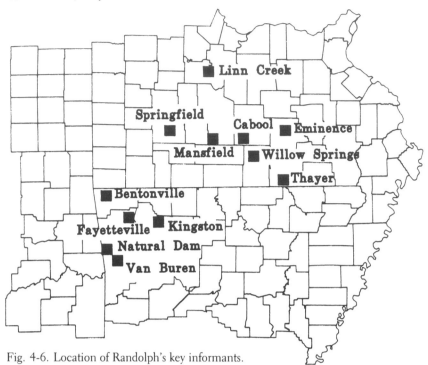

Fig. 4-6. Location of Randolph's key informants.

festivals; however, by the time they were completed, he had become disenchanted with the folk festival concept—he said they were nothing more than Chamber of Commerce boosterism projects.[18] Nevertheless, he made worthwhile contacts with performers (each festival selected a ballad singer, banjo picker, and guitarist to represent its area) and members of the audience (800 attended the Eureka Springs affair). Although Randolph's folk song data do not indicate this, his list of folk song informants from southwest Missouri and northwest Arkansas was expanded due to participation in these events during the peak years of his collection period.

A fourth process may have been at work in affecting the folk song pattern in the Ozarks. Several authors contend that Ozark folk culture, including music, had begun to retreat and disappear by the mid-1920s when Randolph began his folk song fieldwork.[19] They maintain that twentieth-century technology—the three Ts (trains, telephones, and tourism)—were taking their toll on the folk practices of Ozarkians and had brought most of the region's inhabitants into mainstream American culture. Even Randolph declared in 1931 that the Ozark folk were rapidly being assimilated into the popular-culture mode.[20] And Sauer, while not commenting on its effect, noted in

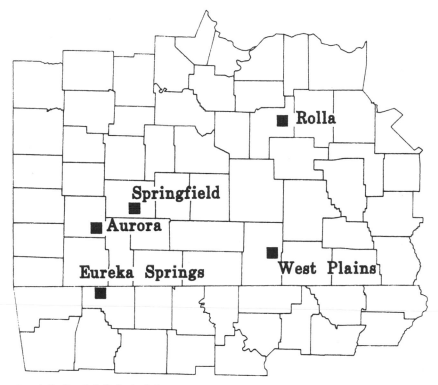

Fig. 4-7. Ozark folk festival sites.

1920 that the Missouri Ozarks had been well dissected by both main lines and branch lines of several railroad companies.[21]

The most dramatic thesis regarding Ozark culture of the 1920s was proposed by a geographer, W. A. Browne. He contended that Ozark folk culture had retreated into the extremely isolated section of the Ozark highlands and was confined to only three counties in southern Missouri by the outbreak of World War I.[22] Therefore, one might argue that folk music as a component of Ozark folklife was rapidly disappearing by the time Randolph began his fieldwork in 1920. Undoubtedly, the uneven distribution of Ozark folk song materials was affected by the improved transportation and communication facilities that were changing the Ozark folk-cultural landscape.

The fifth point concerning folk song distribution centers on the question of settlement patterns in the Ozarks. Bordered by French and German settlements in the eastern and northern Ozarks and the Cherokees in the western Ozarks, the ethnic core of the Ozarks was predominantly white, Anglo-Saxon Americans who had migrated from the Appalachian Mountain sections of eastern Kentucky and Tennessee as well as western North Carolina and Virginia.[23] The French established settlements in the eastern Ozarks in the 1730s with the founding of Ste. Genevieve along the Mississippi River in 1732. They pushed further westward when lead deposits were discovered at Mine La Motte (Madison County) and at Old Mines (Washington County).[24] In the 1840s and 1850s, German Catholics and Lutherans settled in the northern and eastern Ozarks, mixing with the French in the latter area. German communities dotted the landscape of the counties that bordered the Missouri River to the south and the Mississippi River to the west. Town names such as Rhineland, Holstein, New Offenberg, and Friedheim were common. German was the "mother tongue" in a twenty-county area in the northern and eastern Ozarks of Missouri from Benton to Bollinger.[25] The western Ozark portion in northeastern Oklahoma was Cherokee country. They had been forced to move to Indian Territory during the first half of the nineteenth century from their original homeland in the southeastern United States. A "cultural fault line" existed between the Americans in northwest Arkansas and the Cherokees in northeastern Oklahoma based on ethnic variance and historical considerations.[26]

In contrast, the central and western Ozark counties of Missouri and northwestern counties of Arkansas were settled by old-stock Americans who migrated from the southern Appalachian states in the 1820s.[27] As Randolph noted in 1931, these were "nearly all old-timers of English stock, descended from the early colonists."[28] The folk music heritage of these settlers differed from the French, German, and Native American groups surrounding it. These transplanted hillfolk brought a body of folk music that has been described as "the oldest Anglo-American folksongs" and very similar to "what one would find in the Appalachians."[29] The northern, eastern, and western Ozarks, therefore, preserved a different kind of folk music that apparently was of little interest to Randolph. As stated in the first volume of *Ozark Folksongs*, he preferred the old British ballads and American songs that were a part of the cultural baggage brought by the Appalachian migrants who settled the central and southern Ozark counties.[30]

Summary

In summary, a variety of cultural forces related to space and time affected the distribution of folk songs in the Ozarks. The first three processes were associated with Randolph's folk song collection activities during the 1920–40 period: (1) places of residence, (2) favorite informant locations, and (3) folk festival sites. It appears that where Randolph lived during the twenty-year time span (Pineville, Galena, Pittsburg, and Day) influenced the folk song data. Because of the transportation matter, he was somewhat bound to place. The location of key informants was also a contributing factor in the large number of folk songs found in certain Ozark counties (e.g., Greene in Missouri and Washington in Arkansas). And the connections he made through the folk festival outlets helped to expand his collection in those areas where the events were held. The remaining two questions were beyond Randolph's personal experiences. The settlement matter occurred primarily before Randolph's collection period but obviously influenced the type of folk song that appealed to him. It seems to have restricted his folk song territory to those counties where the old-stock Americans from Appalachia lived. The retreat of folk culture concept may also have been a limiting influence and one that Randolph admitted himself. A number of folklorists and geographers of the time suggested that traditional Ozarks culture was on the decline and had retreated to the more rugged Ozarks interior—a factor that may have had an impact on the Randolph collection area.

One might speculate that the folk song data are skewed because of Randolph's parapatetic wanderings: the informants were confined to a handful of "favorites" and the folk festivals represented a mere five sites in the Ozarks. Moreover, some might suggest that Randolph's bias for the "old-time" songs of the Appalachian migrants, while excluding the other ethnic music of the region, were inhibiting factors in the folk song collection process. Similarly, Randolph may have used the folk culture retrenchment idea to his advantage by not seeking informants outside his "home" areas.

Recognizing these limitations, this analysis of the folk song data from a geographic perspective provides another piece to the cultural puzzle of the Ozarks. Like Joan Miller's folk tale study, it offers further evidence in helping to understand the interlocking phenomena within the cultural matrix of a region seemingly neglected by American cultural geographers.

Conclusions

Geographers are familiar with the Ozarks as a physical region, but it is apparent that more study is needed on its cultural geography, especially its folk culture. Are there other traditional materials available for cooperative study between cultural geographers and folklorists such as Miller's follow-up study on Ozark folklore? [31] As Sauer suggested in 1941:

There are lesser lines of historical fieldwork, the place names that have connotation of olden days, folk customs and dialect turns that reveal traditions of times when tradition was a living part of the economy, the memories that still belong to the oldest members of the group.[32]

What geographic approaches may be used to analyze traditional materials of the Ozarks? Several approaches and potential research topics on folklife in general have been outlined by Kip Lornell and Ted Mealor including definition of folk culture regions, cultural diffusion of folk traits, and cultural integration of folk elements.[33] More specifically, how can Ozarks folk music be studied from different geographic perspectives (e.g., the role of place in Ozark folk music or its impact on later generations of musicians from the region)?

Data on nonmaterial culture such as folk tales and folk songs are scarce. Though the Randolph data are not perfect, they do afford cultural geographers and folklorists an opportunity to work more closely on traditional materials. Miller's 1968 study on the Ozarks bridged that gap in what Zelinsky described as "one of the rare explicitly geographic ventures into American folklore."[34] This was one of the major purposes of the Society for the North American Cultural Survey (now the North American Culture Society) when it was founded in 1974 at Pennsylvania State University upon the urging of Zelinsky, a cultural geographer, and Bill Nicolaisen, a folklorist.

Finally, a great deal of discussion has occurred in recent years concerning the cultural convergence theory. Cultural homogenization appears to continue despite efforts directed toward the multiculturalism concept. As we march toward the next century, I contend that regardless of how academics view Ozark culture, a folk music will remain intact and continue to thrive in the region. It will retain its vital role in Ozark folklife and remain as significant to the region as it did to Randolph some sixty years ago:

> The songs of a people certainly cast a singular light upon the life and culture of that people, and no study of the Ozark hillfolk can possibly be complete without consideration of the Ozark folk songs.[35]

Notes

1. Curtis F. Marbut, "The Physical Features of Missouri," *Missouri Geological Survey* 10 (1896); Nevin M. Fenneman, *Physiography of the Eastern United States* (New York: McGraw-Hill, 1938); and William D. Thornbury, *Regional Geomorphology of the United States* (New York: John Wiley and Sons, 1965).

2. Carl O. Sauer, *The Geography of the Ozark Highland of Missouri* (New York: Greenwood Press, 1968).

3. Russel L. Gerlach, *Immigrants in the Ozarks: A Case Study in Ethnic*

Geography (Columbia: University of Missouri Press, 1967), and Milton Rafferty, *The Ozarks: Land and Life* (Norman: University of Oklahoma Press, 1983).

4. E. Joan Wilson Miller, "Ozark Culture Region as Revealed by Traditional Materials," *Annals of the Association of American Geographers* 58 (1968), pp. 51–77.

5. Miller's eleven-county folk culture region was based on the distribution of 383 folk tales and the location of 147 informants drawn from Randolph's *Who Blowed Up the Church House? and Other Ozark Folk Tales* (New York: Columbia University Press, 1952), *The Devil's Pretty Daughter and Other Ozark Folk Tales* (New York: Columbia University Press, 1955), *The Talking Turtle and Other Ozark Folk Tales* (New York: Columbia University Press, 1957), and *Sticks in the Knapsack and Other Ozark Folk Tales* (New York: Columbia University Press, 1958).

6. The four volumes of *Ozark Folksongs* were originally published by the State Historical Society of Missouri from 1946 to 1950. It has been described as one of the most comprehensive regional collections of folk songs ever published. The first volume includes British Ballads and Songs, the second covers Songs of the South and West, the third includes Religious Songs and other Items, and the fourth focuses on Humorous and Play Party Songs. The second edition of *Ozark Folksongs* was published by the University of Missouri Press in 1980.

7. Robert Cochran, *Vance Randolph: An Ozark Life* (Urbana: University of Illinois Press, 1985).

8. W. K. McNeil, "Introduction," in *Ozark Folksongs* by Vance Randolph (Columbia: University of Missouri Press, 1980), pp. 9–28.

9. Cochran, *Vance Randolph: An Ozark Life*.

10. Ibid., p. 67.

11. Ibid., p. 169.

12. Norm Cohen (ed.), *Ozark Folksongs* (Urbana: University of Illinois Press, 1982).

13. Ibid.

14. Cochran, *Vance Randolph: An Ozark Life*, p. 164.

15. Robert Cochran, telephone interview, September 15, 1990.

16. Cohen, *Ozark Folksongs*.

17. McNeil, "Introduction."

18. Cochran, *Vance Randolph: An Ozark Life*.

19. Charles M. Wilson, *Backwoods America* (Chapel Hill: University of North Carolina Press, 1935); Lucile Morris, *Bald Knobbers* (Caldwell, Idaho: Caxton Printers, 1939); and Catherine S. Barker, *Yesterday Today: Life in the Ozarks* (Caldwell, Idaho: Caxton Printers, 1941).

20. Vance Randolph, *The Ozarks: An American Survival of Primitive Society* (New York: Vanguard Press, 1931).

21. Sauer, *The Geography of the Ozark Highland of Missouri*.

22. W. A. Browne, "Some Frontier Conditions in the Hilly Portion of the Ozarks," *Journal of Geography* 28 (1929), pp. 181–88.

23. Miller, "Ozark Culture Region as Revealed by Traditional Materials."

24. Walter A. Schroeder, *The Eastern Ozarks* (Bloomington, Ill.: McKnight and McKnight Publishing Company, 1967).

25. According to the WPA *Guide to 1930s Missouri*, singing and performing music permeated family life and social functions in the French settlements: "music loving Creoles gathered night after night for the pure joy of singing together." They sang tragic ballads like "Le Retour Funeste," the story of a mother who accidentally murdered her son, as well as love ballads such as "L'Amant Malheureux."

26. Russel L. Gerlach, "Rural Religions and Ethnic Groups as Cultural Islands in the Ozarks of Missouri" (unpublished Ph.D. dissertation, University of Nebraska, Department of Geography, 1974).

27. Leslie Hewes, "Oklahoma Ozarks as the Land of the Cherokees," *Geographical Review* 32 (1942), pp. 269–81, and Leslie Hewes, "Cultural Fault Line in the Cherokee Country," *Economic Geography* 19 (1943), pp. 136–42.

28. Gerlach, *Immigrants in the Ozarks*.

29. Randolph, *The Ozarks: An American Survival of Primitive Society*.

30. Cohen, *Ozark Folksongs*, xix.

31. Randolph, *Ozark Folksongs*.

32. E. Joan Wilson Miller, "Ozark Superstitions as Geographic Documentation," *The Professional Geographer* 24 (1972), pp. 223–26.

33. Carl O. Sauer, "Foreward to Historical Geography," *Annals of the Association of American Geographers* 31 (1941), p. 16.

34. Christopher Lornell and Theodore W. Mealor, "Traditions and Research Opportunities in Folk Geography," *The Professional Geographer* 35 (1983), pp. 51–56.

35. Wilbur Zelinsky, *The Cultural Geography of the United States* (Englewood Cliffs, N.J.: Prentice-Hall, 1973), p. 108.

36. Randolph, *The Ozarks: An American Survival of Primitive Society*, p. 222.

Geography on Record: Origins and Diffusion of the Blues

Thomas Arkell

A discerning collection of blues records can act as a vinyl stratigraphy of North America's black population, reflecting the development of a people and of how it responded to the environmental changes that were thrust upon it. The diffusion of blues music, from the west coast of Africa to North America, across the Atlantic to Europe, and back down to Africa, reflects the triangular pattern of the slave trade. Within America, the birth of the blues in the Mississippi Basin and its diffusion north mirror the movement of Africans from the plantations of the rural South to the urban North. The evolution of the sound of the blues reflects their suffering, emancipation, and continuing problems in the cities of America.

Blues is the culmination of several different strands of traditional African-American music born in the American South but with its ancestral origins on the west coast of Africa. It is estimated that between 1680 and 1786 more than two million Africans were shipped across the Atlantic by the British slave trade. With them they brought few material possessions, but they brought intangible elements of their African culture. One of the most important aspects of this culture was music.

The instruments of the New World were unfamiliar to the slaves, and their tribal music found expression in vocal chants and the rhythmic banging of work implements. Several types of Negro folk music emerged from these foundations in the seventeenth and eighteenth centuries.

Reprinted by permission from *Geographical Magazine* 63 (1991): 30–34.

From the black church evolved "spiritual" folk music, which was based on Anglo-Protestant hymns and adapted to suit black traditions and to reflect the slaves' predicament. These religious chants preserved the antiphonal character of the collective song from West Africa.

The secular equivalent to the "spiritual" song was the "work song" of loggers and track liners. A famous medium for this adapted tribal music was the penitentiary chain gang, of which the members would rattle and beat their manacles to make a loud, rhythmic base for their chantings. The chants shared the antiphonality of black spiritual music and its West African predecessor, but the words of the songs expressed the trauma and oppression of the slave population. Love, travel, and death were common themes later adopted by blues music.

In addition to these group songs, workers singing sadly to themselves in the cotton plantations or crying across the fields to fellow slaves gave rise to a type of song known as the "holler." This, liberally structured and modal in character, was the precursor of the solo blues song.

The slaves' music was influenced by the cultures with which it came into contact, such as the folk music of the Irish, English, and Scottish settlers and the francophone Cajun music from the Louisiana swamps. The Anglo-Irish ballad, in vogue during the nineteenth century, was absorbed by popular black culture and is still evident in the repertoire of blues singers today.

The adoption of the ballad was roughly contemporaneous with the American Civil War, which brought about the abolition of slavery in 1863. Where the spiritual song, the work song, and the holler were all products of bondage, tied and subordinated to religious ceremony, the ballad, which traditionally told stories, could be used to express the slaves' new found freedom, recounting tales of victories over erstwhile masters. It was through the ballad that black folk heroes, such as John Hardy and Joe Turner, were created.

By the turn of the century, the fusion of these traditions of black and white folk music was complete. It produced an embryonic form of the blues—a twelve-bar folk tune, the name of which came from the Victorian expression "to have the blue devils," meaning to have a fit of depression or melancholy. Its geographical hearth in America's Deep South corresponded with the fertile cotton-producing plains of the Mississippi Basin, bound by the Appalachian Mountains and the Ozark Plateau to the north, the Everglades to the south, and the arid interior of Texas to the west. The cotton zone stretched from east Texas through Louisiana, Mississippi, Alabama, and Georgia, to the coast of South Carolina, and also followed the course of the Mississippi River northward as far as Memphis, and included parts of Arkansas. Throughout this zone there was a large slave population with a flourishing tradition of black folk music and a well-established church—hence its familiar name

"Bible Belt." Ethnomusicologists believe the musical nucleus was the triangle among the Mississippi towns of Natchez, Jackson, and Greenville, and that Memphis was a possible center of propagation (Fig. 5-1).

Although economic hardship meant that former slaves were usually tied sharecroppers on plantations in the South, their nominal liberty led to a gradual diffusion of their musical culture. Communications routes, especially the railways, the Mississippi River, and highways 49 and 61, served as corridors for this diffusion, as songsters traveled among public dances and medicine and minstrel shows. Their repertoire was varied, consisting of ballads, religious songs, ragtime, and blues, usually played on a banjo or an improvised string instrument (succeeded by the guitar and the harmonica).

The first generation of bluesmen was born in the 1880s and was recording between the mid-1920s and the late 1930s (Fig. 5-2). Their music was known as "rural" or "country" blues. Varying geographical and cultural contexts led to the emergence of differing regional styles. Alabama remained tied to its

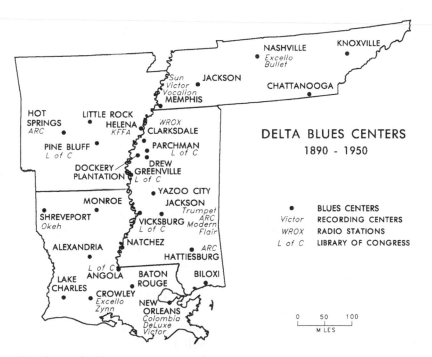

Fig. 5-1. Delta blues centers (1890–1950). *Source*: Paul Oliver, *The Story of the Blues* (New York: Chilton Book Company, 1973).

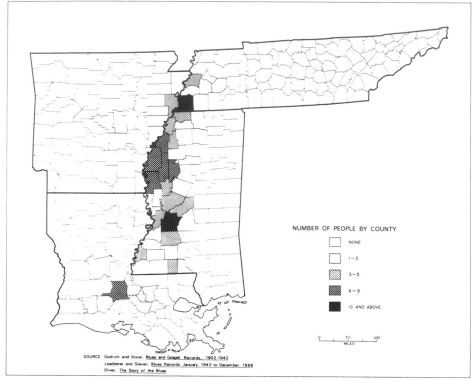

Fig. 5-2. Recorded blues musicians (1890–1940). *Source*: Godrich and Dixon, *Blues and Gospel Records, 1902–1942*; Leadbitter and Slaven, *Blues Records: January, 1943 to December, 1966*; Oliver, *The Story of the Blues*.

gospel traditions (exemplified by Clifford Gibson and Jaybird Coleman), while the Memphis style was more influenced by the secular traditions that preceded the blues. Memphis blues blended the "songster" tradition with string bands, and rhythm sections consisting of washboards and jugs, and was typified by Gus Cannon's Jug Stompers. The Mississippi delta had its own brand of blues known as the delta blues, which was characterized by the "bottleneck" or slide guitar used by Bukka White, Charley Patton, and Robert Johnson. In Texas, western Louisiana, and Arkansas, the blues remained heavily influenced by the cotton-field holler, exemplified by Blind Lemon Jefferson and Huddie "Leadbelly" Ledbetter. Meanwhile, on the Atlantic coast and in the Appalachian foothills of Georgia and South Carolina, blues was more influenced by the white rural "hillbilly" tradition, which inspired the music of Blind Willie McTell, Sonny Terry, and Brownie McGhee.

Like many other popular musical traditions, the blues was a creative

Beale Street in Memphis (photo courtesy of Jim Curtis).

response to oppression, but it lacked the anger and aggression of its contemporary, the Irish rebel song; and subsequent oppression-induced styles, including punk rock, which developed in urban Britain in the 1970s. Early blues also lacked the overt revolutionary flavor of its Caribbean cousin—another musical response to the slave trade—which developed into reggae. In contrast, the blues was characterized by a tone of resignation. But this apparent submission to Western and Christian ideals concealed the revolutionary character of the music. Jahn Janheinz writes of blues in *Munta: The Outline of the New African Culture*: "Melancholy is a mask—the lament hides the protest."

Early bluesmen addressed political issues most critical to them, however, including injustice, police discrimination, and conditions in jails and for chain gangs. Guitar Welch's "Electric Chair Blues" and Furry Lewis's "Judge Harsh Blues" are good examples of penitentiary songs with political overtones. Strikes, job layoffs, and unemployment were covered by Doctor Ross in "General Motors Blues," while the principles of American democracy were satirized in Leadbelly's "Bourgeois Blues." Prohibition was also a common target—Sonny Boy Williamson II and Peetie Wheatstraw were particularly vociferous in their demands for whisky.

Although blues most obviously conveyed immediate, personal experiences, it was also supposed to represent the collective class consciousness of the wider community. The music was usually performed to a racially and socially homogeneous audience and dealt with themes such as poverty, inflation, and the extreme misery of living conditions in the Deep South. Big Bill Broonzy's "Plow Hand Blues" and J. B. Lenoir's "Born Dead" are bitter testimonies of the hardships endured.

The Great Depression of the 1930s caused mass migrations in America. Sharecroppers left the southern plantations in the thousands and moved northward and westward in search of employment in the cities. Their music went with them. The general pattern of migration was thus: from the central southern states to the large urban centers by the Great Lakes; from the southeastern states to New York; and from Texas, Louisiana, and Arkansas to Los Angeles and Oakland. Midwestern cities, such as St. Louis and Kansas City, were staging posts along the migration routes, while Chicago became a pole of attraction for black artists from all over the South.

The growth of recording studios and the increasingly widespread use of the radio enabled the blues to reach an ever-wider audience as a definitive form of music and the expression of the black community. But, having crossed geographical boundaries, regional styles merged into a single national form.

By this time blues music had achieved a foothold on American musical culture. It had already played a significant role in the development of jazz in New Orleans and had begun to influence white popular music, including bluegrass in Kentucky and western swing in Texas. Cajun music was also influenced by the blues.

The first recorded style was classic blues—played by W. C. Handy and Bessie Smith, which developed in bars in the black quarters of Chicago, St. Louis, and Harlem. Its roots were firmly in the earlier rural blues of southern country festivals, but it incorporated elements of jazz, giving it a distinct character. As the 1920s drew to a close, classic blues was on the decline and the predecessor of urban blues was rising in its place. This style, known as "barrelhouse," was influenced by the piano music of the logging camps in the southwestern states and emerged when musicians ceased their migratory search for employment and settled in the urban centers of the North and the Midwest.

Urban blues developed out of another large wave of migration from the South during the postwar years. Muddy Waters, Elmore James, Howlin' Wolf, and John Lee Hooker were among the migrants who imported the Mississippi style to Chicago and Detroit, while Lightnin' Hopkins and Jimmy Witherspoon were the pioneers of a Texo-Californian style in Los Angeles.

In its new urban environment, the blues began to take on a new form. Larger audiences necessitated the use of electric amplification (popularized by T-Bone Walker), and the music became harder and grittier, reflecting its industrial surroundings. The lyrics told of employment discrimination and house-market manipulation, which had created a black underclass. Jimmy Wilson's "Tin Pan Alley" and Juke Boy Bonner's "Lyons Avenue" outline the extent to which society had degenerated in black districts of New York and Houston.

Urban blues, in turn, branched into rhythm and blues (R&B), which drew on swing and jump jazz rhythms. R&B—exemplified by the music of Bo Diddley, Jackie Wilson, and B. B. King, and which diversified into soul, funk, and other styles—is considered to be the progenitor of rock and roll.

The reawakening of a black identity and the campaigning for civil rights during the 1960s provided an unprecedented opportunity for the blues to become a vehicle for political lobbying. This niche, however, was filled by the more palatable soul music, which had become more integrated into the American social system. As a result, soul began to replace blues as the principal musical expression of the North American black. Many former urban blues musicians, including Ray Charles and James Brown, defected to soul, while gospel singers such as Aretha Franklin and the Staple Singers moved increasingly further from blues.

Meanwhile blues spread across the Atlantic to Britain, where white artists, namely Alexis Korner and John Mayall, began developing their own form of R&B. British blues was typified by Eric Clapton and early Fleetwood Mac—both spawned by John Mayall's Bluesbreakers. Later, bands such as the Blind Hobo Jug Stompers drew directly on rural blues, while other variations of R&B, including southern rock (popularized by the Allman Brothers Band), persisted in the South, where tastes were more conservative.

Despite a gradual decline in the popularity of blues, musicians from many disciplines have recently become more interested in its origins. American and European compositions have been laced with African rhythms and chants. Simultaneously, the influence of the blues has come full circle back to Africa, where musicians have blended it—in its highly evolved form—with their own traditional forms. The music of Ali Farka Toure (known as the "John Lee Hooker of Mali") is a model example of this hybrid style. Similarly, in other African countries, especially Zaire, an Afro-Brazilian fusion is in vogue.

But, after a century of evolution, blues is seen by the disaffected youth of America as an inadequate means to convey their discontent. As a musical tradition that has been absorbed and accepted by the surrounding white majority, many blacks feel that blues no longer offers a sufficient platform for a protesting minority. Black Americans are also abandoning the blues owing to its association with their unhappy past and because they feel the need to liberate themselves from the music's apparently closed and repetitive structure. Blues clubs have lost their role as the social and cultural centers of the black inner city. The new generation is embracing rap music, which is more aggressive and addresses the problems of racism and class. Nonetheless, blues has spanned three continents and has transected barriers of age, culture, race and, to a lesser extent, language. The simple and natural rhythms, derived from African tribal music, still have a wide appeal and will continue to influence music throughout the world.

6

The Geography of Zydeco Music

Robert Kuhlken and Rocky Sexton

I never thought I'd ever hit Europe, but I know one thing: the way
I was playin' that accordion it was goin' to go somewhere . . . I
know what I had goin' was goin' to go somewhere.[1]

Zydeco music is a unique blend of Afro-American and Afro-French traditions indigenous to southwest Louisiana. Born out of close interaction between the Cajun (white) and Creole (black) populations of Louisiana, zydeco music developed into a distinctive genre when it received a healthy dose of rhythm and blues influence from the urban areas of east Texas.[2] Its current popularity as dance music is directly tied to the past when house dances were the primary form of entertainment and interaction for rural Creoles. These gatherings featured music that was a precursor to modern zydeco, which contributed to its development.

Methodology

Music can be a cultural trait possessing distinctive spatial attributes. Folk and ethnic music in particular often exhibit a strong regional identity. George Carney has spearheaded efforts by cultural geographers to recognize and chart the distribution and diffusion of the many forms of American music and notes a curious lack of attention to this aspect of the cultural landscape.[3]

Reprinted by permission from the *Journal of Cultural Geography* 12 (1991): 27–38.

We examine here the concept of a hearth area for zydeco music by utilizing a cultural-historical approach in delineating its origins within the Creole area of southwest Louisiana. Following the example of a simple yet effective model utilized by Carney, birthplace and residence maps of notable zydeco musicians give an indication of the diffusionary movement of the music.[4] Although the core area remains quite definitive, the residential relocations of musicians follow the general trend in Creole population movement and hence may be viewed as factors in its diffusion. Subsequent diffusion can be attributed to the commercial recording and distribution of the music and the national and international concert tours of zydeco musicians. The locations of clubs, dance halls, and church halls where zydeco music is featured reveal another glimpse into its geography.

Origins of Zydeco

Although possibly stemming from African roots, the term zydeco is most often attributed to the folk expression "Les haricots sont pas sales" (The beans are not salted).[5] This saying reflects hard times, with the connotation that people are so poor they cannot even afford to put salt pork in their beans. Zydeco is a musical style that arose out of a mutual acculturation process in Louisiana, when African and Afro-Caribbean music came into contact with European styles and instrumentation. The primary example of this process occurred in the prairie region of southwest Louisiana where Cajuns and Creoles represent the two main ethnic groups.

During the first few decades of this century Cajun and Creole music were very similar. Within this context zydeco music emerged due to a retention of African melodic and rhythmic styles popular with black audiences. John Roberts notes how African-derived Creole elements often transformed white music.[6] By blending in African rhythms, Creole musicians created highly syncopated versions of traditional Cajun songs, leading Daniel Wolff to comment in 1988 that "to this day, Cajun music and zydeco remain distinct—the major difference between the two being racial."[7] In addition it was during this same period (1920–40) that Creole performers began to be influenced by blues music.[8]

An earlier form of zydeco, called la-la, or simply French music, utilized the same instuments as Cajun music. The fiddle, which came into Louisiana from Canada after 1755 by way of the Acadian diaspora, was the standard lead instument.[9] Mary Wilson reports that "the fiddle was used by Afro-American musicians as the primary instrument—and at times the lone instrument—for entertainment."[10] Although some elderly Creole musicians still favor the fiddle, it is rare in contemporary zydeco.

Zydeco music now features the accordion, which arrived in south Louisiana sometime during the latter part of the nineteenth century. Most scholars feel it was introduced by German or midwestern settlers who came to this area after the Civil War.[11] Geographer Malcolm Comeaux places the accordion in the Louisiana landscape during the 1880s, although an earlier introduction (1830) has been suggested by Florence Borders.[12] The typical model was a diatonic accordion with one row of buttons, which was adopted by both white and black musicians. Availability of the accordion was enhanced by mail-order outlets, and it soon displaced the fiddle as a lead instument.[13] These two instuments, along with the *tit fer*, or triangle, constitute what folklorist Nicholas Spitzer has termed the "original triumvirate of Cajun folk music."[14]

When zydeco emerged from its Cajun-related roots and began to be influenced heavily by rhythm and blues, the simple diatonic accordion was no longer adequate. As Alan Grovenar notes, "With the migration of Creoles to urban areas, such as Lake Charles and Houston, the more versatile piano accordion replaced the one-row model."[15] Blues scholar Paul Oliver attributes the preference for the piano accordion to its capability to tackle "blues in many keys."[16] And because zydeco is first and foremost dance music, the accordion served admirably as lead instument: "Its resonating, high volume was ideal for noisy dance halls."[17]

The washboard has replaced the triangle as a rhythm instrument and has evolved in south Louisiana into the *frottoir* or rubboard, worn on the chest like a breastplate. The frottoir is the signature instrument of zydeco music. Barry Ancelet and Mathe Allain have suggested its antecedents: "Rasps and notched gourds used in Afro-Caribbean music were replaced by washboards, called *frottoirs*, rubbed with thimbles, spoons, or bottle openers."[18] Spitzer relates how the modern version of this instument "became popular in the 1930s when sheetmetal was introduced to the area for roofing and barn siding."[19] Currently frottoirs are manufactured in Lafayette, Louisiana, by the Champagne Sheet Metal Company, which has shipped orders all over the country as well as to Nova Scotia and Japan.[20]

Zydeco within Black Creole Culture

The term Creole, as used here, refers to the Afro-French inhabitants of southwest Louisiana and their relatives in Texas and California. These people are the result of biological and cultural mixing that has been occurring since the beginning of the eighteenth century. The process within Louisiana started on French- and Spanish-owned plantations of the lower Mississippi Valley, where masters often freed their "colored" offspring. Children of these African/European unions came to be known as the *Gens de Couleur Libre* or Free People of Color. Acculturation was accelerated by the Haitian Revolution, which caused an influx of French, slaves, and *Gens de Couleur Libre* into Louisiana. An example of this immigration was the year 1809 when 1,828 whites, 1,978 *Gens de Couleur Libre*, and 1,991 slaves arrived in New Orleans.[21]

By the dawn of the Civil War, the *Gens de Couleur Libre*, or Creoles as they were called, and other African Americans, had penetrated into the prairie region of Louisiana. There the Creoles came into further contact with Acadians, Spanish, Germans, and Native Americans. By the beginning of the twentieth century, many African Americans had been heavily influenced by the French culture of the region. Most of these people spoke French, attended Catholic churches, and participated in small-scale agriculture, raising crops such as cotton, sugarcane, yams, and rice.

In rural areas prior to the introduction of modern innovations such as electricity, radio, and automobiles, entertainment forms were of a less complex nature. In southwest Louisiana one activity that provided an open forum for communal gatherings was the house dance. This setting facilitated interaction in the form of singing, dancing, eating, and visitation. Most house dances occurred on weekends and were frequented by people living within a few miles of the host location. The bands comprised local musicians who were compensated with a few dollars collected by "passing the hat," charging a small admission, or selling refreshments.[22]

Music at dances was provided by bands that played the precursor to zydeco music. These groups often would consist of only an accordion player accompanied by a rubboard or frottoir. A larger band might include string instruments such as the fiddle and guitar, along with the tit fer. Lyrics were sung in French, the dominant language in the area at the beginning of this century. Dances included polkas, mazurkas, two-steps, and *valses*. In some areas a more African-influenced, upbeat version of the two-step was used. This dance was called a "la-la," and eventually the term came to be applied both to house dances in general and to the music played at these functions. Other French and/or African words used to designate house dances were *un bal, un soire, un gumbo, un diverti,* and *un zydeco*.

Later in the twentieth century traditional Creole culture was affected by urbanization and modernization. Improved roads and availability of automobiles made travel much easier. The introduction of innovations such as radio, movie theaters, and eventually television resulted in forms of entertainment that served as a lure away from traditional activites like the house dances.

Outmigration Patterns

Outmigration from southwest Louisiana is generally considered a World War II and postwar phenomenon. With the onset of American involvement in the war, an immediate need for labor developed in areas where ships, munitions factories, and military bases were under construction. The ship-building industry that developed in the Beaumont–Port Arthur–Houston area of Texas, for example, was a strong lure to the Creoles of adjacent Louisiana. Aircraft and munitions factories in southern California likewise resulted in an outmigration from the prairie region.[23] At the close of the war many Creoles chose to remain in these areas.

A specific example of outmigration was reported from the town of Frilot Cove, St. Landry Parish.[24] Of thirteen adults questioned about the locations of their siblings the following replies were given: thirty-seven siblings were reported living in Frilot Cove, twenty-two lived elsewhere including those in California (five), Houston (three), Michigan (two), Beaumont (one), and Arkansas (one).

Emergence of Modern Zydeco

As Creoles began to leave Louisiana for more urban settings the traditional music they took with them was influenced by urban blues music. This process reached its peak in the post–World War II urban areas and is personified by Clifton Chenier, the late "King of Zydeco." Chenier was born in 1925, the son of a musician and sharecropper, in Opelousas, the center of Louisiana Creole country. In 1947 he moved to Lake Charles, then in 1958 to Houston, where he became heavily influenced by blues music. It is Chenier who popularized the term zydeco and specifically linked it to his music, which ranged from blues sung in French and accompanied by an accordion and frottoir, to more traditional Afro-French songs. Thus it can be seen that zydeco developed out of a rural Afro-French tradition with a blues influence that became more pronounced due to outmigration and urbanization of Creoles.

It is in this context that dance halls and clubs began to emerge as commercial enterprises in contrast to the earlier house dances which had been communal, nonprofit affairs. Despite a more commercial, adult-

El Cid O's Zydeco Club in Lafayette, Louisiana (photo courtesy of Rocky Sexton and Robert Kuhlken).

oriented setting, many clubs and dance halls have retained something of a family, or at least a familiar, atmosphere. As in the past, group interaction occurs against a backdrop of zydeco music, a musical form with roots in the prairies of southwest Louisiana.

Carriers for Diffusion

Several specific indicators of diffusion may be examined in order to document the spread of zydeco music from its hearth area. Following the example of a spatial representation utilized by Carney for bluegrass and country music, we have located the birthplaces and subsequent places of residence for fifteen notable zydeco musicians, all born in the Creole area of southwest Louisiana (Fig. 6-1). Residential relocation has mostly occurred in east Texas and California (Fig. 6-2). Since most zydeco performers were not able to become full-time professional musicians in southwest Louisiana, the wage opportunities offered by the Texas Gulf Coast area and California prompted this migrational pattern. Their music was appreciated by the Creole populations living in these areas; thus, zydeco music was not abandoned. Zydeco has remained functional within the Creole culture, and continues to nurture it in a contemporary setting.

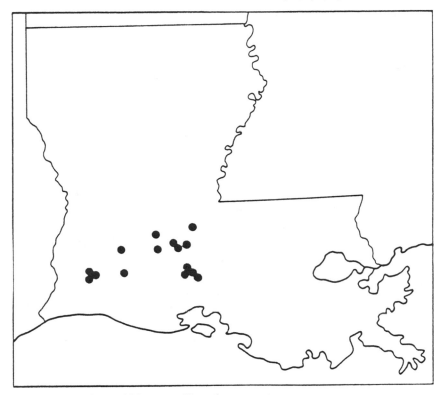

Fig. 6-1. Birthplaces of fifteen notable zydeco musicians.

Obviously, the hearth area remains well defined, judging from the number of musicians who still reside and perform there. Support for the music *in situ* takes the form of patronage at concerts and dance halls, radio air time as well as entire morning radio programs devoted to zydeco, and perhaps most significantly, an annual festival that takes place in the rural community of Plaisance, Louisiana. The Zydeco Festival began in 1982 and consists of a full roster of bands taking the stage one after another in a twelve-hour continuous celebration. Its location in the heart of the hearth exerts considerable centripetal force and reflects the strength of zydeco music as a nonmaterial culture trait.

One of the primary vehicles for diffusion of music is the actual movement of musicians as they perform at a number of locations during a concert tour. The first extraterritorial exposure of a large non-Creole audience to live zydeco took place when Chenier appeared at the Berkeley Blues Festival in 1966. In 1967 he played concerts in San Francisco and Los Angeles, and in

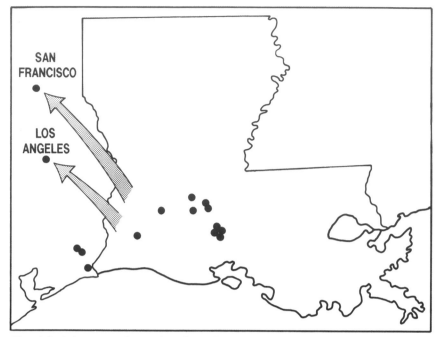

Fig. 6-2. Subsequent places of residence for fifteen notable zydeco musicians.

1969 he appeared at the Ann Arbor, Michigan, Blues Festival and also went on a European tour. In the liner notes to one of Chenier's albums, record producer and folklorist Chris Strachwitz has written:

> In the fall of 1971 Clifton Chenier and his band played a series of concerts, clubs, and dances on the west coast. Two nights they were booked to play for the French-Creole population of the Bay area which has remained a tight-knit group since moving out here from Louisiana. The dances were held in St. Mark's Hall in Richmond, California.[25]

After the 1971 tour Chenier's popularity soared. He began to wear a crown on stage, calling himself the "King of Zydeco." John Broven writes that "During the seventies Clifton Chenier's name became synonymous with zydeco."[26] After many successful concert tours during the 1970s and 1980s, Chenier made one of his last appearances at the 1987 Zydeco Festival in Plaisance.[27] His death soon after deprived the world of a soulful and masterful musician who was justifiably proud of his contributions to and representation of Creole culture.

National and international concert tours have served to spread zydeco around the world, bringing the experience of this infectious dance music to large numbers of people who may never get the opportunity to travel to Louisiana. Artists such as Rockin' Dopsie, Nathan Williams, Willis Prudhomme, Terrance Simien, Queen Ida (based in San Francisco), and Buckwheat Dural have all toured extensively. Zydeco bands are frequently featured in the larger blues festivals around the nation, such as those in San Francisco and Chicago.

Zydeco music has been well received in Europe ever since Chenier first toured there in 1969, with stops in London, Paris, Copenhagen, Oslo, and Vienna. Its popularity overseas has increased dramatically since then. Rockin' Dopsie and Fernest Arceneaux have both toured Europe. Simien completed a successful tour of Switzerland in 1987 and followed with a tour of North Africa in 1989. Indeed, the demand for this music prompted the following liner notes by Jeff Hannusch on an album by BooZoo Chavis:

> One of the surprising musical trends of the 1980s has been the sudden international acceptance of zydeco. Once a style of music whose popularity was confined to southwest Louisiana, today zydeco commands worldwide attention and is considered by many to be the most exciting brand of ethnic music in America. [28]

Recently, a unique and intentional form of international diffusion of zydeco music took place when Delton Broussard and the Lawtell Playboys, from Louisiana's St. Landry parish, traveled to the Seychelles Islands, off the east coast of Africa, to perform several concerts for the native Creole population. [29] In this manner zydeco is beginning to serve not only as a form of entertainment but also as a link between Creoles of Louisiana and other such populations that emerged during the colonial era.

Perhaps the most effective carrier of diffusion of zydeco has been the commercial recording and widespread distribution of the music on records, tapes, and lately, compact digital discs. Early forms of zydeco recordings by Douglas Bellard, Amede Ardoin, and others were strictly for regional distribution. Beaumont musician Clarence Garlow had a few minor hits in the early 1950s, paving the way for two back-to-back releases that began the commercial success of recorded zydeco: "Paper in My Shoe" by BooZoo Chavis in 1954, followed by Chenier's "Ay-Tete-Fee" in 1955. [30] The ultimate success of recorded zydeco has led one reviewer to comment that "we have reached a point where it seems like zydeco artists monopolize the ethnic category in the Grammy awards." [31]

Until recently, as national labels have attempted to capitalize on the growing popularity of this music, the commercial recording and distribution of most zydeco have been shepherded by two independent labels: Chris Strachwitz's Arhoolie Records in El Cerrito, California, and Floyd Soileau's *Maison de Soul* in Ville Platte, Louisiana. Strachwitz produced some of Chenier's first recordings, as well as those of other east Texas artists during the early 1960s, some of which are now being reissued. He notes a demand for recorded zydeco among the major east and west coast market areas, with San Francisco somewhat stronger than Los Angeles.[32] Soileau has been recording both Cajun and Creole musicians since the late 1950s and feels that the recorded music plays a very important part in keeping the culture intact. While over half of the *Maison de Soul* releases are sold within the major zydeco market area between New Orleans and Houston, larger cities elsewhere also provide a market. St. Louis and especially Atlanta, where an emerging Creole community exists, appear particularly strong.[33]

Further evidence for the successful transplantation and viability of the music is presented in a map of nightclubs, dance halls, and church halls that regularly feature zydeco (Fig. 6-3). Again, the core area remains strong, but east Texas and the San Francisco Bay area are also represented, revealing the popularity of the music among Creole residents in those locations.[34] Houston is particularly visible, not only due to several zydeco clubs, but because the Catholic churches there encourage the music's traditional function within Creole culture as a way to foster solidarity and group cohesion. As Grovenar relates:

Fig. 6-3. Location of night clubs, dance halls, and churches that regularly feature zydeco music.

Today most Catholic churches in Houston with large Creole memberships hold zydeco dances. Zydeco is welcomed by the Catholic churches not only because the dances are an important source of revenue, but they allow Creoles to preserve their heritage by meeting family and friends, eating Creole food, and listening and dancing to traditional music.[35]

It is this kind of setting that hearkens back to the house dances of rural southwest Louisiana where zydeco originated and therefore allows the music to reassert its functional role in a new urban context.

Discussion

From its origins amid the prairies of southwest Louisiana, zydeco music has spread to other areas of the country, most notably California and east Texas. It is now recognized as "the major ethnic style in far southeast Texas."[36] Los Angeles holds an annual Cajun and Creole festival featuring zydeco musicians. In the San Francisco Bay area, St. Mark's Hall in Richmond has been the scene of regular zydeco dances for many years.

That this music is the expression of a living dynamic culture may be seen from the continuing attempts at stylistic innovation and assimilation of newer forms. The influence of jazz, for example, is apparent from the many bands that now include a saxophone in their line-up. In 1977, Chenier was having fun with what one reviewer termed "zydisco."[37] Strachwitz remembers that it was always a problem during recording sessions to get Chenier to stick to the older forms of zydeco but praised his sense of innovation: "Clifton is not only a unique artist in the zydeco field, but he is a jazzman, an endless improviser."[38]

Today's leading musicians continue to experiment. Ben Sandmel reports that "some popular zydeco artists, such as Buckwheat Dural and Terrance Simien, have begun to draw heavily on contemporary urban soul sources, to the consternation of purists."[39] A perennial crowd pleaser at the zydeco festival in Plaisance is any of several different versions of a soul-inspired dance tune originally known as the "Harlem Shuffle." Various bands now include this tune in their repertoire and have transformed it with zydeco rhythm and new lyrics into the "zydeco shuffle."

As indicated by the data, zydeco music is a recent phenomenon in terms of widespread popularity outside of Creole communities. Its significance should not be viewed solely in terms of the number of concerts performed or records sold, although commercial acceptance has helped to legitimize the musical form, resulting in an economic incentive for the preservation and spread of zydeco.

Despite exposure outside of the core area, zydeco music is still associated with an Afro-French or Creole cultural tradition. The recent rise in zydeco's popularity is matched with an upsurge of Creole ethnic identity at both the public and personal level. Ann Savoy has expressed this development:

> The black Creole culture is rich and is growing in its appreciation of its modern zydeco music. Creole musicians look with pride and optimism at their culture today, and zydeco is taking the world by surprise. [40]

One elderly Creole during an interview remarked that zydeco "brings back the old system" in reference to revitalization of traditional Creole culture. Just as Cajun music has served to foster cultural solidarity among the white French of southwest Louisiana, zydeco music is playing a powerful role in the development of a modern Creole identity.

Notes

1. Clifton Chenier, interview in Ann Savoy, ed., *Cajun Music: A Reflection of a People* (Eunice, La.: Bluebird Press, 1984), p. 381.

2. The term Creole is problematic because in the past both blacks and whites utilized the designation. Unlike New Orleans where a certain amount of controversy still continues over usage of the term, in present-day southwest Louisiana, Creole is only applied to persons of Afro-French descent.

3. George Carney, ed., *The Sounds of People and Places: Readings in the Geography of American Folk and Popular Music* (Lanham, Md.: University Press of America, 1987), and George O. Carney, "Geography of Music: Inventory and Prospect," *Journal of Cultural Geography* 10 (Spring/Summer 1990), pp. 35–48.

4. George Carney, "T for Texas, T for Tennessee: The Origins of Country Music Notables," *Journal of Geography* 78 (November 1979), pp. 218–25, and George Carney, "Bluegrass Grows All Around: The Spatial Dimensions of a Country Music Style," *Journal of Geography* 73 (April 1974), pp. 34–55.

5. Barry Ancelet, "Zydeco/Zarico: Beans, Blues, and Beyond," *Black Music Research Journal* 8 (March 1988), pp. 33–49.

6. John Roberts, *Black Music of Two Worlds* (New York: Praeger, 1972), p. 55.

7. Daniel Wolff, "Clifton Chenier," *The Nation* 246 (March 19, 1988), p. 390.

8. Nicholas Spitzer, *Zydeco and Mardi Gras: Creole Identity and Performance Genres in Rural French Louisiana* (unpublished dissertation, University of Texas, Department of Anthropology, 1986), p. 337.

9. Ann Savoy, ed., *Cajun Music: A Reflection of a People* (Eunice, La.: Bluebird Press, 1984), p. 4.

10. Mary Wilson, *Traditional Louisiana French Folk Music: An Argument for Its Preservation and Utilization as a State Cultural Heritage* (unpublished dissertation, University of Pittsburgh, Department of Music, 1977), p. 67.

11. Steven Del Sesto, "Cajun Social Institutions and Cultural Configurations," in *The Culture of Acadiana: Tradition and Change in South Louisiana*, ed. by Steven Del Sesto and Jon Gibson (Lafayette: University of Southwestern Louisiana, 1975), pp. 1–11; and Nicholas Spitzer, "Zydeco," in *Encyclopedia of Southern Culture*, ed. by Charles Wilson and William Ferris (Chapel Hill: University of North Carolina Press, 1989), pp. 1037–38.

12. Malcolm Comeaux, "The Cajun Accordian," *Louisiana Review* 7 (Winter 1978), pp. 117–28, and Florence Borders, "Researching Creole and Cajun Musics in New Orleans," *Black Music Research Journal* 8 (November 1988), pp. 15–31.

13. Nicholas Spitzer, Review of Savoy, *Cajun Music: A Reflection of a People*, in *Journal of Country Music* 11 (June 1987), pp. 47–50.

14. Mary Wilson, quote by Spitzer, p. 91.

15. Alan Grovenar, *Meeting the Blues* (Dallas, Tex.: Taylor Publishing, 1988), p. 141.

16. Paul Oliver, "Clifton Chenier," in the *New Grove Dictionary of American Music*, ed. by H. Hitchcock and S. Sadie (New York: Grove's Dictionaries of Music, 1986), p. 414.

17. Ben Sandmel, "Allons Danser: Cajun and Creole Bands Are Conserving Native Music," *The Atlantic* 260 (July 1987), p. 88.

18. Barry Ancelet and Mathe Allain, *Travailler, C'est Trop dur: The Tools of Cajun Music* (Lafayette, La.: Lafayette Natural History Museum Association, 1984), p. 4.

19. Spitzer, 1989, p. 1038.

20. Interview with Kenneth Champagne, Lafayette, Louisiana, March 13, 1990.

21. Alcee Fortier, *A History of Louisiana* (New York: Manzi, Joyant & Co., 1904).

22. Lauren Post, *Cajun Sketches from the Prairies of Southwest Louisiana* (Baton Rouge: Louisiana State University Press, 1962).

23. Increasing urbanization and westward migration of the black population in the United States during the first half of the twentieth century was documented by John Fraser Hart, "The Changing Distribution of the American Negro," *Annals Association of American Geographers* 50 (March 1960), pp. 242–66. Black migration from Louisiana, especially to California and Texas, during the 1950s is graphically presented on a map in George Davis and Fred Donaldson, *Blacks in the United States: A Geographic Perspective* (Boston: Houghton Mifflin, 1975), p. 46. See also James Allen and Eugene Turner, *We the People: An Atlas of America's Ethnic Diversity* (New York: Macmillan, 1988), pp. 147–48.

24. Joseph Jones, *The People of Frilot Cove: A Study of a Racial Hybrid Community in Rural South Central Louisiana* (unpublished thesis, Louisiana State University, Department of Sociology, 1950), p. 64.

25. Chris Strachwitz, liner notes on Clifton Chenier, *Live at a French Creole Dance* (Arhoolie 1059).

26. John Broven, *South to Louisiana: The Music of the Cajun Bayous* (Gretna, La.: Pelican Publishing, 1987), p. 113.

27. Walter Liniger, "From the Blues Archive: Video Footage of Clifton Chenier's Appearance at the 1987 Zydeco Festival," *Living Blues* 81 (May 1989), p. 55.

28. Jeff Hannusch, liner notes on Boo Zoo Chavis, *Zydeco Homebrew* (Maison de Soul 1028).

29. Suz Redfearn, "From Lawtell to the Garden of Eden," *Wavelength* 11 (November 1988), p. 4.

30. Broven, pp. 108–10.

31. Ron Weinstock, "Book reviews (Ancelet, Broven, Savoy, Hannusch)", *Living Blues* 74 (January 1987), p. 44.

32. Telephone interview with Chris Stachwitz, Oakland, California, March 15, 1990.

33. Interview with Floyd Soileau, Ville Platte, Louisiana, March 13, 1990.

34. Macon Fry, "In Search of the Zydeco Dance Halls," *Wavelength* 13 (April 1990), p. 68.

35. Grovenar, p. 141.

36. Larry Willoughby, *Texas Rhythm, Texas Rhyme: A Pictorial History of Texas Music* (Austin: Texas Monthly Press, 1984), p. 77.

37. Jim DeKoster, "Review of Chenier's *Classic Clifton*, (Arhoolie 1082)," *Living Blues* 48 (March 1980), p. 30.

38. Broven, quote by Chris Strachwitz, p. 113.

39. Sandmel, p. 90.

40. Savoy, p. 306.

Spatial Perspectives on the Field Recording of Traditional American Music: A Case Study from Tennessee in 1928

Christopher Lornell

Although the printed documentation of traditional American music began in earnest during the late nineteenth century, less than sixty years have passed since the mounting of the first wide-scale attempts to aurally preserve this music.[1] This preservation was not undertaken by scholars nor erudite enthusiasts but by commercial record companies such as Okeh, which in 1923 issued the first "hillbilly" record by an Atlanta-based musician, Fiddlin' John Carson. The response to Carson's record, "The Little Old Log Cabin In The Lane" and "The Old Hen Cackled And The Rooster's Going To Crow" (Okeh 4890), was so positive that within a matter of months Okeh and other companies were rushing other hillbilly musicians into the studios to try to cash in on their newfound commercial success. A similar phenomenon had occurred in Afro-American music in 1920 when Okeh issued "Crazy Blues" and "It's Right Here For You" (Okeh 4169) by cabaret singer Mamie Smith. This was the first blues record issued by a black singer, although it would be another four years before the more traditional country blues singers had the opportunity to make records.

One of the initial problems faced by these companies was recruiting music talent. While based in large northern cities, most of these companies operated regional offices. The executives in the North were confounded by the puzzle

Reprinted by permission from the *Tennessee Folklore Society Bulletin* 47 (1981): 153–59.

of locating people who performed very exotic music in a remote section, both physically and culturally, of the country. They very logically turned to their regional offices, hoping that the southern company officials would be able to find suitable musicians for this rapidly expanding market.

This plan helped to promote two practices already existing in the American music industry. The first was the use of A&R (Artist and Repertory) men who functioned as talent scouts, producers, and financial consultants to the musicians. The second practice involved the use of portable recording equipment and engineers to record musicians in temporary studios—a field recording—rather than sending the musicians to the permanent studios in the North. These two practices fed upon one another, and by the late 1920s most of the major American record companies were using A&R men, frequently in conjunction with their field recording sessions.

These intriguing aspects of the early recorded history of traditional American music have been recognized in numerous articles and books published over the past twenty years.[2] Geographers, on the other hand, have tended to overlook the wealth of primary data generated by the many recordings of American folk music made during the 1920s and 1930s. A few articles by cultural geographers have appeared in such journals as the *John Edwards Memorial Foundation Quarterly* and the *Journal of Geography*.[3] The majority of these have been republished in George O. Carney's compendium *The Sounds of People and Places: Readings in the Geography of Music* (Washington, D.C.: University Press of America, 1978). Most of these articles focus upon more current trends in music, such as bluegrass or rock and roll, leaving the lode of primary data from the 1920s and 1930s virtually untouched. The intent of this article is to expand the geographical perspective on this period and style of music through an examination of two field recording sessions held by the Victor Company in Memphis and Bristol, Tennessee, between August and November 1928.[4] This examination concentrates on the musicians themselves and how they came to participate in these particular sessions, and, most importantly, on the distances they traveled to the sessions.

In August 1928 the Victor Company began one of their biannual trips to the South. This trip began in Memphis and ended in Bristol, Tennessee, in November with intermediate stops in Nashville (ten days) and Atlanta (eleven days). At each of these temporary studios, Victor recorded a wide array of musicians representing diverse types of music: blues, jazz, semiclassical, popular hotel orchestras, and country string bands.

Many traditional musicians were recorded during this trip including the Binkley Brothers' Clodhoppers (Nashville) and the Georgia Yellowhammers (Atlanta), two highly regarded string bands. Such well-known blues singers as

Furry Lewis (Memphis) and Blind Willie McTell (Atlanta) and obscure religious groups as Blind Benny Paris & Wife (Atlanta) and Hamp Reynolds Sacred Harp Singers (Atlanta) were also recorded on this swing through the South. This article focuses on the two sessions held at the extreme ends of Tennessee and will be restricted to traditional musicians about whom biographical data are available. This final stipulation eliminates such enigmas as Charlie Kyle, who recorded in Memphis, and the Smith Brothers from the Bristol session.

The Memphis Session

Memphis was often visited by Victor and other record companies during the mid-to-late 1920s in search of musicians. The session under scrutiny here, August 27 through September 24, 1928, marked the third visit to Memphis by Victor. This is an important fact because it helps account for the large number of musicians from Memphis who recorded during this session, as well as the extended period Victor remained in town. Many of the musicians recorded at this session had, in fact, already recorded for Victor, including Memphians Frank Stokes, Dan Sain, Jim Jackson, the Memphis Jug Band, Elder Richard Bryant, and Gus Cannon. These musicians, plus newcomers Furry Lewis, Robert Wilkins, Reverend Sutton E. Griggs, and Reverend E. S. (Shy) Moore, were probably all originally recommended by either Will Shade, a member of the Memphis Jug Band, or Charlie Williamson of the Beale Street Frolic Orchestra. These men had themselves recorded for Victor and served as talent scouts during subsequent field trips. Their scouting chores for Victor in Memphis presented few problems, as the city was teeming with musical talent of all sorts.

The other blues musicians from outside the Memphis area were Tommy Johnson and Ishman Bracey from the Jackson/Crystal Springs section of Mississippi as well as Ashley Thompson and Noah Lewis, who recorded with Cannon's Jug Stompers, from near Ripley, Tennessee. They all had recorded for Victor earlier in 1928 and were returning for a follow-up session. Their initial contact with Victor came in a variety of ways. Johnson and Bracey, for example, were both sent up by H. C. Spier, a furniture store operator from Jackson, Mississippi, who was a part-time scout for a number of record companies during the 1920s. Lewis and Thompson, on the other hand, were semiregular members of Cannon's group, though they traveled to Memphis sporadically to play music and spent most of their time out in the country.

It is more difficult to pinpoint how the other groups of traditional musicians ended up at this Victor session in Memphis. Ida May Mack, Bessie Tucker, and K. D. Johnson, for instance, were Afro-American blues singers from Dallas about whom very little is known. The same is true for Dr. Smith's Champion Hoss Hair Pullers, a group from Calico Rock, Arkansas, that gained a small measure of fame playing on a Hot Springs, Arkansas, radio station during the mid-1920s. It can only be presumed at this time that these groups were either approached by Victor dealers or scouts who suggested that they travel to Memphis to participate in this session.

These suppositions are, in fact, supported by the circumstances under which the Taylor-Griggs Louisiana Melody Makers recorded in Memphis for Victor. This group, which was based in Arcadia, Louisiana, began broadcasting over KWKH in nearby Shreveport in the mid-1920s and quickly gained a solid local following. In their home town the local Victor record dealer, Ed Conger, suggested they follow up their local successes by recording. Conger, in turn, placed them in contact with Ralph Peer, who was Victor's principal A&R man for the entire South. Peer personally auditioned the group and asked them to travel to Memphis for the next Victor field session.[5]

The Bristol Session

A similar background and set of stories can be cast for the musicians who participated in the Victor session held in Bristol, Tennessee, between October 27 and November 4, 1928. Many of the musicians had been previously recorded by Victor and, as in Memphis, were making their second appearance on record. This specific session was almost certainly organized by Ralph Peer, who, during the previous year in Bristol, had used an unusual technique to attract talent. During his stay in 1927, Peer placed an article in the local paper announcing that Victor was in town seeking musicians. This announcement was in addition to the usual practices of contacting local record dealers and music stores. On the basis of his successful 1927 trip, which resulted in the first recordings by two of America's most important country singers, Jimmie Rodgers and the Carter Family, Peer returned to Bristol.[6]

It is not entirely clear which of Peer's techniques succeeded in attracting all the musicians to the 1927 session, but it could be that the success of Rodgers and the Carter Family in conjunction with local publicity attracted some nearby musicians for the session in autumn 1928. This would help account for the presence of such obscure groups as the Smyth County Ramblers, a string band based, quite likely, in Smyth County, Virginia, some thirty to forty miles northeast of Bristol. Peer's earlier trip to Bristol could also have attracted the attention of Clarence Greene, an expert old-time fiddler and guitarist from nearby Elizabethton, Tennessee, who recorded two sides at this session. An interview with Harry Gay reveals that he and Steve Tarter, the only black musicians to record at this session, performed their blues for Victor because of the publicity that was generated in their home town of Johnson City, Tennessee, located some thirty miles from Bristol.[7]

The reasons why certain other musicians recorded at this session are well known. The most graphic example is provided by Ernest V. Stoneman and his friends and family. Stoneman was one of the first country singers to record, first for Okeh in 1924 and in later years for a number of other companies. Stoneman, a native of Galax, Virginia, signed a five-year contract with Peer in 1925 and switched from Okeh to Victor when Peer made that same lateral move in 1927. Apparently at Peer's suggestion, Stoneman brought a number of local musicians with him to Bristol, and they recorded together in various combinations.

The other musicians recorded at this session had all participated in previous Victor field sessions and were probably invited back on the strength of their initial performances. It is not entirely clear how their first recording opportunities for Victor came about, but this group included the Carolina Twins (Gwen Foster and Dave Fletcher from Shelby County, North Carolina) as well as a large contingent from Corbin, Kentucky (Alfred G. Karnes and Ernest Phipps and Congregation).

Conclusions

This background information should clarify the various reasons why these musicians participated in these two field recording sessions. Recording traditional music was at this time still in its infancy and no comprehensive system for scouting this talent had evolved, a fact that remains true to this day. Most of these musicians made a few records and returned home to pursue their full-time occupations while retaining music as a sideline. But for the opportunity to record, people are willing to travel long distances, which is clearly true of the musicians who trekked from Dallas, Texas, to Memphis.

This factor of distance points out one of the interesting contrasts between the two sessions: musicians traveled longer distances to record in Memphis and, while the reasons are not entirely clear, they may include variables such as transportation linkages and the location and dates for other Victor field sessions. Another variable affecting the distances musicians traveled might be the locations of the Victor record dealers who, as demonstrated earlier in this article, often acted as talent scouts in their sales area.

A second fact is that the Memphis field session attracted more musicians, many of whom were from Memphis. This can be explained by the presence of the two active talent scouts located within the black community in Memphis who naturally drew upon their friends and acquaintances as a source for musicians. Over three-fourths of the Americans from the Memphis session were Afro-American, while in Bristol, located in a stronghold for Anglo-American music, only two blacks recorded. The fact that Memphis had more musicians participating can be accounted for by their extended stay, which was probably precipitated by their good fortune on previous trips.

Another spatial aspect of these sessions is the dearth of musicians from certain areas of Tennessee and surrounding states. The area between Memphis and Bristol is totally vacant, which is significant because it points up the area from which Victor drew for their Nashville session held in late September and early October. Nearly every group recorded in Nashville was from Middle Tennessee. By holding sessions in each of the three sections of Tennessee—the Delta, the Plateau, and the Mountains—Victor followed a clear pattern of drawing upon musicians located, for the most part, near their recording nodes.

The spatial considerations—home locations of the musicians, the distances they traveled to record, and the regions each session drew musicians from—are all illustrated by the SYMVU map accompanying this article (Fig. 7-1). This computer-generated map also helps to support the contention that field recording sessions of traditional music served as at least temporary nodes for functional cultural regions. Such regions are based not so much on cultural homogeneity, the basis for folk culture regions, as on the more pragmatic consideration of commerce. The Victor company was in business to sell records and make money, and they were primarily interested in recording

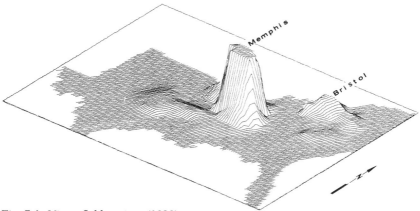

Fig. 7-1. Victor field sessions (1928).

musicians whose product was important traditional music, for which we are most grateful today, but their paramount goal was to find musicians whose records would sell. The recording centers in this study served as nodes for those regions, central points where the activity of recording the music was coordinated and directed. Such functional cultural regions were extremely flexible and variable, and shifted each time the major companies moved their studios to cities such as Memphis, New Orleans, Atlanta, Charlotte, or Louisville.[8]

More work on the nature of these functional cultural regions and their relationship to traditional music and field recording sessions needs to be undertaken before any definitive statements can be made, but it would appear that field sessions tended to reflect the indigenous music for areas within 100 or so miles surrounding the node. This preliminary study only hints at the parameters of this way of examining traditional music. It takes into account only two field sessions out of dozens, and only a few of the possible variables, such as the presence or absence of permanent A&R men, the willingness and ability of musicians to travel, the location of the record dealers who served as part-time scouts, and the distribution and trade area served by the Bristol newspaper in 1927, that could affect the structure of each session. All these factors work in combination to present a fascinating historical and spatial study, the nature of which cultural geographers are just now beginning to explore.

Notes

1. See, for example, W. F. Allen, C. P. Ware, and L. M. Garrison, *Slave Songs of the United States* (New York: A. Simpson & Company, 1867), and Bernard Katz, *The Social Implications of Early Negro Music in the United States* (New York: Arno Press and the *New York Times*, 1969) for African American scholarship; and James Francis Child, *The English & Scottish Popular Ballads Volumes 1–5* (Boston: Houghton Mifflin and Company, 1882–94) for Anglo-American scholarship.

2. For example, R.W.M. Dixon and J. Godrich, *Recording The Blues* (London: Studio Vista, 1970) or Bill C. Malone, *Country Music USA* (Austin: University of Texas Press, 1968) pp. 33–79.

3. For example, A. Doyne Horsley, "The Spatial Impact of White Gospel Quartets in the U.S.," *JEMF Quarterly* 15 (Summer 1979), pp. 91–99, and Larry Ford, "Geographical Factors in the Origin, Evolution and Diffusion of Rock and Roll Music," *Journal of Geography*, 70 (November 1971), pp. 455–64.

4. This information is available in Brian Rust, *The Victor Master Book*, Vol. 2 (Stanhope, N.J.: Walter C. Allen, 1970).

5. For more information on this group, see Tony Russell, "Music in Arcadia: The

Story of the Taylor-Griggs Louisiana Melody Makers," *Old Time Music* 24 (Spring 1977), pp. 8–16.

6. For more specific information on this session, see Charles K. Wolfe, "Ralph Peer At Work: The Victor 1927 Bristol Sessions," *Old Time Music* 5 (Summer 1972), pp. 10–15.

7. Kip Lornell and Roddy Moore, "Tarter and Gay Revisited," *Juke Blues* 8 (Spring 1987), p. 21.

8. For more information on functional cultural regions, see Terry Jordan and Lester Rowntree, A *Thematic Introduction to Cultural Geography* (New York: Harper and Row, 1979), pp. 13–15.

T for Texas, T for Tennessee: The Origins of American Country Music Notables

George O. Carney

Historians, sociologists, and folklorists have claimed for some time that there were regional patterns in the origin of music styles and that preferences for types of music varied from place to place.[1] Geographers, however, have only recently begun to investigate the spatial and temporal implications of music,[2] even though several well-known cultural geographers have suggested that music may be used to analyze basic processes of cultural change through space and time and that more studies of nonmaterial culture are needed to understand human behavior.[3]

To date, most research on geographical aspects of music has focused on country music in the United States, particularly the spatial diffusion of outdoor festivals and radio stations, perception of places through country music song titles and lyrics, and spatial interaction exhibited by country music audiences as they migrate in and out of Nashville.[4] But what about the individuals who have created this style of American music? Where do the performers, composers, and publishers originate? Are they country folk, as one might expect, or are they city dwellers? Does the South, generally acknowledged as the culture hearth of country music, produce the greatest numbers of country performers and writers? Finally, have the origins of country artists changed over time? This study considers these questions by examining the spatial and temporal dimensions of the origins of country music notables—those performers, composers, publishers, and executives who have made significant contributions to the field of country music since the late nineteenth century.[5]

Reprinted by permission from *The Journal of Geography* 78 (1979): 218–25.

Country Music

Defined as a "hybrid," country music grew from Anglo-Celtic ballads that were transplanted to the rural South during the colonial period and gradually absorbed various vocal and instrumental influences of that social environment. From the eighteenth through the early part of the twentieth century, country music gained little acceptance either from the world of musical culture or from the realm of academic scholarship. Music appreciation devotees, whose experience was limited historically to imported European classical or similar music, could see no merit in American rural music. During this time, some professional musicians and musicologists, supported by the well-to-do classes, endeavored to educate the American populace to the values of "good" music through concerts, recitals, and music appreciation courses. This "highbrow" group attempted to convince Americans that European classical music was something that all should enjoy, whereas they denounced country music, an indigenous sound of America, as "lowbrow."[6]

The opposition to rural music might have persisted in America, had it not been for the emergence of radio. During the 1920s radio became a widely popular and inexpensive diversion for millions of rural people.[7] The radio revolutionized the musical tastes of Americans and was important in the discovery of country musicians. Additionally, the phonograph industry, stimulated by a decline in sales of records during the Depression and by the competition of radio, began to search for new marketing outlets. Such music executives as Ralph Peer of Okeh Records realized that a market might exist among America's rural population; therefore, he arranged the recording of music of some early country performers, including Fiddlin' John Carson, Jimmie Rodgers, and the Carter Family.[8]

Despite the introduction of country music talent via radio and phonograph, knowledgeable commentators of the 1920s and 1930s predicted that country music would ultimately lose all popular appeal.[9] As recently as 1943, Tennessee's governor asserted that country music, the Grand Ole Opry, and Roy Acuff were bringing disgrace to the state of Tennessee.[10] Today, however, country music is performed in the White House, listened to by astronauts in outer space, studied in universities, and heard from Moscow to Tokyo. Country music exhibits no discernible evidence of disappearing from American life but rather continues to reach a growing audience. Despite the increasing complexity and urbanization of modern America, country music almost daily increases in popularity among all socioeconomic classes. Much more than a sound, country music is popular because it is a manner of viewing or reflecting on life. To many people, it has been a way of life itself. As country music composer John D. Loudermilk has stated, "We need dialogue . . . I want to tell the world how the guy in the filling station feels. It's vital that people know how he feels."[11]

Information Sources

Several listings of notable contributors to country music have been published in recent years. Five of these sources have provided the data for this study: *Country Music Who's Who; The Country Music Encyclopedia; A History and Encyclopedia of Country, Western and Gospel Music; Encyclopedia of Folk, Country, and Western Music;* and *Country Music, U.S.A.*[12] Although some sources include a wide range of information, the most often provided and most reliable are date and place of birth. These are the primary data analyzed in this treatment of country music notables. Of course, a person may be born in one location but reared in quite a different one. Studies of migrants indicate, however, that people, whenever possible, tend to move to a neighborhood inhabited by people from the same or similar places. For example, Harlan County people moving to Detroit often settle near others who are also from eastern Kentucky.[13] Moreover, living in a new environment with different cultural norms often intensifies the sentimental attachment to the area from which people have moved.[14] "Born in Harlan County" may tell us more about the upbringing of a person than the fact that he or she "grew up in Detroit." Thus, place of birth is not only the most readily available information, but also the best single indicator of a performer's heritage.

In assembling the list of notables, I did not add or delete anyone because of my evaluation of their significance. All persons associated with country music, including singers, instrumentalists, songwriters, publishers, and recording executives, were included in the study. Each person was counted separately except those kin habitually working together, such as the Willis Brothers, who were only counted once. Kin who have separate careers as performers, such as the Monroe Brothers, were counted individually. Merging the lists from the five sources gave a total of 593 persons with known birthplace and birth date.

Rural and Urban Origins of Notables

To establish the rural or urban background of country music notables, I compiled a list of all those from cities with populations of 50,000 or more by the end of the decade in which the notable was born.[15] There were ninety-four notables, or 16 percent of the total of 593, born in cities of that size (Table 8-1). Of the forty notables born before 1900, none originated in a city with at least 50,000 population. During the first decade of the twentieth century, three of thirty-four (9 percent) were born in urban centers–Atlanta, St. Louis, and Chicago. From 1910 to 1919, fourteen of 130 (11 percent) originated in urban areas. During the 1920s and 1930s, a greater proportion of notables—twenty-two of 141 and twenty-nine of 179, amounting to 16 and 22 percent, respectively—were urban born. Data for the period since 1940 indicate a leveling off of urban-born notables (fifteen of sixty-nine, or 22 percent).

Although the proportion of country music notables born in large cities is greater for recent decades than earlier ones, such younger stars as Tanya Tucker, Johnny Rodriquez, and Barbara Fairchild are from places with less than 50,000 population. Representative of those notables born since 1940, Tucker hails from Seminole, Texas (5,007 population), Rodriquez was born in Sabinal, Texas (1,554 population), and Fairchild is a native of Knobel, Arkansas (339 population). Should this trend continue, small towns and rural areas will produce roughly three of every four notables, and country music will still be provided mainly by country-born musicians in the future.

The spatial pattern of urban-born country music notables reveals a regional dominance. Sixty-seven of the ninety-four urban-born notables were native to cities located in the South.[16] Nashville (eleven), Atlanta (eight), Oklahoma City (six), Houston (five), and Birmingham (four) account for slightly more than one-half of the cities of origin in the South. The remaining thirty-three notables were born in cities ranging from San Antonio in the Southwest to Charleston in the lowland South to Huntington in the upland South.

Regional Production of Notables

The South has been, and still is, the cradle of country music. The distribution pattern of birth places of country music notables features a crescent-shaped arc beginning with the upland sections of West Virginia and Virginia, continuing south to encompass most of the upland Southeast, and moving westward to the black prairie of east Texas (Fig. 8-1). This contiguous group of states, often referred to as the "fertile crescent of country music," contains approximately 29 percent of the total population of the United States. It has provided 77 percent of the country music notables or over three times the number that would have resulted if all four census regions had shared equally in their origins (Table 8-2). At the other extreme, the urban and industrial Northeast (New England, New York, New Jersey, and Pennsyl-

Table 8-1. Origin of Country Music Notables, by Size of City and Period of Birth

City Size (population)	Period of Birth						
	Pre-1900	1900–1909	1910–1919	1920–1929	1930–1939	1940–Present	Total
50,000 or less	40 (100%)	31 (91.0%)	116 (89.0%)	119 (84.5%)	139 (78.0%)	54 (78.0%)	499 (84.0%)
50,001–100,000	0	0	2 (1.5%)	5 (3.5%)	12 (6.5%)	1 (1.5%)	20 (3.5%)
100,001–250,000	0	1 (3.0%)	6 (4.5%)	9 (6.0%)	10 (5.5%)	10 (14.5%)	36 (6.0%)
250,001–500,000	0	0	4 (3.0%)	7 (5.0%)	10 (5.5%)	3 (4.5%)	24 (4.0%)
500,001–1,000,000	0	1 (3.0%)	1 (1.0%)	1 (1.0%)	1 (0.5%)	1 (1.5%)	5 (1.0%)
Over 1,000,000	0	1 (3.0%)	1 (1.0%)	0	7 (4.0%)	0	9 (1.5%)
Total	40	34	130	141	179	69	593

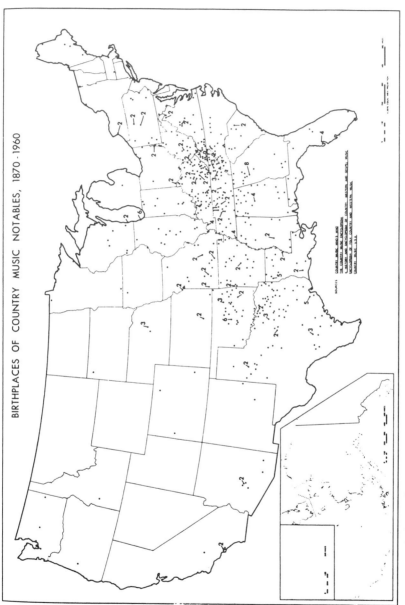

Fig. 8-1. Birthplaces of country music notables (1870–1960).

Table 8-2. Region of Birth of Country Music Notables, by Decade

Region	Pre-1900	1900–1909	1910–1919	1920–1929	1930–1939	1940–Present	Total
South	33 (82.5%)	31 (91.0%)	98 (75.0%)	110 (78.0%)	134 (75.0%)	54 (74.0%)	457 (77.0%)
North Central	7 (17.5%)	3 (9.0%)	23 (18.0%)	19 (13.5%)	34 (19.0%)	6 (9.0%)	92 (15.5%)
Northeast	0	0	5 (4.0%)	6 (4.25%)	5 (3.0%)	5 (7.0%)	21 (3.5%)
West	0	0	4 (3.0%)	6 (4.25%)	6 (3.0%)	7 (10.0%)	23 (4.0%)
Total	40	34	130	141	179	69	593

vania), the most populous region, has contributed only twenty-one notables, thirteen of whom were born in Pennsylvania. Thus, the Northeast is the most significantly underrepresented of all four regions, having produced only 3.5 percent of all country music notables.

Country music has always been popular in the Midwest and the Great Plains.[17] The region, however, has generated only ninety-two of the 593 notables (15.5 percent). This record is better than that of any other region outside the South; however, the majority of the notables were born in the southern parts of Missouri, Illinois, Indiana, and Ohio, areas more closely linked culturally to the South than to the Midwest.

The West, comprising the Rocky Mountains and the Pacific states, has yielded relatively few notables until recent years. Obviously, most of the performers who now reside on the West Coast are immigrants from east of the Rocky Mountains. Others such as Merle Haggard, a native of Bakersfield, California, are offspring of Dust Bowl refugees who migrated from Oklahoma, Texas, and Arkansas during the 1930s.[18]

The South: Fertile Crescent of Country Music

While 77 percent of all country music notables hail from the South, the talent output is not equally distributed throughout the region. Texas leads in total production with seventy-eight country music notables, followed by Kentucky and Tennessee with seventy and sixty-seven, respectively (Table 8-3). Such total production figures, however, make no allowances for differences in population.

To assess relative production by individual states, one must compensate for variations in total population. Although there are limitations in adopting a constant population to determine the relative production of notables who were born over an eighty-year period, population data for 1930 were chosen to establish a production ratio for the nation and for each of the southern states. By using the 1930 total of almost 123 million residents in the United States and the total of 593 country music notables, we can calculate a national production ratio of one notable per 207,000 residents.

National Production Rate

The same technique can be used to establish a production ratio for any region or state, substituting the appropriate number of notables and the 1930 population. If we assign a value of 1.00 to the national ratio and use it as a

Table 8-3. Production of Country Music Notables, by State in the South

	Number by Period of Birth						Total Number	Population 1930 (in millions)	Total Production Index
	Pre-1900	1900–1909	1910–1919	1920–1929	1930–1939	1940–Present			
Texas	3	9	15	14	26	11	78	5.8	2.78
Kentucky	2	10	28	10	19	1	70	2.6	5.60
Tennessee	8	2	18	22	10	7	67	2.6	5.36
Oklahoma	1	0	10	5	15	3	34	2.4	2.93
Virginia	7	2	0	12	10	2	33	2.4	2.84
Arkansas	1	1	8	2	10	6	28	1.8	3.22
Alabama	0	3	4	14	4	2	27	2.6	2.16
Georgia	4	2	1	5	8	4	24	2.9	1.71
North Carolina	3	1	5	6	7	1	23	3.2	1.49
West Virginia	1	0	6	8	4	3	22	1.7	2.68
Louisiana	0	1	0	4	10	2	17	2.1	1.68
Mississippi	1	0	1	3	5	4	14	2.0	1.45
Florida	0	0	2	3	3	4	12	1.4	1.79
South Carolina	2	1	0	1	3	0	7	1.7	0.85
Maryland	0	0	0	1	0	0	1	1.6	0.13
Delaware	0	0	0	0	0	0	0	0.2	0.00
Total	33	32	98	110	134	50	457	36.8	2.57

norm, a production index value can be determined for any region or state by comparing its ratio with that for the nation. Thus, a state that has produced twice as many notables per capita (i.e., one per 103,500 residents) would have an index value of 2.00 and one that has turned out only half as many notables (i.e., one per 414,000) would have an index value of 0.50.

The sixteen southern states, with a 1930 total population of 36.8 million and a production of 457 country music notables, have an index value (2.57) that is approximately two and one-half times the national average (Table 8-3). All states within the South have contributed more than the national norm with the exception of South Carolina (0.85), Maryland (0.13), and Delaware (0) (Fig. 8-2). The leading states in terms of this population index are clearly Kentucky (5.60) and Tennessee (5.36), both of which have produced more than five times the national average. Arkansas (3.22), Oklahoma (2.93), and Virginia (2.84) rank ahead of Texas (2.78), which is only slightly above the southern region as a whole.

The majority of Tennessee's output occurred prior to 1930, well before the founding of the Grand Ole Opry and the emergence of Nashville as a recording center.[19] Most of Tennessee's notables, such as Uncle Dave Macon, Roy Acuff, and Clarence Ashley, were born in the state's eastern upland section where country music was nurtured during those early stages of development. Except for recent years, Kentucky's contribution has been considerable. In the 1910–19 decade, it produced more notables than any other state, regardless of population size. Like Tennessee's performers, Kentucky's notables, such as Merle Travis and Loretta Lynn, were born primarily in the Appalachian east where coal mining, the dominant economic activity, was influential in the development of country music themes.[20]

During the entire period, Texas spawned the greatest number of notables. The 1930s proved to be a rich decade for Texas production, and a high output has continued in recent years with the development of Austin as a center for the "progressive" style of country music. Many of the performers associated with the rise of the Austin Sound, including Willie Nelson, Waylon Jennings, and Don Williams, were born in the Lone Star State.[21]

Virginia ranks fifth in both total output (33) and index value (2.84). The state's contribution through time has been erratic; its most productive years occurred before 1900 and between 1920 and 1939. The movement of indigenous performers, such as the Carter Family, Pop Stoneman, and Kelly Harrell (all of whom were born in the southwestern hill country), into the commercial country music stream contributed to the predominance of the early years. The 1920s and 1930s were productive decades for Virginia because of the birth of numerous performers associated with the development

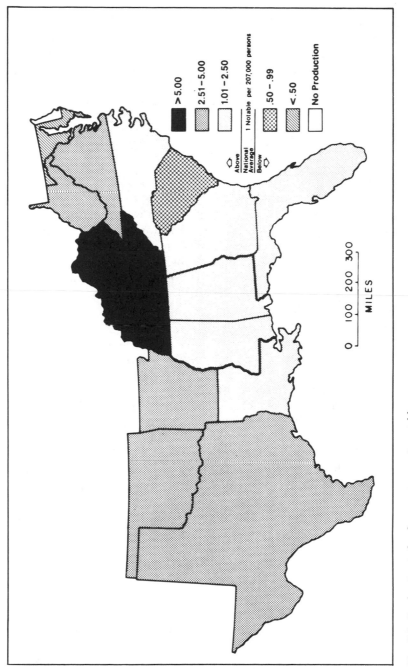

Fig. 8-2. Production index for country music notables.

Above
National
Average
Below

>5.00

2.51–5.00

1.01–2.50

1 Notable per 207,000 persons

.50–.99

<.50

No Production

0   100   200   300

MILES

of the bluegrass style of country music; these performers included the Stanley Brothers, the McReynolds Brothers, and Mac Wiseman.

Georgia, like Virginia, supplied several performers during the formative years of country music. Although the state ranks eighth in total production (24) and falls below the South as a whole on the index (1.71), north Georgia was a fertile source for many of the pre-1900 notables such as Fiddlin' John Carson, the first country music performer to have his selections recorded and marketed on a commercial basis in 1923, and the Skillet Lickers (Gid Tanner, Riley Puckett, and Clayton McMichen), one of the first rural string bands to be recorded.[22]

Arkansas is sixth in total production (28), but its index value (3.22) is third among the southern states. Over one-half of Arkansan performers originated in the Ozark-Ouachita section of the state, an area composed primarily of transplanted mountaineers from Appalachia who carried their appreciation of country music with them as they moved westward.[23] Peak production for Arkansas occurred during two decades, 1910–19 and 1930–39. The earlier decade included the birthdates of such notables as Patsy Montana, one of the first female stars; patriotic songster Elton Britt; and cowboy vocalist Jimmy Wakely. During the latter decade, several contemporary stars like Johnny Cash, Charlie Rich, and Jim Ed Brown were born.

West Virginia ranks low in total output (22); however, when one considers its population, it rates above the South as a whole with a 2.68 index value. Fifteen of the state's twenty-two notables, including Jimmy Dickens, Wilma Lee and Stoney Cooper, and Hawkshaw Hawkins (all from the Clinch Mountain section of the state), were born before 1930.

Alabama (2.16), Louisiana (1.68), and North Carolina (1.49) fall below the regional norm of the South. Over one-half of Alabama's production of twenty-seven notables took place in the 1920s, an era when Hank Williams, the Louvin Brothers, and Sonny James were born. The 1930s was a profitable decade for Louisiana when ten, including Faron Young, Jerry Lee Lewis, and Floyd Cramer, of its total output of seventeen were born. North Carolina's contributions were almost equally distributed throughout the period from 1910 through 1939. Western North Carolina was an especially prolific area for noted instrumentalists such as Earl Scruggs, who revolutionized banjo picking, and Doc Watson, who accomplished the same for the flat-top guitar.

In relation to their population, Florida (1.79), Mississippi (1.45), and South Carolina (0.85), all on the periphery of the fertile crescent of country music, have made few contributions to the genre. Maryland has produced only one performer, and Delaware none; although they are defined as southern states by the U.S. Census Bureau, both states are clearly beyond the range of the fertile crescent.

Oklahoma ranks fourth in both index value (2.93) and total output (34). The state is an interesting case because its production of notables is highly concentrated in the 1910–19 and 1930–39 decades. From an inspection of the biographies of Oklahoma-born notables, one learns that the first decade was the birth period of many performers who became prominent playing the western swing style of country music, such as Spade Cooley, and the singing cowboy stylists, such as Johnny Bond.[24] Notables born in Oklahoma during the second decade usually migrated from the state with their parents in reaction to either the Dust Bowl of the 1930s or the attraction of World War II defense work. Several female notables who rose to fame during the resurgence of country music in the 1960s fall into this category. Bonnie Owens, former wife of both Buck Owens and Merle Haggard, migrated west to Bakersfield. Wanda Jackson, Norma Jean, Molly Bee, and Jean Shepherd were also born in the 1930s and migrated from Oklahoma to either the West Coast or Nashville.[25]

Summary and Conclusions

Although recent trends indicate that higher percentages of country music notables are urban born, their origins have been more common in rural areas and in urban centers with populations of less than 50,000. Country music's audience is national, but it has been and continues to be performed, composed, and produced primarily by individuals born in the fertile crescent of country music, a region of the South that ranges from the mountains of West Virginia to the prairies of east Texas. Even a majority of urban-born notables have originated in southern cities such as Atlanta, Nashville, Birmingham, and Oklahoma City. The evidence suggests that while it has been relatively easy for the appreciation of country music to diffuse around the world, the ability to make the music successfully has not been as easily exported beyond the bounds of this fertile crescent.

Although beyond the scope of this study, a qualitative evaluation of country music notables would seem to be a potentially fruitful research undertaking for cultural geographers interested in music. For most regions and states the research would be difficult because the cultural influences are complex and biographical data are spotty at best, yet the results would provide a further dimension to the geographical analysis of music. Several questions might be asked:

1. Are the states with high total output and high index value also the homes of the most innovative performers?

2. Where has the exposure to other types of music, such as blues, gospel, jazz, cajun, and mariachi, been the most influential in shaping a performer's style?

3. Are there still regional variations in country music styles despite the homogenizing influences of commercial music that have been at work for over fifty years?

4. How important is the nasal twang of the southern accent that is reflected not only in the singing styles of the performers but in their instrumental sounds as well?

5. What are the effects of the country music tradition? How does it affect children who are born and reared in a culture area where country music is habitually heard on the radio and played in the home?

Alan Lomax, the noted folklorist, has stated that music is the most conservative of all cultural traits.[26] Thus the music composed, performed, and heard by Americans is one of the best indicators of cultural patterns in the United States. Music therefore represents an important research opportunity as we engage in the "unfinished task" of cultural geography.[27]

Notes

1. Bill C. Malone, *Country Music, U.S.A.* (Austin: University of Texas Press, 1968), pp. 3–12; Alan Lomax, *Folk Songs of North America* (Garden City, N.Y.: Doubleday, 1960), pp. xv–xvii; Charlie Gillett, *The Sound of the City: The Rise of Rock'n'Roll* (New York: Outerbridge and Dienstfrey, 1970), pp. 1–2.

2. For a collection of research works on the geography of music, see George O. Carney, ed., *The Sounds of People and Places: Readings in the Geography of Music* (Washington, D.C.: University Press of America, 1978).

3. Wilbur Zelinsky, *The Cultural Geography of the United States* (Englewood Cliffs, N.J.: Prentice-Hall, 1973), pp. 107–8; Peter Hugh Nash, "Music and Environment: An Investigation of Some of the Spatial Aspects of Production, Diffusion and Consumption of Music," *Canadian Association of University Schools of Music Journal* 5 (1975): 42–43; and Marvin W. Mikesell, "Tradition and Innovation in Cultural Geography," *Annals of the Association of American Geographers* 68 (1978): 11. For Fred Kniffen's observations concerning music as a cultural trait worthy of study, see Charles F. Gritzner, "Country Music: What's That 'Caterwauling' All About?" in *The Sounds of People and Places: Readings in the Geography of Music*, ed. George O. Carney (Washington, D.C.: University Press of America, 1978), p. 68.

4. For example, see George O. Carney, "Bluegrass Grows All Around: The Spatial Dimensions of a Country Music Style," *Journal of Geography* 73 (1974): 34–55; George O. Carney, "From Down Home to Uptown: The Diffusion of Country-Music Radio Stations in the United States," *Journal of Geography* 76 (1977): 104–10;

Tamara and Larry K. Stephenson, "A Prologue to Listening," *Antipode* 5 (1973): 12–16; and Ben Marsh, "Sing Me Back Home: A Grammar of the Places in Country Music Song" (M.S. thesis, Pennsylvania State University, 1976).

5. Various names are used to designate persons who are prominent in the field of country music. These include artist, star, performer, composer, publisher, and executive—terms that are used interchangeably in the text. The neutral term "notable" is derived from Richard A. Peterson and William R. F. Phillips, "Notables of Mid-Century: How They Are Viewed," *Social Forces* 44 (1966): 408–17.

6. For an excellent introduction to the early history of country music, see Archie Green, "Hillbilly Music: Source and Symbol," *Journal of American Folklore* 78 (1965): 204–28; and Charles F. Gritzner, "Country Music: A Reflection of Popular Culture," *Journal of Popular Culture* 11 (1978): 857–64.

7. "All States Broadcast Except Wyoming," *Literary Digest* 75 (1922): 29; and Edmund de S. Brunner, *Radio and the Farmer* (New York: Radio Institute of Audible Arts, n.d.), p. 5.

8. The role of the radio and phonograph industry in preserving and reviving the country music tradition is discussed in Charles Seeger, "Music and Class Structure in the United States," *American Quarterly* 9 (1957): 281–95; D. K. Wilgus, "Country-Western Music and the Urban Hillbilly," *Journal of American Folklore* 83 (1970): 157–79; and Malone, *Country Music, U.S.A.*, pp. 33–78.

9. For an example of this dire prediction, see B. A. Botkin, "Folk and Folklore" in *Culture in the South*, ed. William T. Couch (Chapel Hill: University of North Carolina Press, 1934), pp. 567–79.

10. Elizabeth Schlappi, "Roy Acuff—A Smoky Mountain Boy" in *Country Music Who's Who*, ed. Thurston Moore (Denver: Heather Enterprises, 1972), H-79-64.

11. Carney, *Sounds of People and Places*, p. 319.

12. Thurston Moore, ed., *Country Music Who's Who* (Denver: Heather Enterprises, 1972), G2-20; Melvin Shestack, ed., *The Country Music Encyclopedia* (New York: Thomas Y. Crowell, 1974); Linnell Gentry, ed., *A History and Encyclopedia of Country, Western, and Gospel Music* (Nashville: McQuiddy Press, 1969); Irwin Stambler and Grelun Landon, eds., *Encyclopedia of Folk, Country, and Western Music* (New York: St. Martin's Press, 1969); and Malone, *Country Music, U.S.A.*

13. See, for example, James S. Brown and George A. Hillery, Jr., "The Great Migration, 1940–1960" in *The Southern Appalachian Region*, ed. Thomas R. Ford (Lexington: University of Kentucky Press, 1962), pp. 54–78; Robert Coles, *The South Goes North* (Boston: Little Brown, 1971); and Harvey M. Choldin, "Kinship Networks in the Migration Process," *International Migration Review* 7 (1973): 163–76.

14. This process has been identified by Lewis M. Killian, *White Southerners* (New York: Random House, 1970); Harry K. Schwarzweller, James S. Brown, and J. J. Mangalam, *Mountain Families in Transition: A Case Study of Appalachian Migration* (University Park: Pennsylvania State University Press, 1971); and Todd Gitlin and Nanci Hollander, *Uptown: Poor Whites in Chicago* (New York: Harper & Row, 1971).

15. According to the U.S. Bureau of the Census, a city with a population of 50,000 or more is a necessary component of an SMSA (Standard Metropolitan Statistical Area). This figure is used as the breakpoint for rural/urban in this study.

16. For the purpose of this study, the South is defined as the sixteen states comprising the Southern Census Region. See *County and City Data Book 1972*, p. xii.

17. D. K. Wilgus, "An Introduction to the Study of Hillbilly Music," *Journal of American Folklore* 78 (1965): 195–96.

18. Bill C. Malone and Judith McCulloh, eds., *Stars of Country Music: Uncle Dave Macon to Johnny Rodriquez* (Urbana: University of Illinois Press, 1975), pp. 326–39.

19. The relatively recent emergence of the Grand Ole Opry and the Nashville music industry is discussed in Charles K. Wolfe, *The Grand Ole Opry: The Early Years, 1925–1935* (London: Old Time Music, 1975); and James Blumstein and Benjamin Walter, eds., *Growing Metropolis: Aspects of Development in Nashville* (Nashville: Vanderbilt University Press, 1975), pp. 341–57.

20. For example, see the Merle Travis album *Folksongs from the Hills*, Capitol AD 50, which includes his compositions of "Dark as a Dungeon" and "Sixteen Tons," and Loretta Lynn, *Coal Miner's Daughter* (New York: Warner Books, 1976).

21. Malone and McCulloh, *Stars of Country Music*, pp. 437–41.

22. Norm Cohen, "Fiddlin' John Carson: An Appreciation and a Discography," *JEMF Quarterly* 10 (1974): 138–56; and Norm Cohen, "The Skillet Lickers: A Study of a Hillbilly String Band and Its Repertoire," *Journal of American Folklore* 78 (1965): 229–44.

23. Frank L. Owsley, "The Pattern of Migration and Settlement of the Southern Frontier," *Journal of Southern History* 19 (1945): 147–76.

24. Malone, *Country Music, U.S.A.*, pp. 145–83.

25. Ibid., pp. 286–92.

26. Alan Lomax, *Folk Song Style and Culture* (Washington, D.C.: American Association for the Advancement of Science, 1968), pp. 117–69.

27. The identification of cultural geography as an "unfinished task" is from Mikesell, "Tradition and Innovation in Cultural Geography," p. 16.

Okie from Muskogee: The Spatial Dimensions of Oklahoma Country Music

George O. Carney

Country music is one of the greatest cultural resources and most valuable exports of Oklahoma. The state has produced performers, composers, and company executives who have significantly shaped the country music industry since statehood in 1907. One need only to mention native-born performers like Spade Cooley, Floyd Tillman, Hoyt Axton, and Reba McEntire to demonstrate the impact of Oklahoma on various substyles of American country music. Moreover, the list of performers born outside Oklahoma but with strong Oklahoma ties is endless. Most notable are Bob and Johnnie Lee Wills, Gene Autry, Hank Thompson, and Roy Clark.

Recently Oklahoma historians have recognized Oklahoma's role in the evolution of American country music.[1] Cultural geographers, however, have thus far neglected this important element in the culture complex of the state even though several well-known cultural geographers have suggested that music may be used to analyze basic processes of cultural change through space and time and that more studies of nonmaterial culture are needed to understand human behavior.[2]

To date, most research on geographical aspects of music has focused on country music at the national scale, particularly the spatial diffusion of outdoor festivals and radio stations, perception of places through country music song titles and lyrics, and spatial interaction exhibited by country music audiences as they migrate in and out of Nashville.[3] A more recent

Reprinted by permission from the *Arkansas Journal of Geography* 3 (1987): 11–17.

study, which also followed the national scale trend, examined the spatial and temporal dimensions of the origins of country music personalities (performers, composers, and executives) who had made significant contributions to the field of country music since the late nineteenth century.[4]

This research deviates from the national scale trend by analyzing biographical data on Oklahoma-born country music personalities and answering several questions concerning their spatial and temporal origins as well as addressing the value of cultural geography studies at the state level.

Based on existing biographical sources,[5] Oklahoma has produced fifty-nine country music personalities, a figure that places it fourth behind Texas, Kentucky, and Tennessee in total output and also fourth behind Kentucky, Tennessee, and Arkansas in per capita production.[6] Distribution patterns suggest that, in general, the eastern half of Oklahoma is the area of highest productivity (Fig. 9-1). More specifically, five major clusters emerge. First, the most significant concentration is located in Oklahoma County and the three contiguous counties to the south and southeast of it—Cleveland, McClain, and Grady. The second core area appears in extreme east central Oklahoma. It encompasses a triangular-shaped district running from Mc-Alester in eastern Pittsburg County to Tahlequah in central Cherokee County to Poteau in northern LeFlore County. A third major cluster is situated along a straight line from Stillwater in central Payne County to Tulsa. A fourth concentration is positioned along a line originating in eastern Pottawatomie County, which follows a northeasterly direction to central Okmulgee County. The last significant pattern is found in a tier of counties adjacent to the Red

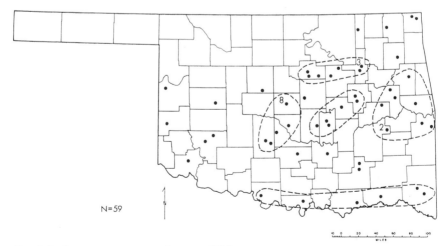

N=59

Fig. 9-1. Country music artists born in Oklahoma.

River from Jefferson to McCurtain. With the exception of Marshall, each has produced at least one personality.

These five groups (42/59) account for more than 71 percent of the total. The bulk of the remaining 29 percent are randomly distributed in the southwestern and northeastern counties. In all likelihood, higher population densities in eastern and central Oklahoma have affected productivity. Eastern Oklahoma, however, has been strongly influenced by the cultural forces of the three states to the east—Missouri, Arkansas, and Louisiana—where country music traditions have historically flourished, especially in the Ozark-Ouachita region of Missouri and Arkansas.

In terms of rural/urban origins, a majority of country personalities were born in communities of 2,500 or less, a figure considered rural by the U. S. Bureau of the Census (Table 9-1). Almost 51 percent (30/59) were included in this category. Rural-oriented towns like Grand (currently a ghost town), Schulter, Tabler, Wade, Braggs, Ripley, Chockie, Centralia, and Roosevelt were representative of this group. Roughly 22 percent (13/59) came from cities classified as Standard Metropolitan Areas (i.e., those with 50,000 or more population). Oklahoma City was the most dominant urban center with eight. Representative of the Oklahoma City group were Tommy Overstreet, Henson Cargill, and Molly Bee. Radio stations WKY and KLPR, during the 1930s and 1940s, provided ample opportunities for the development of local talent by airing live country music performances. Tulsa produced only three country notables, an anomolous statistic considering its country music flavor for the past fifty years. It is the home of KVOO, which carried live country music during its early stages, and was considered to be one of the most powerful stations west of the Mississippi to program country music during the 1930s. Moreover, Tulsa is synonymous with western swing because of the influence of the Wills Family since 1934. One would think with this exposure to country music that Oklahoma's second most populous city would have been more productive.

Table 9-1. Origin of Oklahoma Country Music Personalities (N = 59)

City Size (Population)	Period of Birth					
	1907–1919	1920–1929	1930–1939	1940–Present	N/A	Total
>2,500	9	5	7	4	5	30
2,501–25,000	0	1	5	6	2	14
25,001–50,000	1	0	0	1	0	2
<50,000	1	0	5	5	2	13
Total	11	6	17	16	9	59

Oklahoma's production of country personalities is evenly balanced among three time periods: the immediate poststatehood period of 1907–19, the 1930s, and the post-1940 era. These three time spans account for approximately 75 percent (44/59) of the total. Several of those born in the pre-1920 era were associated with western swing, a popular style during the 1930s. Included were Spade Cooley, dubbed the "King of Western Swing," and two members of the Texas Playboys, Noel Boggs and Smokey Dacus. Approximately 29 percent of the country artists (17/59) were born during the Depression years; however, many migrated from the state with their parents either in reaction to the Dust Bowl or because of the attractions of World War II defense work. Ironically, several who were born in Oklahoma during this decade but realized their potential elsewhere made significant contributions to honky-tonk, a substyle of country music that originated in the dancehalls of Oklahoma and Texas during the 1930s. Merle Kilgore, Dallas Frazier, and Bobby Burnett typify this group. The 1930s also spawned a cadre of Oklahoma women who vied for the title of "Queen of Country Music" during the 1960s when females were finally beginning to achieve equal status with males. Notable examples were Bonnie Owens, Wanda Jackson, Norma Jean, Mollie Bee, and Jean Shephard.

The post-1940s era has continued the 1930s trend of producing female country artists. Prominent examples are Becky Hobbs, Gail Davies, Gus Hardin, and Reba McEntire. Furthermore, performers born in the most recent period represent a variety of country substyles, such as Ray Wylie Hubbard (progressive country), Alan Munde (bluegrass), and Mel McDaniel (honky tonk).

Production decreased in the 1920s, interrupting the three periods of high productivity. Those born during this decade matured during the World War II era and its aftermath and, in all probability, were busily engaged in serving their country or struggling through the rock and roll boom of the 1950s, which dealt a severe blow to country music.

In addition to those bred and born in Oklahoma, the list of country music personalities associated with Oklahoma is a long one. Several Texans migrated north to hone their music skills and make their names as Oklahoma residents. There is Gene Autry, dubbed "Oklahoma's Singing Cowboy," who launched his career on KVOO in Tulsa. Bob and Johnnie Lee Wills found their professional home on KVOO and Cain's Ballroom in Tulsa and spent the most productive years of their careers in Oklahoma. Roger Miller, raised near Erick, was best known for his novelty songs such as "Dang Me," "Chug A Lug," and "King of the Road." Hank Thompson, a premier honky tonk stylist, owns a Sand Springs country music radio station and once sponsored the Hank Thompson School of Country Music at Rogers State College in

Johnnie Lee Wills and the Boys, a western swing band from Oklahoma, perform at the Tulsa State Fair (photo by George Carney).

Claremore. Finally, Roy Clark, a native West Virginian, has become a Tulsa institution.

Conclusions

Guy Logsdon and William Savage, country music historians, indicate that Oklahoma country artists migrated from the state in order to achieve fame and fortune. They are critical of the state for not providing a more conducive climate for the development of individual and group talents. Oklahoma, however, is not an exception because few states with a rural orientation, sparse population, and lack of a major urban center have succeeded in becoming music centers. The allure of major recording studios, more and better performing outlets, and bigger markets has affected the decisions of Oklahoma country musicians to leave. It is not surprising, therefore, that country performers headed to Nashville, Bakersfield, or Austin.

Regardless of their final destination, the question remains: Why has Oklahoma been such a fertile ground for country music personalities? Savage attributes the phenomenon to the rural, white composition of the population that migrated to the state from the upper and lower South more than seventy-five years ago. Country music was an item in their "cultural baggage" brought from the country music hearth. These are the people, according to Savage, who have always played, sung, and listened to country music and still remain loyal fans.[7] Logsdon, a University of Tulsa professor, contends that the early families who migrated to Oklahoma were restless, creative types. He also theorizes that music was a way of getting off the farm, away from rural poverty. "Oklahoma had a high population of tenant farmers and sharecroppers," states Logsdon. The newer generation of performers, Logsdon says, are not moving out of poverty but rather entering a profession. A lot of Oklahomans helped make country music a profession—Bob Wills, Johnnie Lee Wills, and Hank Thompson—where a young person could stand back and say, "Hey, that's what I want to do," concludes Logsdon.[8] Billy Parker, a KVOO disc jockey and successful country artist, believes that Oklahoma has always been a heart-of-the-matter type state. He emphasizes the country tradition in Oklahoma by stating, "We've been country people raised in a country atmosphere."[9] Ray Bingham, head of a country music booking agency in Tulsa, comments that most Oklahomans grew up with country music influences, especially the abundance of live country music radio shows in the state. "Oklahoma has that type of heritage. If you live in St. Louis, for example, you might not have been able to hear all those country radio programs," suggests Bingham.[10]

A second more general question for us as geographers is: Why should cultural geographers devote time and research efforts to the study of the music of a state like Oklahoma? Cultural geographers can profit from studying the music trends and patterns of a state because music is a vital component of culture. Similar to religion, dialect, politics, and economic activities, music geography enhances the understanding of the place-to-place variations within a state and helps shape the character of a place or places. In Oklahoma, for example, country music has reflected the changing life style of the state from brightening the solitary life of the homesteader to providing solace for the displaced rural folk who migrated to the city. Furthermore, one can better comprehend the place-to-place variations in Oklahoma by examining the differences and similarities between an old-time fiddlers' contest at the Greer County Fair and a crowded dance floor at Cain's Ballroom in Tulsa. Recognizing and appreciating the contributions made by the musicians and musical institutions of a state can create a sense of local awareness and, translated correctly, can become a source of pride in place, or regional consciousness (e.g., jazz and Cajun music in Louisiana and country and blues in Tennessee).

Perhaps Oklahoma should take a cue from its neighboring state of Texas, which has established the Institute of Texan Cultures at San Antonio and Sound Archives of the Barker History Center at the University of Texas at

Austin; both of which were featured as repositories of Texas music in a recent issue of *The Texas Humanist* entitled "Texas Music: The Beat Goes On."[11] It includes eleven articles focusing on various forms of Texas music such as blues, country, folk, rock and roll, Mexican-American, and German. In the editorial notes, Marise McDermott states: "Music is a direct form of expression. One can examine in depth various social groups through their music; their ways of life, value systems, aspirations and even their misery. Thus music is a key to understanding history and culture." It appears that Texas is on the road to developing research and resource centers that would be invaluable for the cultural geographers of that state who are interested in charting music origins, identifying culture regions based on music, and tracing diffusion paths of music styles.

It is time Oklahomans reawakened to a seemingly neglected side of their state's culture and paid tribute to those who participated in its development. When the names of Spade Cooley, Otto Gray, or Cowboy Copas are mentioned to young Oklahomans, few grasp their significance to American country music or realize they are Oklahomans. In contrast, political, religious, and sports figures such as Carl Albert, Oral Roberts, and Johnny Bench are easily recognized by Oklahomans. Cultural geographers have a responsibility to teach the youth of the state the multifaceted aspects of their culture, including music.

Alan Lomax, the noted folklorist, states that music is one of the most conservative of all cultural traits and serves as an important indicator of the cultural milieu of an area. With the culture of Oklahoma facing increased homogeneity, music remains an enduring characteristic of its changing lifestyle. Historically, Oklahomans have always reacted against cultural conformity. Perhaps this is because of the rugged individualism of the frontier experience, the rebellious attitude of a youthful state, or the unique mixture of the people who settled there. Oklahomans must retain that spirit of cultural independence and recognize the limitations of cultural conventionality. An Oklahoma cultural renaissance will result in the discovery of the rich and diversified music heritage of the state.

In her colorful history of Oklahoma, entitled *Oklahoma: Footloose and Fancy Free*, Angie Debo wrote: "When it comes to music, Oklahomans are like mockingbirds—more interested in getting it out of their system than in a finished performance."[12]

Oklahoma's country music legacy proves Debo both right and wrong. Right because Oklahomans sang, performed, and wrote music whenever and wherever they could. Wrong because Oklahomans, amateur and professional, have provided us with a multitude of finished performances to form the musical mosaic of our state.

Notes

1. Guy Logsdon, "Hit the Road, Jack!" *Oklahoma Monthly* (February 1976), pp. 7–16, and William W. Savage, Jr., *Singing Cowboys and All That Jazz* (Norman: University of Oklahoma Press, 1983).

2. Wilbur Zelinsky, *The Cultural Geography of the United States* (Englewood Cliffs, N.J.: Prentice-Hall, 1973); Peter Hugh Nash, "Music and Environment: An Investigation of Some of the Spatial Aspects of Production, Diffusion, and Consumption of Music," *Canadian Association of University Schools of Music Journal* 5 (1975), pp. 42–71; and Marvin W. Mikesell, "Tradition and Innovation in Cultural Geography," *Annals of the Association of American Geographers* 68 (1978), pp. 1–16.

3. Larry K. and Tamara Stephenson, "A Prologue to Listening," *Antipode* 5 (1973), pp. 12–16; George O. Carney, "Bluegrass Grows All Around: The Spatial Dimensions of a Country Music Style," *Journal of Geography* 73 (1974), pp. 34–55; Ben Marsh, "Sing Me Back Home: A Grammar of the Places in Country Music Song," (unpublished Master's thesis, Pennsylvania State University, Department of Geography, 1976); and George O. Carney, "From Down Home to Uptown: The Diffusion of Country Music Radio Stations in the United States," *Journal of Geography* 76 (1977), pp. 104–10.

4. George O. Carney, "T for Texas, T for Tennessee: The Origins of American Country Music Notables," *Journal of Geography* 78 (1979), pp. 218–25.

5. Bill C. Malone, *Country Music, U.S.A.* (Austin: University of Texas Press, 1968); Linnell Gentry (ed.), *A History and Encyclopedia of Country, Western, and Gospel Music* (Nashville: McQuiddy Press, 1969); Thurston Moore (ed.), *Country Music Who's Who* (Denver: Heather Enterprises, 1972); Melvin Shestack (ed.), *The Country Music Encyclopedia* (New York: Thomas Y. Crowell, 1974); and Irwin Stambler and Grelun Landon, *The Encyclopedia of Folk, Country & Western Music* (New York: St. Martin's Press, 1984).

6. Carney, "T for Texas, T for Tennessee."

7. Savage, *Singing Cowboys and All That Jazz.*

8. Guy Logsdon, personal interview, Tulsa, Oklahoma, October 1984.

9. Billy Parker, radio station KVOO disc jockey, Tulsa, Oklahoma, personal interview, October 1984.

10. Ray Bingham, country music booking agent, Tulsa, Oklahoma, personal interview, October 1984.

11. Marise McDermott (ed.), "Texas Music: The Beat Goes On" in *The Texas Humanist* 7 (1985), pp. 5–31.

12. Angie Debo, *Oklahoma: Foot-Loose and Fancy-Free* (Norman: University of Oklahoma Press, 1949).

10

Selected Reading and Listening II

Chapter 4

Abrahams, Roger D. A *Singer and Her Songs: Almeda Riddle's Book of Ballads*. Baton Rouge: Louisiana State University Press, 1970.

Carney, George O. *Folk Music of the Ozarks*. Stillwater, Okla.: O.S.U. Publishing, 1990.

Cochran, Robert. *Vance Randolph: An Ozark Life*. Urbana: University of Illinois Press, 1985.

Cohen, Norm (ed.). *Vance Randolph: Ozark Folksongs*. Urbana: University of Illinois Press, 1982.

Randolph, Vance. *Ozark Folksongs*. Columbia: University of Missouri Press, 1980. 4 Vols. (Rev. ed.)

Rayburn, Otto Ernest. *Ozark Country*. New York: Duell, Sloan, and Pearce, 1941.

Almeda Riddle: Ballads and Hymns from the Ozarks (Rounder 0017).

Echoes of the Ozarks. 3-LP set (County 518/520).

I'm Old but I'm Awfully Tough: Traditional Music of the Ozark Region (Missouri Friends of the Folk Arts MFFA 1001).

Music of the Ozarks (National Geographic Society 703).

The Rackensack. 2 Vols. (Ozark Folk Center LP 278/279).

Chapter 5

Baraka, Amiri. *Blues People*. New York: William Morrow, 1963.

Charters, Samuel. *The Bluesmen*. New York: Oak Publications, 1967.

Evans, David. *Big Road Blues: Tradition and Creativity in the Folk Blues.* New York: Da Capo Press, 1987.

Ferris, William, Jr. *Blues from the Delta.* New York: Da Capo Press, 1984.

Keil, Charles. *Urban Blues.* Chicago: University of Chicago Press, 1966.

Oliver, Paul. *The Meaning of the Blues.* New York: Macmillan, 1960.

Shaw, Arnold. *Honkers and Shouters: The Golden Years of Rhythm and Blues.* New York: Macmillan, 1978.

Titon, Jeff Todd. *Early Downhome Blues: A Musical and Cultural Analysis.* Urbana: University of Illinois Press, 1977.

Anthology of Rhythm and Blues (Columbia CS 9802).

Bluebird Blues (RCA LPV 518).

Rare Blues of the '20s (Historical HLP 1-5—4-LP set).

Roots: Rhythm and Blues (Folkways RF-20).

Roots of the Blues (New World-252).

Straighten Up and Fly Right: Rhythm and Blues from the Close of the Swing Era to the Dawn of Rock 'n' Roll (New World-261).

The Country Blues, Vols. 1-2 (Folkways RF 1/9).

The Great Blues Men (Vanguard VSD-25/26).

The Rural Blues: A Study of Vocal and Instrumental Resources (Folkways RF-202).

The Story of the Blues (Columbia CG 30008—2-LP set).

Chapter 6

Spitzer, Nicholas R. "Zydeco and Mardi Gras: Creole Identity and Performance Genres in Rural French Louisiana." Unpublished Ph.D. dissertation, University of Texas-Austin, 1986.

———. "Zydeco." *Encyclopedia of Southern Culture.* Edited by Charles Reagan Wilson and William Ferris. Chapel Hill: University of North Carolina Press, 1989, pp. 1037–38.

Clifton Chenier: *The King of Zydeco Live at Montreaux* (Arhoolie 355).

———. *Bon Ton Roulet* (Arhoolie 1031).

———. *King of the Bayous* (Arhoolie 1052).

———. *Louisiana Blues and Zydeco* (Arhoolie 1024).

———. *Recorded Live* (Arhoolie 1059).

———. *Live at the San Francisco Blues Festival* (Arhoolie 1093).

Zydeco (Arhoolie 1009—Anthology).

Zydeco Live (Rounder 2069/70—2 LPs).

Zydeco: Volume One, The Early Years (Arhoolie 307).

Chapter 7

Wolfe, Charles K. "Ralph Peer at Work: The Victor 1927 Bristol Session" *Old Time Music* 5 (1972): 10–15.

————. *Tennessee Strings: The Story of Country Music in Tennessee.* Knoxville: University of Tennessee Press, 1977.

————. *Kentucky Country: Folk and Country Music of Kentucky.* Lexington: State University Press of Kentucky, 1982.

Are You from Dixie: Great Country Brother Teams of the 1930s (RCA 8417-2-R).

Early Rural String Bands (RCA LPV-552).

Mountain Ballads (County 502).

Old-Time String Band Classics, 1927-1933 (County 531).

Old-Time Southern Dance Music: The String Bands, Vols. 1-2 (Old Timey 100/101).

Smoky Mountain Ballads (RCA LPV-507).

Traditional Country Classics (Historical 8003).

Chapter 8

Green, Douglas B. *Country Roots: The Origin of Country Music.* New York: Hawthorn Books, 1976.

Malone, Bill C., and McCulloh, Judith (eds.). *Stars of Country Music.* Urbana: University of Illinois Press, 1975.

Rogers, Jimmie N. *The Country Music Message: Revisited.* Fayetteville: University of Arkansas Press, 1988.

Shelton, Robert. *The Country Music Story.* New York: Bobbs-Merrill, 1966.

Tosches, Nick. *Country: The Biggest Music in America.* New York: Stein and Day, 1977.

The Smithsonian Collection of Classic Country Music (Edited by Bill C. Malone—8 LPs From 1922 to 1975—R 025).

Chapter 9

Autry, Gene. *Back in the Saddle Again.* Garden City, N.Y.: Doubleday, 1978.

Carney, George O. *Oklahoma's Folk Music Traditions: A Resource Guide.* Stillwater, Okla.: O.S.U. Printing and Publishing, 1979.

Horowitz, James. *They Went Thataway.* New York: Dutton, 1976.

Savage, William W., Jr. *Singing Cowboys and All That Jazz: A Short History of Popular Music in Oklahoma.* Norman: University of Oklahoma Press, 1982.

Townsend, Charles. *San Antonio Rose: The Life and Music of Bob Wills.* Urbana: University of Illinois Press, 1976.

Best of Johnny Bond (Harmony 7308).

Diamond Jubilee Presents Oklahoma Country (Sessions Records ARI 1025).

Gene Autry's Country Music Hall of Fame Album (Columbia CS 1035).

The Best of Cal Smith (MCA-70).

The Best of Cowboy Copas (Starday SLP948).

The Bob Wills Anthology (Columbia 32416).

Jean Shephard's Greatest Hits (United Artists UA-LA 685-G).

Okie from Muskogee (Capitol ST-384).

Part III

Cultural Hearths and Cultural Diffusion of American Folk and Popular Music

11

Country Music and the South:
A Cultural Geography Perspective

George O. Carney

Several cultural geography studies have investigated a variety of culture traits unique to the American South including dialect, house types, national origin, race, traditional economies, politics, folk tales, and diet.[1] Cultural geographers, however, have neglected to study one of the most unique southern culture traits—music—even though cultural historians, folklorists, and sociologists have long recognized that most, if not all, American music originated in the South.[2]

The American South is a land of music. A recent interpretation of the region has described music as the "South's most spontaneous and distinctive form of artistic expression."[3] Music is one of the greatest cultural resources and one of the most valuable exports of the American South. The region has contributed styles, performers, institutions, instruments, and songs that have significantly shaped the entire realm of America's folk and popular music. Of all the music styles originating in the South, which include blues, jazz, Cajun, Tex-Mex, rock and roll, and country, the last named has made the most lasting impact on American music forms. This investigation therefore examines country music in the American South from a cultural geography perspective.

The first section considers the nuclear hearths of country music vocal and instrumental elements, the spread of country music qualities through various diffusion processes, and the barriers encountered in the diffusion process.

Reprinted by permission from the *Journal of Cultural Geography* 1 (1980): 16–33.

The second analyzes the origin and evolution of seven country music substyles: traditional, singing cowboy, western swing, honky tonk, bluegrass, country pop, and country rock.

Hearth Areas of Country Music

Southern white rural music, subsequently called "hillbilly" in the 1920s and "country" in the late 1940s, evolved from the reservoir of folk music brought to North America by Anglo-Celtic immigrants and West African slaves. In its embryonic stages the music was marked by several vocal and instrumental characteristics that were transplanted to colonial America.

Vocally, early country music resembled the "familiar folksong style of Western Europe."[4] Usually solo voiced and instrumentally unaccompanied, it was performed with a rigidly pitched voice, high, rubato, and nasal quality. A large part of the early country music repertory was derived from the great body of Anglo-Scottish-Irish folk songs that existed during the colonial period. Few of these songs were written down because of the age-old tradition of transmitting them orally from performer to performer and from one generation to the next. Furthermore, the press in early America was almost entirely controlled by the clergy, which had no interest in propagating the secularly influenced folk songs. Despite this diffusion barrier, evidence suggests that approximately 100 of the 300-odd traditional British ballads reached the New World.[5]

Ballads that survived the colonial experience ran the gamut from the ridiculous to the tragic; however, the religious-minded colonists preferred the sad and tragic forms over the gay and bawdy types. According to Alan Lomax, the colonial ballads brought together "the sorrowful themes from England, Scotland, and Ireland with little of their gaiety and sensuality."[6] Somber themes have continued to exert a powerful influence over later generations of country singers who use the "love gone bad" lyrics inherited from their British and American ancestors.

Substantial evidence indicates that traditional British ballads were transplanted in three colonial hearths: New England, Mid-Atlantic, and Lower South (Fig. 11-1).[7] Field research reveals that the New England and Mid-Atlantic colonial source areas served as springboards for the spread of the ballad tradition into the Appalachian South, where it became a part of early country music in the first decades of the nineteenth century.[8] Cecil Sharp, an English folklorist, devoted two years (1916–18) to collecting traditional British ballads in the Appalachian sections of North Carolina, Virginia, Tennessee, Kentucky, and West Virginia. He discovered that singing "was

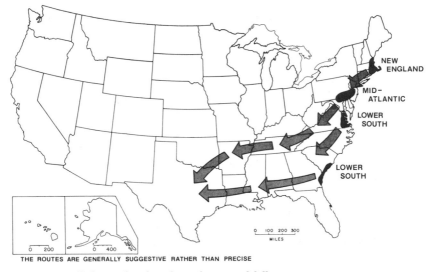

Fig. 11-1. Ballads: Nuclear hearths and routes of diffusion.

almost as universal a practice as speaking" and that the mountaineers still relied heavily on British folk song material carried into Appalachia from the New England and Mid-Atlantic hearth areas.[9] Subsequent field work demonstrated that Appalachian migrants acted as diffusion carriers when they moved westward into the Ozarks by the 1850s.[10] The westward flow of ballads from the Lower South colonial hearth has been documented by the studies of Arthur Palmer Hudson and William A. Owens.[11] In the process of cultural transfer to the New World, ballads were among those music traits selected by colonials that later affected the development of southern white rural music.

A second major force in shaping early country music vocals was the acceptance of harmony singing. It was introduced through the popular church singing schools that originated in New England in the early eighteenth century. The spread of the Yankee idiom was aided by several diffusion agents, including the singing masters who conducted schools in New York, Pennsylvania, and Maryland by the 1750s; evangelistic revival movements, such as the "Great Revival" of 1800 in Kentucky, which swept into Tennessee, the Carolinas, and Georgia during the next decade; and the development of new systems of music notation, especially the "shape-note" tradition, where music notes were shaped differently according to their position in the scale.[12]

The shape-note method gained wide usage throughout rural sectors of the American South because it was easily understood by the musically illiterate and the singing-school master could travel into the more remote areas to teach. The technique entered the South through the Mid-Atlantic hearth area of eastern Pennsylvania (Fig. 11-2). From northwestern Virginia, the scene of the earliest southern shape-note activity, the method diffused as far west as the Ozarks of Arkansas and the Texas hill country.[13] This style of musical instruction became a deeply embedded facet of southern rural music and was largely responsible for the prominence of harmony singing among later generations of country music vocalists. Bill Monroe stated that his ideas for bluegrass harmony were taken from the singing school he attended as a young boy.[14]

Harmony singing preceded the introduction of stringed instruments in the South. For a long period, instruments were difficult to obtain, and in many instances religious attitudes forbade their acquisition, which acted as a cultural barrier to the diffusion process. Country music, therefore, was almost exclusively vocal during its infancy. George Pullen Jackson stated, "the charm of harmony, since it could not be delegated to an instrument, had to be produced vocally."[15] From the solo style of performance associated with balladry, southern white rural music developed a style of harmony that affected both the secular and religious songs of the region.

Southern white rural music was dramatically changed when instruments made their way into the region. One of the earliest instruments used in the rural South was the plucked dulcimer. Although its origins remain unclear, most folklorists agree that many of the dulcimer's characteristics can be traced to the German *scheitholt* and the Scandinavian *langeleik*, stringed instru-

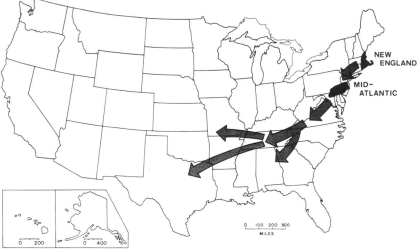

THE ROUTES ARE GENERALLY SUGGESTIVE RATHER THAN PRECISE

Fig. 11-2. Harmony singing—shape-note method: Nuclear hearths and routes of diffusion.

ments of the Middle Ages.[16] Introduced to America in the early 1700s by German settlers in Pennsylvania, the dulcimer diffused from the Mid-Atlantic hearth area to the Appalachian South, where it thrived as an accompanying instrument to ballad singers and became known as the Appalachian or mountain dulcimer (Fig. 11-3).[17] The instrument spread westward in the mid-nineteenth century as Appalachian migrants settled in the Ozark sections of Missouri and Arkansas.[18] The mountain dulcimer eventually lost favor with rural musicians because of its weak volume, which could not compete with the fiddle and banjo in providing music for country dances.

The fiddle, despite being frowned upon by many religious denominations as the "devil's box," provided the chief source of instrumentation at colonial dances including hornpipes (England); schottisches, reels, and strathspeys (Scotland); and jigs (Ireland). According to Charles Gardner, the fiddle took root in the colonial hearth areas of New England and Mid-Atlantic and entered the rural South in the late seventeenth century with the first wave of Scotch-Irish immigration (Fig. 11-4).[19] It was an ideal instrument for the ever-expanding mobile frontiers of the South and was often referred to in nineteenth century as the "royal instrument of the frontier." People moving westward carried the small, compact fiddle in their wagons or in their saddlebags. The fiddler could generally be heard anywhere a crowd gathered, including political rallies, militia musters, house raisings, and barn warmings; and at fiddle contests, which have been held in the South since at least the 1740s.[20]

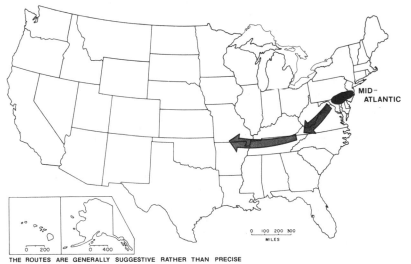

THE ROUTES ARE GENERALLY SUGGESTIVE RATHER THAN PRECISE

Fig. 11-3. Plucked dulcimer: Nuclear hearth and routes of diffusion.

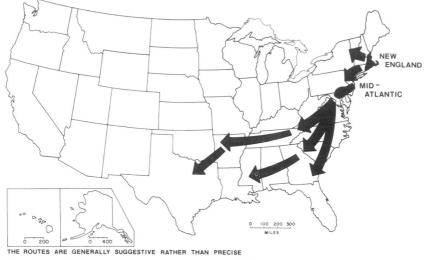

THE ROUTES ARE GENERALLY SUGGESTIVE RATHER THAN PRECISE

Fig. 11-4. Fiddle: Nuclear hearths and routes of diffusion.

The banjo is sometimes called America's only native instrument; however, this description is correct only in the instrument's final state of evolution. Origin of the instrument can be traced back to a West African instrument, the *bania*.[21] Dana Epstein has documented the banjo's association with American blacks as early as 1754; and in Thomas Jefferson's *Notes on Virginia*, published in 1785, he mentions that his slaves played the "banjar."[22] The banjo, therefore, spread from the Lower South nuclear hearth area westward to other portions of the "cotton culture" via the black slave movement (Fig. 11-5). It remained a part of southern black music until the late nineteenth century when white mountain musicians began using it in the development of string bands.[23]

Originally a four-stringed instrument, the banjo was revolutionized in the nineteenth century by a white southerner, Joel Walker Sweeney of Virginia, who added a fifth, or drone, string. The drone string, with its melancholy phrasing, made the five-stringed instrument more acceptable to white rural musicians who used it to accompany their lonely laments. Thereafter, the five-string banjo became the mountain or hillbilly banjo found in the Upland South; whereas the four-stringed instrument became the province of Dixieland or jazz musicians of the Lowland South. Apparently race was an underlying barrier in the slow diffusion of the banjo into early country music.

Information on other country music instruments, such as the guitar and autoharp, is scarce; however, most music historians agree that both appeared in the rural South later than the dulcimer, fiddle, and banjo. During the

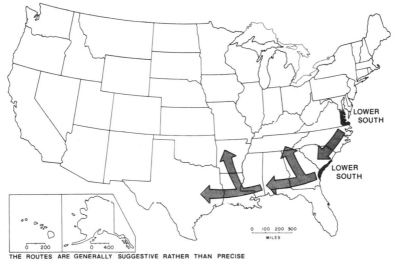

THE ROUTES ARE GENERALLY SUGGESTIVE RATHER THAN PRECISE

Fig. 11-5. Banjo: Nuclear hearths and routes of diffusion.

early nineteenth century, the guitar as well as other cultural items, such as wide-brimmed hats and high-heeled boots, filtered northward from Mexico into Texas where rural blacks mastered the instrument. Long associated with black blues music, the guitar spread from the Texas cotton fields eastward to other sections of the Lowland South, especially with the increased migration of freed blacks following the Emancipation Proclamation of 1864 (Fig. 11-6).

Documentation indicates that southern white musicians did not start using the guitar until the 1880s and widespread occurrence of guitar playing among country performers did not occur until later, when mail-order catalogs advertised the instrument and instruction books.[24] Traditional country musician Hobart Smith states that he did not see his first guitar until the World War I era when a black construction gang laid rails in Saltville, Virginia.[25] Wide adoption of the guitar by rural whites did not occur until racial barriers were broken down. Jimmie Rodgers, Sam McGee, Merle Travis, and Hank Williams, all prominent white country guitarists of the twentieth century, learned to play the guitar by studying the techniques of black friends.

The autoharp entered the rural South via the eastern Pennsylvania nuclear hearth where it was invented in Philadelphia in 1881 by Charles F. Zimmerman, a German immigrant (Fig. 11-7). The Stoneman and Carter families from southwestern Virginia, two of the most prominent groups in early country music, popularized the instrument in the 1920s. The autoharp, originally a parlor instrument, became important to Southern rural music

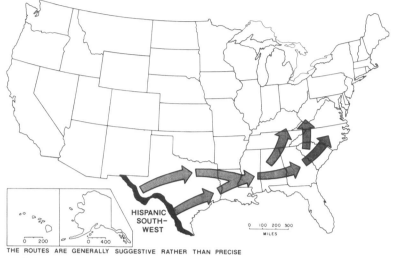

Fig. 11-6. Guitar: Nuclear hearth and routes of diffusion.

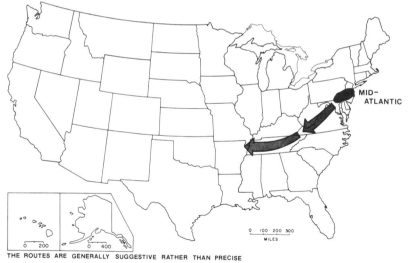

Fig. 11-7. Autoharp: Nuclear hearth and routes of diffusion.

because it was easy to play and conveniently transported from place to place. Diffusion of the instrument was aided by two carriers: door-to-door salesmen who worked for the Alfred Dolge Company, which marketed the autoharp in the early 1900s, and the singing-school masters who used it in local Appalachian and Ozark communities where it became known as the "mountain piano."[26]

Four hearth areas thus served as departure points for the dispersal of the basic vocal and instrumental qualities of country music into the rural South: New England (ballads, fiddle, and harmony singing including the shape-note method); Mid-Atlantic (ballads, fiddle, dulcimer, and autoharp); Lower South (ballads and banjo); and Hispanic Southwest (guitar). In order for these musical innovations to spread throughout the rural South, several diffusion processes occurred including personal contact, human migration, and objectification.[27]

Because music is an easily transported item in the "cultural baggage" of an individual or group, migration in the eighteenth and nineteenth centuries played a key role in the spread of ballads, harmony singing, dulcimer, and fiddle as settlement pushed westward beyond the coastal areas. With the establishment of permanent settlements on the southern frontiers, personal contact was an important diffusion factor as vocalists and instrumentalists shared their songs and picking techniques with neighbors and relatives. As slavery spread westward with the advancement of the "Cotton Kingdom," black migration carried the banjo to other sections of the Lowland South where it was eventually adopted by white musicians via personal contact.

During the latter nineteenth century, the guitar migrated from Mexico into east Texas where blacks began using it to sing the country blues. With the increased migration of freed blacks following the Civil War, the instrument diffused eastward to other sectors of the Lower South. Personal contact between blacks and whites in various forms of employment, such as railroad work, led to the adoption of the instrument by white musicians.

Face-to-face communication was also significant in the diffusion of the shape-note method of singing and the autoharp. Singing-school masters and door-to-door salesmen acted as diffusion agents when they conducted schools and visited potential customers, respectively.

Objectification became an influential element during the later stages of the diffusion process as mail-order catalogs advertised instruments, such as the guitar and autoharp; shape-note hymn books were introduced in the rural South; and the phonograph industry began recording country music performers in the 1920s.

With the addition of new instruments and singing techniques and the diffusion of these innovations throughout the South, it was inevitable that different substyles of country music would emerge over space and through time.

Evolution of Country Music Substyles

The popular perception of country music can best be described as a monolithic type of American music with little difference from performer to performer and few variations from place to place. To some extent, this perception is accurate because country music has become a national music as the forces of cultural homogenization have become greater since World War II. American music styles, like so many of our culture traits, have been subject to a process of blending, mixing, and borrowing, especially during the 1970s. Prior to this amalgamation period, there were distinctive substyles of country music readily identified by areas of origin, innovative performers, and definitive vocal and instrumental characteristics. Based on these criteria, seven substyles of country music have emerged during the twentieth century.

Traditional

The traditional or "old-timey" substyle most clearly resembles the early country music of the eighteenth and nineteenth centuries. It has been conserved most effectively in five pockets of the Upland South: southwestern Virginia, western North Carolina, northern Georgia, middle Tennessee, and northern Arkansas (Fig. 11-8). Early country music, like many of the southern cultural traditions, survived the onslaught of modern communication, transportation, and urbanization in these mountainous areas.

Traditional country music was first recognized by those outside the South during the 1920s when the record industry ventured into the region to audition rural musicians and radio began to program live country music performances. Vocal characteristics used by the singers in these new performing outlets retained a strong ballad influence and the lasting effect of church singing-school harmony. Instrumentally, the "old-timey" musicians continued to rely on the fiddle and banjo combination, or with the addition of a guitar and second fiddle, a rural string ensemble was formed.

Prominent groups and individuals who perpetuated the traditional substyle included the Carter and Stoneman families from southwestern Virginia; Mainer's Mountaineers and Charlie Poole and the North Carolina Ramblers from western North Carolina; Fiddlin' John Carson and Gid Tanner and the Skillet Lickers from north Georgia; Dr. Humphrey Bate's Possum Hunters and Uncle Dave Macon and the Fruit Jar Drinkers from middle Tennessee; and Pope's Arkansas Mountaineers and Dr. Smith's Champion Hoss Hair Pullers from northern Arkansas.[28]

Much of the traditional substyle was lost following World War II because practitioners died, stopped playing, or changed to meet new audience de-

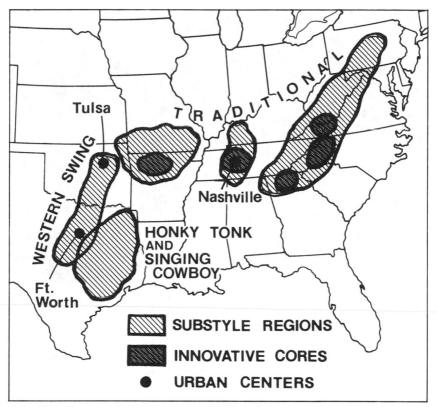

Fig. 11-8. Country music substyles (pre-1945).

mands. The inauguration of the urban folk music movement of the 1960s, however, led to an effort to regain the "old-timey" country sounds of an earlier era. Several young groups have relied upon recordings of the 1920s to recreate the traditional substyle. Among them are the New Lost City Ramblers, Iron Mountain String Band, and the Front Porch String Band.[29] Thus traditional country remains as a viable substyle even though performed by musicians from a different cultural milieu.

Singing Cowboy

In the 1920s a new substyle of country music emerged in east Texas: singing cowboy. The first of the singing cowboy stylists was Carl T. Sprague, who was recorded in 1925. He was followed by the Cartwright Brothers, Goebel Reeves, and Jules Verne Allen—all of whom hailed from east Texas

Waco Johnson Family, a traditional string band, from Mountain View, Arkansas (photo by George Carney).

communities such as Sherman, Waxahatchie, and Alvin (Fig. 11-8). The songs they performed were authentic cowboy music of the late nineteenth century such as "When the Work's All Done This Fall," "The Cowboy's Prayer," and "Following the Cow Trail."[30]

After its humble origins in the 1920s the singing cowboy substyle flourished in the 1930s when more individuals began to record and appear on radio. East Texas produced the singing cowboy performers who made the substyle nationally popular—Gene Autry of Tioga and Woodward Maurice Ritter, better known as "Tex" because of his origins in Panola County, Texas. Both men gained success in the early 1930s by journeying to New York where they became overnight sensations because of their thick Texas accents, cowboy tale telling, and cowboy songs. By the mid-1930s they were making films in Hollywood where they introduced the singing cowboy music to a national audience.[31]

Although this substyle contributed few novel ideas concerning instrumentation or rhythm, it did produce a significant contingent of country singers from the Southwest, especially Texas; a trend that was to follow in later years as the regional emphasis in country music shifted from the Southeast to the Southwest. Furthermore, the music used lyrics that depicted the cultural West and led to the growing usage of the term "western" as a designation of country music. But perhaps its most lasting influence on American country music has been the employment of cowboy phenomena in naming bands and the donning of cowboy fashions. These traditions were carried on in the Southwest by a new substyle that was created there in the 1930s.

Western Swing

Cowboy duds and band names proved to be the only similarities between the singing cowboy and western swing substyles as the latter became one of the most unique forms in American country music history. Several music historians have described western swing as a mixture of musical cultures: traditional country from the Southeast, jazz from Louisiana, and Mexican mariachi from the Rio Grande Valley. Bill Malone states that western swing is clearly "within the country music framework" but was heavily indebted to pop, blues, and jazz.[32] On the other hand, Charles Townsend's exhaustive study of Bob Wills, the creator of western swing, emphatically describes the music as "western jazz" because of its improvisation, two-four beat, and use of jazz instrumentation.[33]

The music began taking shape in the late 1920s and early 1930s when Wills organized a band in Fort Worth, which gained a reputation as being the "cradle of western swing" because the musicians were from the vicinity and local radio stations were promoting the new sound. After moving to Tulsa in the mid-1930s, Wills made country music history by adding horns (reed and brass) to his band, which now numbered from fifteen to eighteen pieces. Other distinctive instrumental ingredients included multiple fiddles playing harmony; a strong rhythm section composed of drums, bass, and tenor banjo; and the jazz-like improvisation of the steel guitar. Wills created western swing for dancing, and it became the "Big Band" sound of the 1930s applied to country music.[34]

Western swing was a distinctively regional phenomenon in terms of its personnel and most intensive popularity. A majority of its performers were native to Texas and Oklahoma, including Wills, who created the sound. During the music's early development, Wills chose Texans such as Tommy Duncan, Leon McAuliffe, Jesse Ashlock, and Al Stricklin, but during the Tulsa years, 1934-42, he relied heavily on Oklahomans such as Smokey Dacus, Zeb McNally, and Eldon Shamblin (Fig. 11-8).

A western swing renaissance occurred in the 1970s with a new generation of enthusiasts such as Asleep at the Wheel and Alvin Crow and the Pleasant Valley Boys; and after Wills's death in 1975, several of his musicians reorganized themselves as the Original Texas Playboys. The resurgence of western swing, according to Malone, was in part a tribute to the regional consciousness of the Southwest. [35] Developing parallel to western swing in the Southwest was a brand of country music known by the social institution in which it was created: honky tonk.

Honky Tonk

After the repeal of prohibition, hundreds of rural musicians found employment in the bars, roadhouses, and taverns of Texas and Oklahoma. These social institutions, collectively referred to as honky tonks, were frequented by farmers, laborers, truck drivers, and oil-field roustabouts who gathered to relax, drink beer, and release their frustration with a round of "hell raising." These activities were coupled with listening and dancing to music.

"Hillbilly Haven," a roadside tavern in the outskirts of a small Oklahoma town, where honky tonk music still flourishes (photo by George Carney).

To overcome the rowdy clientele, the music became louder and a steady, heavy beat was necessary for dancing. A "sock rhythm"—the playing of closed chords, or the striking of all six strings in unison in order to achieve a percussive effect—was applied to the guitar. The string bass, a permanent fixture in all honky tonk bands, provided the heavy beat and the fiddle was heavily bowed for the customer's dancing pleasure. By the end of the 1930s honky tonk bands were adopting the electric guitar, which helped to amplify the music over the noisy atmosphere.[36]

Although many honky tonkers danced, the substyle was essentially lyric-oriented and aimed at working-class listeners. Lyrical content typically dealt with the listener's problems, including drink, illicit love, and divorce. Frequently termed "cryin' in your beer" music, honky tonk titles included "Divorce Me C.O.D.," "Born to Lose," and "It Makes No Difference Now."

In 1935 Al Dexter of Troup, Texas, recorded one of the first songs to carry the term honky tonk in its title, "Honky Tonk Blues." Dexter and other Texas cohorts, such as Ted Daffan, Moon Mullican, and preeminently Ernest Tubb, wrote or recorded songs that were to legitimize the honky tonk sound of the 1930s. The honky tonk substyle suffered in the 1950s from the emergence of rock and roll; however, by the 1960s and 1970s, it was revived by several Texas-born singers such as Ray Price, Johnny Horton, George Jones, Lefty Frizzell, and Buck Owens (Fig. 11-8).[37]

The future of honky tonk depends primarily on how faithful its young exponents, such as Texan Moe Bandy, remain to this "hard country" sound and to the trends in American social patterns. For as long as there is drinking, cheating, and hurting, honky tonk stylists will surely have an audience.

Bluegrass

The only new substyle of country music to emerge in the Southeast in the 1930s was bluegrass, although many of its distinctive characteristics were not added until the late 1940s. Essentially an instrumental music, bluegrass evolved out of the rural string bands of an earlier period. Bill Monroe, the acknowledged creator of bluegrass, used mandolin, guitar, fiddle, and stand-up string bass in his original band when it played on the Grand Ole Opry for the first time in 1939. It was not until 1945, when Earl Scruggs joined Monroe's group, that the five-string banjo became an integral part of the bluegrass ensemble. Scruggs brought to the bluegrass sound the three-finger picking style, which he had learned in his native western North Carolina.[38]

Bluegrass vocals are characterized by a high-pitched solo singing often referred to as the "high lonesome sound." When more than one member sings, the group engages in tight two-, three-, and four-part harmony influenced by the singing-school tradition. The lyrical content of bluegrass songs varies from traditional ballads such as "Pretty Polly" to more modern compositions such as "Proud Mary."

The bluegrass substyle, oddly enough, did not originate in the Bluegrass Basin of Kentucky. A majority of bluegrass performers were born in the hill sections of western North Carolina and Virginia and eastern Kentucky and Tennessee (Fig. 11-9).[39] The label given to this genre of country music was derived from Monroe's band, the Blue Grass Boys, which he named after his native state of Kentucky. Important individuals who helped Monroe shape the substyle were born in the mountains and valleys of the four-state region. Scruggs, whose picking style is still practiced by bluegrass banjoists, was born in Flint Hill, North Carolina; the Stanley Brothers, who first copied the Monroe sound, came from McClure, Virginia; and Lester Flatt, who along

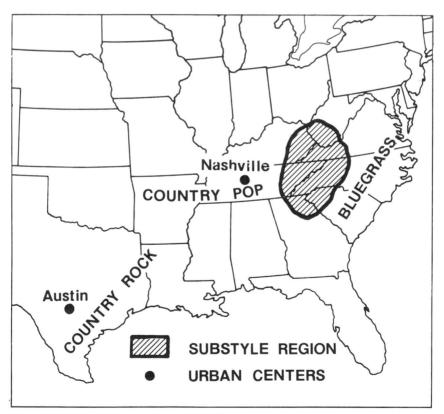

Fig. 11-9. Country music substyles (post-1945).

with Scruggs helped popularize bluegrass, called Overton County, Tennessee his home.

The future of bluegrass as a substyle of country music looks bright because of its appeal to a broad segment of the population—young and old, liberal and conservative, hippie and redneck. Outdoor bluegrass festivals, now numbering over 400, bring together these varied groups to share a similar music preference as they search for a more traditional sound of country music than that offered by Nashville.

Country Pop

The rock and roll phenomenon of the 1950s effected changes in country music. Many country performers were forced to modify their styles to attract a larger audience. Recording executives applied the pressure that set the stage for a closer amalgamation of country and popular music. The success of Hank Williams's compositions of the late 1940s in capturing the popular market created a situation that defied the clearly etched lines of American musical forms. By 1953 country songs recorded by pop entertainers were making inroads on the popular music charts; for example, Williams's "Cold, Cold Heart" recorded by pop artist Tony Bennett sold a million and a half copies.

The country pop sound of the late fifties and early sixties was a product of Nashville (Fig. 11-9). The most influential personality in shaping the country pop sound was Chet Atkins, guitarist par excellence and chief of RCA Victor's country music division on Nashville Row. He created a distinctive instrumental pattern referred to as the "Nashville Sound." Characterized by a "relaxed, tensionless feeling and a loose, easygoing beat," the "Nashville Sound" little resembled other forms of country music.[40] The fiddle and steel guitar were abandoned and replacing them were electric guitars and piano, both of which provided a cool, uptown quality to the music. Floyd Cramer, who joined Atkins in forming the new sound, provided the tinkly piano background and sat in on most of the successful recordings made in the country pop category. And although group singing has consistently been a part of country music, it had never been of the trained, professional quality offered by the Nashville choruses such as the Jordanaires and the Anita Kerr Singers. Paralleling these developments in Nashville was the introduction of an alternative substyle by a group of musicians in Austin, Texas, where the "Nashville Sound" was rejected.

Country Rock

Austin, Texas, had been the scene of a small but enthusiastic colony of musicians since the 1930s, but the first major focus of activity for local musicians was the Armadillo World Headquarters, founded in 1970 in an old national guard armory. Originally a rock music outlet, it increasingly featured country entertainers who appealed to both country and rock audiences. Most of the performers consisted of local Austin musicians or only those recognized in Texas such as Kinky Friedman and the Texas Jewboys, Frieda and the Firedogs, and Asleep at the Wheel. Concurrent with the Armadillo World activity was the change in programming by several Austin radio stations. KOKE announced an intention to play all kinds of country music from traditional to honky tonk, but its selections leaned heavily toward rock-influenced material, especially that produced by Austin-based entertainers (Fig. 11-9).[41]

It was not until 1972, however, when Willie Nelson moved from Nashville to Austin, that the "Austin Sound" began to achieve national recognition. Nelson, a respected composer of country songs, returned to his native state where he had been exposed to a variety of country music, including western swing and honky tonk, as a young musician. His earlier experiences with a number of musical cultures allowed him to be more receptive to the rock forms and musicians already on the Austin scene.

Also willing to capitalize on the rock-oriented Austin movement was Waylon Jennings, a native Texan, who had been influenced by the rock and roll idiom of the fifties when he played bass for Buddy Holly's band. He has promoted his association with Austin by emphasizing the western outlaw image and the easy-going Texas life style in such songs as "Ladies Love Outlaws" and "Luckenbach, Texas."[42]

As the new decade opens, the country rock substyle will likely retain its popularity because of its youthful adherents. The fusion of country and rock will continue to occur as country-oriented rock musicians experiment and rock-oriented country performers are receptive to change.

Summary and Conclusions

The South has been, and still is, the cradle of country music. The region has produced 77 percent of all the country music notables (performers, composers, publishers, and executives) over the last one hundred years. Country music's audience is national, but it has been and continues to be performed, composed, and produced by individuals born in the so-called "fertile crescent" of country music, an area running from the mountains of West Virginia to the prairies of east Texas.[43] Almost without exception, the superstars of today come from the poorest of southern rural backgrounds including Charley Pride, whose humble black sharecropper origins are not radically different from those of Johnny Cash, the son of an Arkansas tenant farmer; or Merle Haggard, the rebel child of an Okie family; or Doug Kershaw, who eked out a living on a Louisiana bayou houseboat; or Loretta Lynn, who is still proud of being a "coal miner's daughter."

During its infant stages, country music was nurtured in the Southeast and diffused westward with migration to the Southwest. The traditional substyle, the foundation for all of country music, endured until the twentieth century when a further mixing of musical cultures occurred primarily because of various types of migration: region to region and rural to urban. Since 1930 the Southwest has become the dominant area for the creation of distinctive country music sounds. Four of the seven substyles emerged in Oklahoma and Texas: singing cowboy, western swing, honky tonk, and country rock.

Four of the seven substyles developed prior to 1945 were associated with rural origins: traditional, singing cowboy, western swing, and honky tonk. Two of the three recent substyles originated in urban centers—Nashville and Austin. The third, bluegrass, evolved from the traditional substyle of southern Appalachia but received much of its impetus from urban devotees in the 1950s and 1960s. Of the urban centers, Nashville had been identified as an important focal point for country music since the 1920s when the Grand Ole Opry opened its doors and eventually stood as the "mecca" of country music. Austin, on the other hand, emerged fifty years later as a geographic center for country music principally because of rebellion against Nashville's monopoly over country music. Urban centers may continue to play an increasingly important role in the evolution of country music substyles. Bakersfield and Tulsa, for example, have drawn talent and executives away from the Nashville industry.

Several factors must be considered if new country music substyles are to be created in the future: (1) activity by young people who are more willing to experiment and improvise than adults, (2) emergence of urban or regional centers outside Nashville, (3) rejection by listeners of the Top Forty format of the "Big Country" metropolitan radio stations that program primarily the Nashville-produced music, and (4) input from new cultural groups to a music that has been the most WASP-ish male-dominated form of American music. Included would be further influence from blacks like Charley Pride, Chicanos like Freddie Fender, Cajuns like Doug Kershaw, Jews like Kinky Friedman, and women like Loretta Lynn.

There may lie in the future a prepackaged, processed, and franchised single type of American country music with no difference from place to place or performer to performer; however, this cultural geographer believes that the older substyles will never die because of the vitality and distinctiveness they hold and the continued role that the American South will play in the evolution of country music.

Notes

1. Wilbur Zelinsky, "Where the South Begins: The Northern Limits of the Cis-Appalachian South in Terms of Settlement Landscape," *Social Forces* 30 (December 1951), pp. 172–78; Fred Kniffen, "Folk Housing: Key to Diffusion," *Annals of the Association of American Geographers* 55 (December 1965), pp. 549–77; Terry G. Jordan, "The Imprint of the Upper and Lower South on Mid-Nineteenth Century Texas," *Annals of the Association of American Geographers* 57 (December 1967), pp. 667–90; Gordon R. Wood, *Vocabulary Change: A Study of Variation in Regional Words in Eight of the Southern States* (Carbondale: Southern Illinois University Press, 1971); E. Joan Wilson Miller, "The Ozark Culture Region as Revealed by Traditional Materials," *Annals of the Association of American Geographers* 58 (March 1968), pp. 51–77; and Sam B. Hilliard, "Hot Meat and Cornpone: Food Habits in the Ante-Bellum South," *Proceedings of the American Philosophical Society* 113 (February 1969), pp. 1–13.

2. Bill C. Malone, *Country Music, U.S.A.* (Austin: University of Texas Press, 1968), pp. 3–12; Alan Lomax, *Folk Songs of North America* (Garden City, N.Y.: Doubleday, 1960), pp. xv–xvii; and Charlie Gillett, *The Sound of the City: The Rise of Rock 'n' Roll* (New York: Outerbridge and Dienstfrey, 1970), pp. 1–2.

3. Bill C. Malone, *Southern Music/American Music* (Lexington: University Press of Kentucky, 1979), p. ix.

4. Alan Lomax, "Folk Song Style," *American Anthropologist* 61 (December 1959), pp. 931–32.

5. Francis James Child, *The English and Scottish Popular Ballads* (Boston: Houghton Mifflin, 1882–98).

6. Lomax, *Folk Songs of North America*, p. 196.

7. These terms have been variously used by cultural geographers to describe source areas for American culture. See, for example, Wilbur Zelinsky, *The Cultural Geography of the United States* (Englewood Cliffs, N.J.: Prentice-Hall, 1973), pp. 117–33 and Terry G. Jordan and Lester Rowntree, *The Human Mosaic: A Thematic Introduction to Cultural Geography* (New York: Harper and Row, 1979), p. 10.

8. Bruno Nettl, *An Introduction to Folk Music in the United States* (Detroit: Wayne State University Press, 1960), p. 39.

9. Cecil Sharp, *Folk Songs From the Southern Appalachians* (London: Oxford University Press, 1917), pp. xxv–xxvi.

10. Vance Randolph, *Ozark Folksongs* (Columbia: The State Historical Society of Missouri, 1950).

11. Arthur Palmer Hudson, *Folksongs of Mississippi and Their Background* (Chapel Hill: University of North Carolina Press, 1936), and William A. Owens, *Texas Folk Songs* (Dallas: Texas Folklore Society, 1950).

12. H. Wiley Hitchcock, *Music in the United States: A Historical Introduction* (Englewood Cliffs, N.J.: Prentice Hall, 1974), pp. 9–22.

13. George Pullen Jackson, *White Spirituals in the Southern Uplands* (Chapel Hill: University of North Carolina Press, 1933), pp. 15–16, 22–26.

14. Personal interview with Bill Monroe, January 14, 1973, Enid, Oklahoma.

15. Jackson, p. 427.

16. Hortense Panum, *Stringed Instruments of the Middle Ages* (London: W. Reeves, 1939), pp. 263–91.

17. Charles Seeger, "The Appalachian Dulcimer," *Journal of American Folklore* 72 (January-March 1958), pp. 40–51.

18. Lynn and Mary Catherine McSpadden, *Mountain Dulcimers in the Ozarks* (Mountain View, Ark.: The Dulcimer Shoppe, 1977), p. 1.

19. Charles Gardner, "Anglo-American Fiddling Styles: Core Regions and Diffusion" (unpublished manuscript, Stephen F. Austin State University, Department of Geography), 1979.

20. Irving L. Sablosky, *American Music* (Chicago: University of Chicago Press, 1971), pp. 35–51.

21. Nettl, p. 56.

22. Dana Epstein, "The Folk Banjo: A Documentary History," *Ethnomusicology* 19 (September 1975), pp. 347–71.

23. John Greenway, Liner Notes, *Banjo Songs of the Southern Mountains*, Riverside RLP 12-610.

24. Hitchcock, p. 39.

25. Malone, *Country Music, U.S.A.*, p. 14.

26. A. Doyle Moore, "The Autoharp: Its Origin and Development from a Popular to a Folk Instrument," *New York Folklore Quarterly* 19 (December 1963), pp. 261–74.

27. Various diffusion processes affecting music were discussed by Larry Ford in his seminal study, "Geographic Factors in the Origin, Evolution, and Diffusion of Rock and Roll Music," *Journal of Geography* 70 (November 1971), pp. 455–64. The term "objectification" includes music books, catalogs, and recordings.

28. Norm Cohen, "Early Pioneers," in *Stars of Country Music*, ed. Bill C. Malone and Judith McCulloh (Urbana: University of Illinois Press, 1975), pp. 3–39.

29. Eric Davidson, liner notes, *The Iron Mountain String Band: An Old Time Mountain String Band*, Folkways Records FA 2473.

30. John I. White, "Carl T. Sprague: The Original Singing Cowboy," *J.E.M.F. Quarterly* 6 (Spring 1970), pp. 32–34, and liner notes, *Authentic Cowboys and Their Western Folksongs*, RCA Victor LPV-522.

31. Information on Autry and Ritter is taken from Douglas B. Green, "Gene Autry" in Malone and McCulloh, pp. 142–56, and Johnny Bond, *The Tex Ritter Story* (New York: Chappell, 1976).

32. Malone, *Southern Music/American Music*, p. 81.

33. Charles Townsend, *San Antonio Rose: The Life and Music of Bob Wills* (Urbana: University of Illinois Press, 1976), pp. 53–67.

34. Ibid., pp. 98–111.

35. Malone, *Southern Music/American Music*, p. 149.

36. Robert Shelton, *The Country Music Story* (Indianapolis: Bobbs-Merrill, 1966), pp. 124–25.

37. Malone, *Country Music, U.S.A.*, pp. 168–70.

38. Bob Artis, *Bluegrass* (New York: Hawthorn Books, 1975), pp. 22–26.

39. For a complete discussion of vocal and instrumental characteristics of bluegrass as well as the origins of bluegrass performers, see George O. Carney, "Bluegrass Grows All Around: The Spatial Dimensions of a Country Music Style," *Journal of Geography* 73 (April 1974), pp. 34–55.

40. Paul Hemphill, *The Nashville Sound: Bright Lights and Country Music* (New York: Simon and Schuster, 1970), pp. 47–54.

41. Bill C. Malone, "A Shower of Stars: Country Music Since World War II," in Malone and McCulloh, pp. 437–41.

42. For a more thorough discussion of the "Austin Sound," see Jan Reid, *The Improbable Rise of Redneck Rock* (Austin: Heidelburg Publishers, 1974).

43. George O. Carney, "T for Texas, T for Tennessee: The Origins of American Country Music Notables," *Journal of Geography* 78 (November 1979), pp. 218–25.

Bluegrass Grows All Around: The Spatial Dimensions of a Country Music Style

George O. Carney

Historians, sociologists, and folklorists have claimed for some time that regional patterns existed in the origin of music styles and that preferences for types of music varied from place to place.[1] Geographers, however, have only recently begun to investigate the spatial implications of music,[2] even though a noted sociocultural geographer has suggested that folk music is a potential topic for analyzing "basic processes of cultural change through space and time."[3] This study attempts to answer some important questions about the geographical aspects of bluegrass, a particular style of country music. The points to be considered include: (1) the spatial distribution of bluegrass musicians, (2) the human-environmental relationship that exists among bluegrass musicians, (3) the annual migratory routes that the musicians follow, (4) the origin and diffusion of the outdoor bluegrass festivals, and (5) the location of places that present bluegrass music on a regular basis.

The Role of Music in American Culture

Americans enjoy numerous styles of music for a variety of reasons. For many, there appears to be an identification with a certain lyrical content, whereas others listen to a particular instrumental sound that is pleasing to

Reprinted by permission from *The Journal of Geography* 73 (1974): 34–55.

their ears. Music has become a cultural trait that is a summing up of many of the familiar patterns of life including family, love, conflict, and work. These life-style experiences, which are expressed in music, give a place its special character. And as the noted folklorist Alan Lomax has stated: "The map sings."[4] From the chanteys and ballads of the Atlantic seaboard to the blues rolling up and down the Mississippi, music has become an integral segment of American culture.

Country music may be defined as a mixture of Anglo-Scot-Irish ballads that were transplanted to America during the colonial period, which gradually absorbed the influences of American social experiences as expressed through song. However, it was not recognized by people outside the rural environment until the twentieth century when the phonograph and radio industry began to feature country talent. One of the styles of country music that emerged during the 1930s was bluegrass, a sound created by Bill Monroe of Rosine, Kentucky.

Bluegrass Music

It has been referred to as "mountain soul music," "ole time pickin' and singin,'" and "folk music in overdrive," but regardless of the popular description, bluegrass is an important ingredient in the country music repertoire. Both the scholarly folklore journals and the popular literature have recently focused on the importance of bluegrass in American society.[5]

Vocally, the bluegrass style is characterized by a high-pitched, emotional sound that is an outgrowth of Scottish bagpipe music and the church singing schools.[6] The instruments include a five-string banjo (played in a three-finger picking style), fiddle, flat-top guitar, mandolin, and stand-up string bass. The two most distinctive features of bluegrass are the use of the banjo as a lead instrument and the nonelectric, unamplified sounds of the instruments.

The term "bluegrass" is derived from the name of a band of musicians, the Blue Grass Boys, who were organized by Monroe in the 1930s. Having originated from Kentucky, it was natural that Monroe, the "father of blue-grass," should name his group after his native state. "I wanted to represent my home state of Kentucky so I took the name 'Blue Grass Boys,'" explains Monroe.[7]

The Performer and Place

Although Monroe labeled his sound "bluegrass," he was born in the Pennyroyal Basin Region of western Kentucky rather than the Bluegrass

Region of central Kentucky. And according to a 1964 study, more than 95 percent of bluegrass musicians were southerners, like Monroe, and at least 80 percent came from southern Appalachian states.[8] More recent data indicate that the percentage of bluegrass performers originating in the South remains high (approximately 70 percent); but as the sound becomes more widely known outside the traditional four-state bluegrass region of Kentucky, Tennessee, Virginia, and North Carolina, bluegrass musicians are being produced farther to the west and north (Fig. 12-1). The "big-name" performers, such as Monroe, Earl Scruggs from Shelby, North Carolina; Lester Flatt from Sparta, Tennessee; and Ralph Stanley from Stratton, Virginia; still originate from the four-state area. On the other hand, the nontraditional bluegrass states of South Carolina, Alabama, Texas, and Ohio are supplying an increasing number of musicians (Table 12-1).

The production of bluegrass performers will continue to remain high in the aforementioned four-state region of Appalachia. The music is a direct descendant of the early hillbilly string bands that were developed in the area, especially the western sections of North Carolina and Virginia. This was the home base for such groups as Charlie Poole and the North Carolina Ramblers, Mainer's Mountaineers, and the Stoneman Family. The instrumental qualities of bluegrass likewise originated in mid-Appalachia. The three-finger picking style, which is so prominent in bluegrass today, was

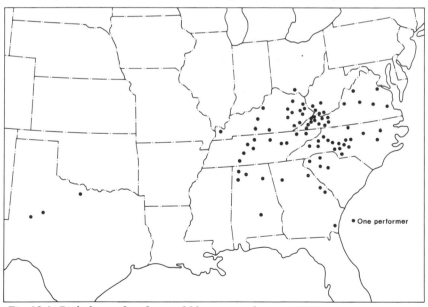

Fig. 12-1. Birthplaces of professional bluegrass performers (1972).

Table 12-1. Bluegrass Performers by State and City or County

North Carolina

1. Middlesex
2. Leaksville
3. Salisbury
4. Rocky Mount
5. Troy
6. Wingate
7. Charlotte
8. Bakersville
9. Lexington
10. Marshall
11. Spruce Pine
12. Flint Hill
13. China Grove
14. Sherrill's Ford
15. Lenoir
16. Greensboro
17. Deep Gap
18. Durham

Virginia

1. Scottsville
2. Galax
3. Pound
4. Bear Branch
5. Pocahontas
6. Richmond
7. Marion
8. Coeburn
9. Providence Forge
10. Mt. Jackson
11. Big Spraddle
12. McClure
13. Alexandria
14. Grayson County
15. Grate City
16. Crimora
17. Big Rock

Kentucky

1. Jenkins
2. Bowling Green
3. Jackson
4. Barren County
5. McAndrews
6. Paducah
7. Rosine
8. Boonscamp
9. Hyden
10. Pikeville
11. Grayson
12. Louisa
13. Leburn
14. Louisville

Tennessee

1. Overton County
2. Kingsport
3. Sneedville
4. Nashville
5. Westmoreland
6. Madison
7. Knoxville
8. Emory Gap
9. Lyles
10. Lawrenceburg

West Virginia

1. Baisden
2. Sandlick
3. Duhring

4. Clear Creek
5. Jolo

Georgia

1. Atlanta
2. Brunswick
3. Tignall

4. Lincolnton
5. Richmond Country

South Carolina

1. Spartanburg
2. Pickens

3. Union
4. Buffalo

Alabama

1. Gadsden
2. Montgomery
3. Lawrence County

4. Sheffield
5. Florence

Ohio

1. Ashland

2. Portsmouth

Texas

1. Wichita Falls
2. Anson

3. Big Springs

Source: *Blue Grass Summer. Muleskinner News.* Elon College, North Carolina.

developed in and around Shelby, North Carolina, by Snuffy Jenkins and Smith Hammett. This picking tradition was passed down to the well-known banjoist Earl Scruggs, who has perfected and introduced the technique to national audiences.[9] And because this area is still primarily rural, both in population and thought, bluegrass will remain popular among musicians and listeners due to its affirmation of old rural values including fundamentalist religion, strong family relationships, and the other "old-time" aspects of the nonindustrial South.[10]

The roots of bluegrass are not only indicated by the origins of the performers but also by the strong sense-of-place consciousness that is revealed when one examines the names of bluegrass bands and the titles of standard bluegrass tunes. In many cases, the performers utilize a local physiographic feature as the basis for naming their group. This identification with place is exemplified by the Blue Grass Boys, Clinch Mountain Boys, Foggy Mountain Boys, Sunny Mountain Boys, and Shenandoah Valley Cut-Ups among the older groups who came from the original bluegrass hearth. There appears to be a strong affinity for place as well as an intense relationship between man and the land existing in the perceptions of bluegrass musicians. This place name concept for band titles has apparently been perpetuated to the younger groups outside the South such as the Bear Creek Valley Boys, Sawtooth Mountain Boys, and the White Oak Mountain Boys (Table 12-2).

In addition to band names, several standard bluegrass tunes indicate place names in their titles. Those songs that pertain to locations within the South include: "Blue Moon of Kentucky," "East Virginia," "Pike County Break-down," "Flint Hill Special," "Rocky Top," "Knoxville Girl," "Black Mountain Rag," "Across the Blue Ridge Mountains," "Cumberland Gap," "Natchez Under the Hill," and "Banks of the Ohio" (Fig. 12-2). Listeners tend to identify with the lyrics and melody associated with the description of the above places and therefore have demanded them over long periods of time. This accounts for the songs' popularity as bluegrass favorites.[11] The country person with the increased mobility of this century was the last to experience the breakup of home and community. Many of these popular bluegrass tunes reflect the changing status of the rural population as they express a yearning for or remembrance of a vanishing place and past.

Migration of the Music and Musicians

With the extended mobility of the American population and the newer vehicles of communication and transportation, bluegrass music has migrated to other sections of the country. Like southern culture as a whole, the bluegrass sound has moved away from its traditional origins. One explanation for the growth of bluegrass during the late 1950s and early 1960s outside the South was the music's increased popularity among young participants in the folksong "revival." In 1959 the Osborne Brothers appeared at Antioch College in Yellow Springs, Ohio and thus became the first band to perform for a northern college audience. During the 1960s such schools as Harvard, Yale, Oberlin, Illinois, the University of California at Los Angeles and at Berkeley, and the University of Chicago staged performances by major bluegrass bands.[12]

The "folk song renaissance" of the 1970s has rejuvenated interest in bluegrass. Both younger and older groups are gaining stature as concert

Table 12-2. Places Named in Bluegrass

Band Names

The Blue Grass Boys (Kentucky)
Kentucky Mountain Boys (Kentucky)
Pine Hall Ramblers (Kentucky)
The Kentuckians (Kentucky)
The Ohio River Valley Boys (Kentucky)
The Turkey Creek Boys (Kentucky)
The Foggy Mountain Boys (Tennessee)
The Sunny Mountain Boys (Tennessee)
The Smoky Mountain Travelers
  (Tennessee)
The Boys from Shiloh (Tennessee)
The Nashville Grass (Tennessee)
The Clinch Mountain Boys (Virginia)
Shenandoah Valley Cut-Ups (Virginia)
The Virginia Boys (Virginia)
Arbuckle Mountain Boys (Oklahoma)
Kiamichi Mountain Boys (Oklahoma)

Illinois River Folk (Oklahoma)
Current River Drifters (Missouri)
Ozark Mountain Trio (Missouri)
Stone Mountain Boys (Ohio)
The Appalachian Grass (Ohio)
The Free State String Band (Maryland)
The New Potomac Bluegrass Boys
  (Maryland)
The Bear Creek Valley Boys (California)
Styx River Ferry (California)
White Oak Mountain Boys
  (Massachusetts)
Pine River Valley Boys (Michigan)
The Garden State Ramblers (New Jersey)
The Sawtooth Mountain Boys (Oregon)
The Bluegrass Texans (Texas)

Song Titles

"My Rose of Old Kentucky"
"Kentucky Mandolin"
"Blue Moon of Kentucky"
"Kentucky Waltz"
"I'm Going Back to Old Kentucky"
"Kentucky" You Are the Nearest Thing
  to Heaven That I've Seen"
"Banks of the Ohio"
"Knoxville Girl"
"East Virginia"
"Foggy Mountain Top"
"Foggy Mountain Breakdown"
"Sourwood Mountain"
"Pike County Breakdown"
"Hills of Roane County"
"Arkansas Traveler"
"Black Mountain Rag"
"Cripple Creek"
"Mississippi Sawyer"
"Natchez Under the Hill"
"Salt Creek"

"Flint Hill Special"
"Rocky Top"
"Georgia Piney Woods"
"Cane River"
"Texas Gallop"
"Blue Ridge Mountain Blues"
"Shenandoah"
"Across the Blue Ridge Mountains"
"Going Back to Harlan"
"Going to Georgia"
"Goin' Up Caney"
"Roanoke"
"In and Around Nashville"
"Columbus Stockade Blues"
"Clinch Mountain Backstep"
"Stony Creek"
"Tennessee"
"Think What You've Done" (Virginia)
"White Dove" (Virginia)
"The Wreck of the Old Ninety-Seven"
  (Lynchburg and Danville, Virginia)

Source: Band Titles, *Bluegrass Unlimited*, 1968–1972. Song Titles, Dennis Cyporyn, *The Bluegrass Songbook* (New York: Macmillan, 1972), Index.

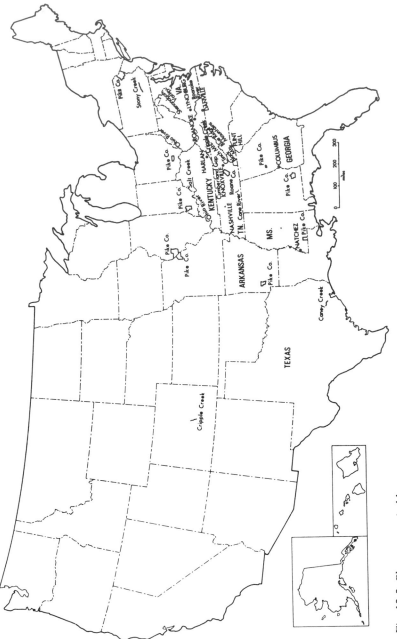

Fig. 12-2. Place names in bluegrass songs.

performers on the college circuit. In 1972, bluegrass was presented at various college and university locations throughout the country (Fig. 12-3). The educational institutions represent different functions including law schools (New York University), art galleries (Yale University), private liberal arts colleges (St. Olaf), gigantic state universities (University of Wisconsin), and state colleges (Humboldt State). Bluegrass is attracted to the Ivy League (Harvard), prestigious southern schools (Vanderbilt and Emory), the Midwest (Western Illinois and Oklahoma State), the Rocky Mountain region (University of Utah), and the extensive University of California system (Davis, Santa Cruz, and Irvine). As rock music wanes, country music, in the form of bluegrass, is catching on among the students. To some degree, it is a fad, but for the majority of students, bluegrass is appreciated for its noncommercialized nature and the sophisticated techniques of playing bluegrass instruments. The college concert stage, however, is less the home of bluegrass performers than the outdoor park festivals found across the country.

Since 1965 one of the major factors for the diffusion of bluegrass has been the rapid increase in the number of outdoor festivals held annually. The festivals, which feature both amateur and professional musicians, are held on large tracts of land that provide ample parking and camping facilities, roofed stages, and shaded wood benches for seating. Shows generally run for three or four days and nights at a cost of approximately $9–12 per person. One of the major highlights of the occasion is the "jamming" that occurs twenty-four hours a day. Local and

Fig. 12-3. College and university concerts (1972).

visiting musicians, good and bad, form groups spontaneously to experiment with new ideas, compare instruments, and "trade licks."

The first outdoor event was the Roanoke Bluegrass Festival, which took place at Cantrell's Horse Farm near Fincastle, Virginia, on Labor Day weekend in 1965. From that small beginning, bluegrass festivals in 1972 numbered approximately 180 and are presented each year, from early spring to late fall, originating from Connecticut to California (Figs. 12-4,5,6). The major concentrations of festivals tend to be clustered in the mountain and hill country sections of Virginia, North Carolina, Tennessee, Kentucky, West Virginia, and Pennsylvania. Festivals, however, have occurred in all but thirteen of the continental United States. Approximately 56 percent of the total number of festivals held from 1965 to 1972 took place within a 400-mile radius of the origin in the mountain section of western Virginia (Fig. 12-7). The basis for bluegrass popularity in the Appalachian region lies in the introduction of stringed instruments during colonial times and the rural population that has tended to conserve the "old-timey" music exemplified in bluegrass.

Beyond the bluegrass core area located in the Appalachian Mountains, a cluster of festivals have emerged in the hill country of southern Missouri, northern Arkansas, eastern Oklahoma, and eastern Texas, with the first major outdoor festival west of the Mississippi produced at Hugo, Oklahoma, in 1969. The mountainous setting may, in part, account for the growth of festivals in this area, but, more importantly, the people and their ancestors in

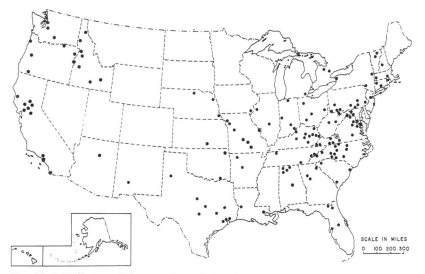

Fig. 12-4. Diffusion of bluegrass festivals (1965, 1966). *Source*: Peggy Logan, *Muleskinner News*, Elon College, North Carolina.

Fig. 12-5. Diffusion of bluegrass festivals (1969). *Source*: Peggy Logan, *Muleskinner News*, Elon College, North Carolina.

Fig. 12-6. Diffusion of bluegrass festivals (1972). *Source*: Peggy Logan, *Muleskinner News*, Elon College, North Carolina.

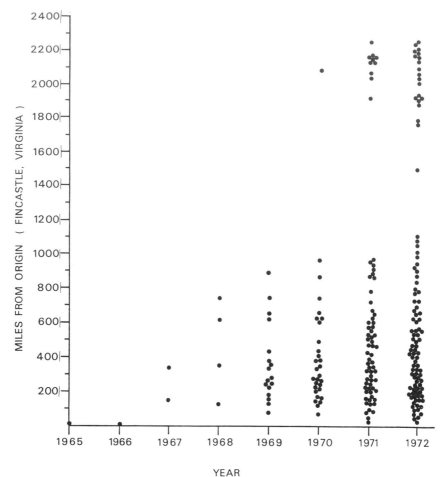

Fig. 12-7. Bluegrass festivals (1965–1972), miles from origin.

the four-state region have migrated from the Appalachian states. They transported their appreciation for bluegrass across the Mississippi.

Population mobility likewise is the factor that accounts for a third concentration of festivals along the West Coast. The rural populace of the Central Valley of California came primarily from the "Dust Bowl" sections of Oklahoma, Arkansas, and Texas during the 1930s.[13] The Pacific Northwest has a sizable population of southerners who immigrated there for a variety of reasons including military service during World War II; employment opportunities, especially in logging; and the beckoning of friends and relatives from southerners who had already located there.[14] The movement of people from these areas, where "old-timey" country music was a life-style trait, has stimulated the growth of festivals in the Far West. Bluegrass has thus spanned the country because people cared enough to preserve the original Appalachian sound even though they were on the move.

The rural nature of bluegrass becomes even more striking when the size of festival cities is examined. Proof are 77 of the 179 (43 percent) festivals which took place in small towns of 2,500 population or less, a figure which the U.S. Bureau of the Census regards as the delineation between rural and urban. The town size of this category ranges from a population of 25 at Pipestem, West Virginia, to 2,429 at Troy, North Carolina. Another 77 (43 percent) festivals were held in urban centers numbering 2,500 to 49,999 with Hodgeville, Kentucky (2,562) and Yakima, Washington (45,588) representing the lowest and highest population points in a medium classification. The remaining 25 (14 percent) festivals were found in SMA's (urban places of 50,000 or more population). Only Los Angeles, Philadelphia, and Houston ranked as metropolitan centers holding festivals.

In addition to the appeal that the outdoor festival holds among rural dwellers, another factor that makes it a small-town phenomenon is the necessity for a significant amount of space to accommodate parking, camping, and seating. It appears also that festivals are attracted to small towns located in areas with such well-known recreational facilities as Myrtle Beach, South Carolina; Lake Ozark, Missouri; and Disney, Oklahoma, near the Lake of the Cherokees.

Whether large or small, the 179 sites throughout the country create a demand for bluegrass musicians to travel from place to place during a festival season. During 1972, Monroe, who is now sixty-two years old and the acknowledged creator of the bluegrass sound, traveled roughly 12,200 miles to twenty-nine festival sites located in 18 states, primarily in the South and Midwest[15] (Fig. 12-8). Not only does Monroe play at festivals, he also promotes them as a business venture. He and his son James sponsor festivals located at Bean Blossom, Indiana; Cosby, Tennessee; McKinney, Texas; Jackson, Kentucky; Henderson, Colorado; and Chatom, Alabama. Monroe's week-long affair at Bean Blossom took shape in 1967, one of the first festivals launched after Fincastle. On his ninety-acre park near this Indiana hamlet of 100 people lying forty-five miles south of Indianapolis, fans numbering in the thousands flock east from California and south from Canada.[16]

The 21,773-mile migration route of the Lewis Family, a well-received bluegrass gospel group from Lincolnton, Georgia, presents a contrast to Monroe's circuit. Whereas the Blue Grass Boys performed at the major festivals, the Lewis Family made sixty-eight stops in seventeen states, playing and singing for people at high school gymnasiums, city auditoriums, and churches, as well as at the outdoor events.[17] The majority of their appearances were confined to the South,

Fig. 12-8. Migration route of Bill Monroe (1972). *Source: Bluegrass Unlimited* (Burke, Virginia: 1972).

especially the Appalachian sections of North Carolina and Virginia (42.6 percent). Their less-frequent appearances outside the South took them primarily to shows like the "Shindig in Barn" at Lancaster, Pennsylvania, where they performed four times in 1972 (Fig. 12-9).

The Osborne Brothers from Hyden, Kentucky, performed eighty-four times in twenty-two states during 1972 (Fig. 12-10). The shows took them approximately 25,289 miles, or around the world, with visits to a significant number of states outside the South including such diverse areas as Rhode Island, Michigan, and Nebraska. The circulation pattern of the Osbornes indicates that more planning goes into their yearly schedule than for the Lewis Family. Their widespread appeal can be attributed to the more "progressive" style of their band, which includes several tunes usually not considered standard bluegrass numbers such as "Take Me Home, Country Roads" and "Shelly's Winter Love," written by folk-pop artist John Denver and honky tonk stylist Merle Haggard, respectively.[18] They have likewise deviated from the traditional bluegrass instrumental arrangement by adding a set of drums and clearly strive for the "cool" stage behavior of jazz musicians. The Osborne Brothers have recorded "Bluegrass Music's Really Gone to Town,"[19] which denotes pride in the recognition of bluegrass by middle- and upper-class northerners and manifests a further trend of bluegrass music.

Bill Monroe ("Father of Bluegrass") and the Bluegrass Boys perform at one of the many outdoor bluegrass festivals held each summer (photo by George Carney).

Location of Bluegrass Music on a Regular Basis

The respectability that bluegrass has gained among northerners can be ascribed in part to its acceptance by the "folk music" intellectual-academician type, such as Alan Lomax, who has called bluegrass the "freshest sound" in American folk music.[20] A further indication of bluegrass music's growing acceptance by the "folk music" coterie is the attention paid to it by the Folkways Recording Company. This company has always catered to a limited audience and has specialized primarily in recordings by well-known city singers like Pete Seeger. In 1959, however, Folkways released an album entitled *Mountain Music: Bluegrass Style*, which featured little-known bands from the southeastern United States.[21] The notes of this album were written by Mike Seeger, a member of the famous Seeger folk music family, and one of the most competent musicians among the urban folk fanciers.

Seeger's interest in bluegrass paralleled that of another northern urbanite,

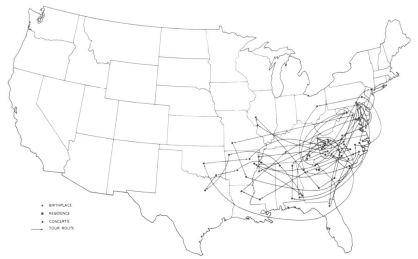

Fig. 12-9. Migration route of the Lewis Family (1972). *Source: Bluegrass Unlimited* (Burke, Virginia: 1972).

Fig. 12-10. Migration route of the Osborne Brothers (1972). *Source: Bluegrass Unlimited* (Burke, Virginia: 1972).

Ralph Rinzler, who came out of a well-to-do New York family to devote most of his life to the study and performance of bluegrass music. An expert mandolinist who played for a time with a city bluegrass group called the Greenbriar Boys, Rinzler devoted considerable study to the career of Bill Monroe.[22] He now serves in an influential music role as director of the performing arts for the Smithsonian Institution and has been instrumental in the establishment of the annual Festival of American Folklife held in Washington, D.C., each Fourth of July holiday. Needless to say, Rinzler has generously sprinkled bluegrass throughout this event since becoming director.[23] With such prestigious folk music influentials supporting the "high lonesome sound," the demand for bluegrass on a regular basis among musically inclined urbanites in metropolitan areas of the North and Far West has flourished. And because bluegrass has received a degree of intellectual admiration from Lomax and Seeger, the country music style is now welcomed regularly on the urban college and university campuses. However, bluegrass has become confined to a various assortment of indoor facilities due to a lack of space for outdoor festivals in the metropolitan areas (Table 12-3).

Data available in 1968 reveal that thirty-three cities provided bluegrass as a recurring practice with a cluster of restaurants, lounges, and taverns located in and around the Baltimore–Washington, D.C., urban area being the most prominent (Fig. 12-11). Rinzler's presence at the Smithsonian has undoubtedly stimulated interest in bluegrass in this area. Two clubs in this region, "The Shamrock" and "The Red Fox Inn," have presented continuous bluegrass from 1968 through 1972, featuring such groups as The Country Gentlemen. Southern New England (Boston and environs) and Southern California (Los Angeles and environs) accounted for an increase to fifty locations in 1969 (Fig. 12-12). Student coffee houses and pubs appear to be the most popular outlets for bluegrass in these clusters. The number of places remained constant in 1970; but in 1971 there were fifty-seven localities, with most of the growth taking place in North Carolina, particularly Winston-Salem, Charlotte, and Chapel Hill (Fig. 12-13).

By 1972 the number of locations playing bluegrass on a repeated basis had reached ninety-four. The most visible growth points were along the Pacific Coast, especially Oregon and Washington, where bluegrass had never been performed on a continual basis until 1972. Dallas—Fort Worth, Louisville, and Nashville were additional urban centers showing an expansion of bluegrass facilities (Fig. 12-14).

Primarily limited to large urban centers of the Northeast and Far West from 1968 to 1970, permanent bluegrass locations in 1971 began to emerge in small towns of the Middle West and Great Plains such as Haysville, Kansas; Eminence, Missouri; and Shawnee, Oklahoma. Although bluegrass fans in

Table 12-3. Location of Indoor Bluegrass Facilities (1968–1972)

Type of Facility	Location
Restaurants, Cafes	(Captain Mac's Clam Shack in Syracuse, New York; Yesterday's Cafe in Waterbury, Connecticut)
Cocktail Lounges	(Walsh's Lounge in Pittsburgh, Pennsylvania; The Shamrock in Washington, D.C.)
Coffee Houses	(The Enormous Room Coffe House in New Haven, Connecticut; Freight and Salvage in Berkeley, California)
Taverns, Bars, Saloons, Beer Gardens	(Hillbilly Ranch in Boston; Dixie Belle Bar in Detroit)
Pizza Parlors	(The Straw Hat Pizza Palace in Santa Cruz, California)
Theaters	(The Round Table Theater in Louisville, Kentucky)
V.F.W. and American Legion Halls	(V.F.W. Hall in Gallatin, Tennessee; American Legion Hall in Exeter, New Hampshire)
Hotels	(Spring Lake Hotel in Waldorf, Maryland; The Railroad Hotel in Manheim, Pennsylvania)
Civic Centers, Community Buildings	(The Civic Center in Henderson, Tennessee; Community Center in Haysville, Kansas)
Labor Union Halls	(U.A.W. Local 1111 Hall in Indianapolis, Indiana)
Entertainment Complexes	(Disney World in Orlando, Florida; Six Flags over Georgia near Atlanta, Georgia; Opryland, U.S.A. in Nashville, Tennessee; Disneyland in Los Angeles, California)
Exclusive Shopping Areas	(Underground Atlanta)
Churches	(Union Church in Walton, Virginia)

Source: *Bluegrass Unlimited*, 1968–1972.

Fig. 12-11. Diffusion of bluegrass indoor facilities (1968). *Source: Bluegrass Unlimited* (Burke, Virginia: 1968).

Fig. 12-12. Diffusion of bluegrass indoor facilities (1969). *Source: Bluegrass Unlimited* (Burke, Virginia: 1969).

Fig. 12-13. Diffusion of bluegrass indoor facilities (1971). *Source: Bluegrass Unlimited* (Burke, Virginia: 1971).

Fig. 12-14. Diffusion of bluegrass indoor facilities (1972). *Source: Bluegrass Unlimited* (Burke, Virginia: 1972).

these areas have more opportunity to attend the outdoor festivals during the summer than do urban dwellers, there is a deficiency of bluegrass during the winter months. Therefore, devotees have scheduled bluegrass shows every Saturday night at community centers, high school auditoriums, and local cafes. Several state bluegrass associations sponsor monthly shows during the winter at various locations throughout their respective states.

Bluegrass, therefore, seems to have moved "uptown" from "down home" during the past five years due to the various outlets provided in urban areas. It has attracted not only the displaced rural population in urban centers, but as has been shown, it also appeals to many members of the "college set" and to urban intellectuals because of its expert instrumentation and use of traditional material. It appears to be making significant inroads into the broad middle ground between the hillbilly audience and the cultural sophisticates. The middle-class listener, whose primary exposure to music is what he hears on television and movies, has been exposed to bluegrass via television shows like *The Beverly Hillbillies*, which used as its theme "The Ballad of Jed Clampett," provided by Lester Flatt and Earl Scruggs. Another Flatt and Scruggs tune, "Foggy Mountain Breakdown," became nationally popular because of its association with the movie *Bonnie and Clyde*. The musical score from *Deliverance*, an Academy Award nominee for 1972, has generated a nationwide upsurge in bluegrass interest, especially in middle-class viewers.

Summary and Conclusions

The preceding evidence indicates that a geographical analysis of bluegrass music incorporates three of the four traditions associated with the field.[24] Bluegrass developed in an area where physical geography imposed a barrier against cultural contact, especially during the seventeenth and eighteenth centuries. The lack of communication, transportation, and commercialization in the Appalachian South allowed the "old-timey" country music to survive; and gradually the combination of traditional hill-country instruments and way of singing resulted in bluegrass. The relationship between humans and the environment is displayed both in bluegrass band names and song titles. The music has preserved, in the new milieu of popular culture, the strong sense of place consciousness that exists among rural people. Bluegrass musicians take pride in their place of birth, which is epitomized in the names of bluegrass groups. They have consistently utilized lyrics that described places that are familiar to both performer and listener thereby creating a sense of communication between the two.

Within the span of approximately thirty-five years, bluegrass music has migrated from the Appalachian South to all sections of the United States. Performances have occurred in both rural and urban environments from South to North and East to West. The diffusion of outdoor festivals and indoor facilities featuring bluegrass during the past decade manifests an interest among all social classes from the Appalachian hillbilly to the urban intellectual. Describing bluegrass in 1963, Bill Monroe said:

> A lot of the people down on the Grand Ole Opry kids me about bluegrass. They tell it to me . . . like I really started something . . . , when I started bluegrass, that can't be stopped. There's no telling where it's going to go. . . .[25]

Although the "father of bluegrass" was probably referring to style, the last sentence is equally applicable to space as bluegrass continues to move from place to place across the cultural landscape of the United States.

Notes

1. Bill C. Malone, *Country Music, U.S.A.* (Austin: University of Texas Press, 1968), pp. 3–12; Alan Lomax, *Folk Songs of North America* (Garden City, N.Y.: Doubleday, 1960), xv–xvii; and Charlie Gillett, *The Sound of the City: The Rise of Rock 'N' Roll* (New York: Outerbridge and Dienstfrey, 1970), pp. 1–2.

2. Larry Ford, "Geographic Factors in the Origin, Evolution, and Diffusion of Rock and Roll Music," *The Journal of Geography* 70 (1971), pp. 455–64; Richard V. Francaviglia, "Diffusion and Popular Culture: Comments on the Spatial Aspects of Rock Music," in David A. Lanegran and Risa Palm, eds., *An Invitation to Geography* (New York: McGraw-Hill Book Company, 1973), pp. 87–96; and Tamara and Larry K. Stephenson, "A Prologue to Listening," *Antipode: A Radical Journal of Geography* 5 (1973), pp. 12–16.

3. Wilbur Zelinsky, *The Cultural Geography of the United States* (Englewood Cliffs, N.J.: Prentice-Hall, 1973), pp. 107–8.

4. Lomax, op. cit. (see note 1 above), xv. See inside front and back covers of Lomax for musical maps.

5. Neil V. Rosenberg, "From Sound to Style: The Emergence of Bluegrass," *Journal of American Folklore* 53 (1967), pp. 143–50; L. Mayne Smith, "An Introduction to Bluegrass," *Journal of American Folklore* 68 (1965), pp. 245–56; Robert Cantwell, "Believing in Bluegrass," *Atlantic Monthly* 229 (1972), pp. 52–60; David Standish, "Shenandoah Breakdown," *Playboy* 18 (1971), pp. 189–90, 193–94; and Ralph E. Winter, "Awash with Nostalgia," "Bluegrass Festivals' Revive Old-Time Music," *The Wall Street Journal*, October 20, 1972, pp. 1 and 15.

6. Personal interview with Bill Monroe, January 14, 1973, Enid, Oklahoma.

7. Ibid.

8. L. Mayne Smith, "Bluegrass Music and Musicians: An Introductory Study of a

Musical Style in its Cultural Context," unpublished master's thesis, University of Indiana, 1964, p. 16.

9. Louise Scruggs, "History of the 5-String Banjo," *Tennessee Folklore Society Bulletin* 27 (March 1961), pp. 1–5; and Ralph Rinzler, liner notes to *American Banjo "Scruggs" Style*, Folkways FA2314.

10. Rosenberg, op. cit. (see note 5 above), pp. 143–50.

11. For a listing of titles and discussion on this topic, consult Dennis Cyporyn, *The Bluegrass Songbook* (New York: Macmillan, 1972), index and p. 105.

12. Smith, op. cit. (see note 8 above), p. 22.

13. Warren S. Thompson, *Growth and Changes in California's Population* (Los Angeles: The Haynes Foundation, 1955), p. 68.

14. See notes to *Comin' Round the Mountain*, Voyager Recordings VRLP 302.

15. Personal interview with Bill Monroe, July 21, 1973, Disney, Oklahoma.

16. Hubert Saal, "Pickin' and Singin,' " *Newsweek* 75 (1970), p. 85.

17. Personal interview with Wallace and Polly Lewis, August 12, 1973, Hugo, Oklahoma.

18. Osborne Brothers, *Country Roads*, MCA Records DL 75321.

19. Osborne Brothers, *Cuttin' Grass*, MGM E/SE 4149.

20. Alan Lomax, "Bluegrass Background: Folk Music with Overdrive," *Esquire* 52 (1959), pp. 103–9.

21. For a thorough discussion of the vocal and instrumental characteristics of bluegrass music see the notes to *Mountain Music: Bluegrass Style*, Folkways FA 2318.

22. See Rinzler's notes to *The Greenbriar Boys*, Vanguard VRS-9104.

23. *Festival of American Folklife* SI-100.

24. William D. Pattison, "The Four Traditions of Geography," *The Journal of Geography* 63 (1964), pp. 211–16.

25. Transcribed from a tape of a live performance, Worcester, Massachusetts, November 11, 1963, in Smith, op. cit. (see note 7 above), p. 61.

From Down Home to Uptown: The Diffusion of Country Music Radio Stations in the United States

George O. Carney

A wide variety of phenomena, including music and communication, have been topics of recent diffusion research.[1] Generally the focus of such work may be classified as either cultural or technological. The present study, however, examines the diffusion of an innovation that embodies both cultural and technological aspects: the all-country-music AM radio station in the United States. The first section provides background material pertaining primarily to the early centers of country music programming on radio; the second presents an analysis of the diffusion patterns of the all-country-music radio station, focusing particularly upon the years 1971–74; and the third details the factors underlying these patterns. Principal data sources include the *Broadcasting Yearbook, 1971–74*, and the *Radio Station Survey, 1971–74*, of the Country Music Association.

Early Centers of Country Music Broadcasts

Radio stations in the South began programming country music in the early 1920s. Station WSB in Atlanta is acknowledged to have been the first when it featured Fiddlin' John Carson in 1922.[2] In the years following, stations

Reprinted by permission from *The Journal of Geography* 75 (1977): 104–10.

throughout the South and Midwest began featuring country talent.[3] Station WBAP in Fort Worth produced the first barn dance music for radio on 4 January 1923, a year and a half before the WLS National Barn Dance in Chicago and about three years prior to the famed WSM Grand Ole Opry in Nashville. In those early, unregulated days of American broadcasting, WBAP programs, featuring such groups as the Peacock Fiddle Band from Cleburne, Texas, were received by listeners in New York, Canada, Hawaii, and Haiti; and they stimulated a series of country music barn dances that began appearing on radio stations located primarily in the South and Midwest (Fig. 13-1).[4]

Although stations WSB and WBAP had programmed barn dance shows as early as 1922, WLS in Chicago produced the first show to achieve longevity and national recognition. The program began one week after the station went on the air on April 12, 1924. Initially owned by Sears, Roebuck and Company and from 1928 by the *Prairie Farmer* newspaper, WLS aimed much of its programming toward the rural and small-town listener in the Midwest.[5] A group of country-style fiddlers performed on the first program, and the music was so well received that hundreds of requests for various fiddle tunes arrived within the next week.[6] This humble beginning in 1924 led to the development of the popular National Barn Dance, now carried by station WGN in Chicago.

Despite the success experienced by the WBAP and WLS barn dance shows, the Grand Ole Opry, transmitted throughout the southland over Nashville's 50,000-watt station WSM, became the most important country music radio show when it gained network status in 1939. For thirty minutes every Saturday night, sponsored by Prince Albert Tobacco, the National Broadcasting Company carried a segment representative of the larger four-and-a-half-hour show headlined by a famous performer and supported by other acts.[7]

In addition to national shows like the WSM Grand Ole Opry, the 1930s and 1940s witnessed the emergence of regional barn dances sponsored by local radio stations (Fig. 13-1). These included Louisiana Hayride, produced by KWKH in Shreveport; Midwestern Hayride, originating in Cincinnati, and the Boone County Jamboree, originating from Renfro Valley, Kentucky, both supported by WLW in Cincinnati; Jamboree, produced by WWVA in Wheeling; Big D Jamboree, aired by Dallas's KRLD; New Dominion Barn Dance, presented by Richmond's WRVA; Tennessee Barn Dance, aired by WNOX in Knoxville; and the KXLA Hometown Jamboree from Pasadena.[8]

By the mid-1950s only the WSM Grand Ole Opry and WWVA Jamboree were still on the air. It was then, however, that the all-country-music radio station (i.e., one that plays 100 percent country music regardless of the

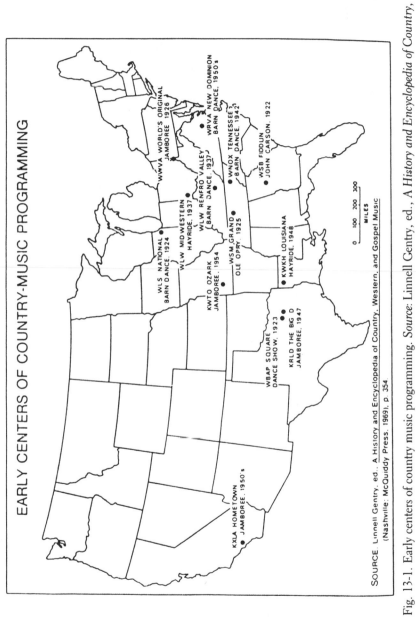

EARLY CENTERS OF COUNTRY-MUSIC PROGRAMMING

WWVA WORLD'S ORIGINAL JAMBOREE, 1926

WRVA NEW DOMINION BARN DANCE, 1950's

WRVA NEW DOMINION BARN DANCE, 1950's

WNOX TENNESSEE BARN DANCE, 1942

WLW RENFRO VALLEY BARN DANCE, 1937

WLS NATIONAL BARN DANCE, 1924

WLW MID WESTERN HAYRIDE, 1937

WSB FIDDLIN JOHN CARSON, 1922

WSM GRAND OLE OPRY, 1925

KWTO OZARK JAMBOREE, 1954

KWKH LOUISIANA HAYRIDE, 1948

WBAP SQUARE DANCE SHOW, 1923

KRLD THE BIG D JAMBOREE, 1947

KXLA HOMETOWN JAMBOREE, 1950's

0   100   200   300
MILES

SOURCE: Linnell Gentry, ed., A History and Encyclopedia of Country, Western, and Gospel Music (Nashville: McQuiddy Press, 1969), p. 354.

Fig. 13-1. Early centers of country music programming. *Source:* Linnell Gentry, ed., *A History and Encyclopedia of Country, Western, and Gospel Music* (Nashville: McQuiddy Press, 1969).

WSM Grand Ole Opry sign on facade of Ryman Auditorium in downtown Nashville (photo by George Carney).

number of hours it is on the air in a twenty-four-hour period) emerged.[9] This movement resulted in more programming of country music on a part-time basis and also burgeoned in its own right.

Diffusion Patterns

Complete data on the locations of all-country-music radio stations first became available in 1971 as a result of the extensive efforts of the Country

Music Association.[10] In that year there were 525 such stations, 12.3 percent of all AM stations operating in 1974 (Table 13-1). They were clustered in several parts of the South and Far West. Significant concentrations were found in the Appalachians from southern Pennsylvania to northern Alabama; the coastal lowland areas of the Carolinas, Florida, and Alabama; Texas with the exception of the Rio Grande Valley; and the Central Valley of California and Willamette Valley in Oregon (Fig. 13-2). In 1971 Texas, North Carolina, Florida, Tennessee, Georgia, Alabama, and Virginia had the greatest number of all-country stations; California, which ranked seventh, contained the only significant number outside the South (Table 13-2). In terms of ratio of all-country to total AM radio stations, the southeastern and south central states of Texas (22.0 percent), Alabama (19.6 percent), Tennessee (18.2 percent), Florida (17.7 percent), and North Carolina (17.4 percent) ranked high (Table 13-2). The highest percentage (27.3 percent), however, was in Nevada. One explanation is that no large-wattage, all-country-music station is dominant in the intermontane region, so each of a large number of small-wattage (5,000 watts or less) stations captures "a small piece of the market pie."[11]

In 1972, 120 stations adopted the all-country format, resulting in a net total (after closings) of 633 stations or 14.8 percent of all AM stations (Table 13-1). Most of the stations adopting the new format were located in southern or border states such as Alabama (9), Florida (8), Georgia (5), Tennessee (6), Arkansas (6), Louisiana (5), Kentucky (7), Oklahoma (9), North Carolina (7), and Texas (5). Together they accounted for 67 of the 127 new stations (Table 13-2). There was also significant expansion outside of the South, particularly in California (8), Washington (5), Indiana (6), Illinois (5), and Michigan (5). In terms of the proportion of AM stations that were all-country, Alabama led with 26.1 percent, followed by Texas (23.8 percent), South Dakota (23.5 percent), Nevada (22.7 percent), Florida (21.7 percent), North Carolina (20.8 percent), and Oklahoma (20.6 percent). The situation in South Dakota is similar to that in Nevada (i.e., a large number of small-wattage country-music stations were established because no large-wattage all-country station dominated the upper Great Plains).[12]

The largest growth occured in 1973, when 143 all-country stations were added, resulting in a total after closings of 764 or 17.8 percent of all AM radio stations (Table 3.1). Considerable increase was again noticeable in the South, particularly in Texas (21), Tennessee (11), Kentucky (9), Alabama (10), and Mississippi (10), for a total of 61 stations. Areas outside the South penetrated by the diffusion included Minnesota with nine new stations and Missouri, Montana, and West Virginia with six each. By 1973 the number of all-country stations in Alabama and Texas had increased to 33.3 percent and 31.1 percent of the total AM stations in each state. Tennessee ranked third

Table 13-1. Radio Station Adoption of All-Country Formats by City Size

City Size	Total AM Stations	Adoptions by 1971		1972			1973			1974			Percentage of Total Adoptions for 1974
		Total	%*	New	Total	%*	New	Total	%*	New	Total	%*	
25,000 or less	2,558	321	12.5	51	372	14.5	65	437	17.1	52	487	19.0	56.9
25,000–50,000	539	67	12.4	31	98	18.2	25	117	21.7	11	128	15.0	15.0
50,001–100,000	413	53	12.8	13	66	16.0	21	87	21.1	16	105	25.4	12.2
100,001–250,000	347	44	12.7	9	53	15.3	16	69	19.9	8	77	22.2	9.0
250,001–500,000	171	23	13.4	3	26	15.2	4	30	17.5	3	33	19.3	3.9
500,001–1,000,000	182	13	7.1	1	14	7.7	4	18	9.9	2	20	10.9	2.3
Over 1,000,000	71	4	5.6	0	4	5.6	2	6	8.5	0	6	8.5	0.7
Total		525			633			764			856		
All-country radio stations as percentage of AM radio stations in 1974 (4,291)			12.3			14.8			17.8			20.0	

Source: *Radio Station Survey*, Country Music Association, Nashville, *Broadcasting Yearbook*, 1971–74; and *City-County Data Book*, 1972.

*These percentages represent the cumulative level of adoption over the total number of AM stations in the respective size categories for 1974.

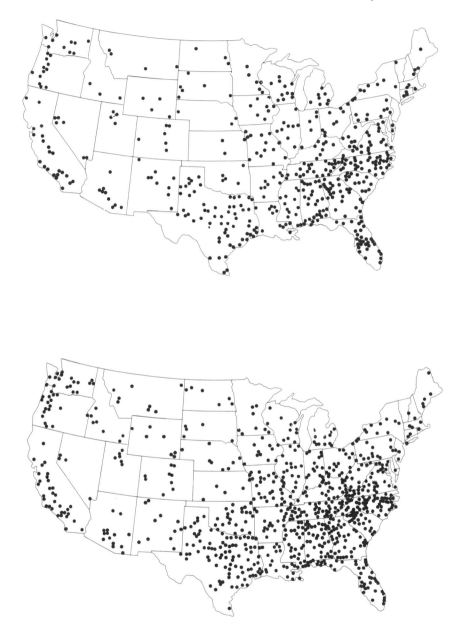

Fig. 13-2. All-country-music radio stations (1971 and 1974). Source: Country Music Association, *Radio Station Survey*.

Table 13-2. Radio Station Adoption of All-Country Formats by State

STATE	TOTAL AM 1974	1971		1972		1973		1974	
		Total All-Country	% of 1974 Total AM	Total All-Country	% of 1974 Total AM	Total All-Country	% of 1974 Total AM	Total All-Country	% of 1974 Total AM
AL	138	27	19.6	36	26.1	46	33.3	41	29.7
AZ	64	10	15.6	11	17.2	10	15.6	10	15.6
AR	84	9	10.7	15	17.9	18	21.4	20	23.8
CA	187	25	13.3	33	17.6	33	17.6	32	17.1
CO	68	6	8.8	8	11.8	8	11.8	10	14.7
CT	39	2	5.1	2	5.1	3	7.7	2	5.1
DE	10	0	0.0	0	0.0	0	0.0	0	0.0
FL	198	35	17.7	43	21.7	45	22.7	44	22.2
GA	177	28	15.8	33	18.6	36	20.3	43	24.3
ID	43	4	9.3	6	13.9	8	18.6	8	18.6
IL	127	8	6.3	13	10.2	13	10.2	17	13.4
IN	87	5	5.7	11	12.6	11	12.6	16	18.4
IA	80	6	7.5	7	8.8	9	11.3	12	15.0
KS	61	3	4.9	5	8.2	5	8.2	6	9.8
KY	110	12	10.9	19	17.3	28	25.5	26	23.6
LA	92	12	13.0	17	18.5	19	20.7	24	26.1
ME	35	3	8.6	1	2.9	4	11.4	5	14.3
MD	50	5	10.0	5	10.0	6	12.0	8	16.0
MA	65	1	1.5	3	4.6	2	3.1	3	4.6
MI	129	9	7.0	14	10.9	18	14.0	16	12.4
MN	92	6	6.5	6	6.5	15	16.3	15	16.3
MS	104	13	12.5	12	11.5	22	21.2	28	26.9
MO	109	16	14.7	19	17.4	25	22.9	36	33.0
MT	40	4	10.0	4	10.0	10	25.0	9	22.5
NE	48	3	6.3	5	10.4	5	40.4	8	16.7
NV	22	6	27.3	5	22.7	4	18.2	4	18.2
NH	27	0	0.0	0	0.0	0	0.0	2	7.4

State									
NJ	39	0	0.0	0	0.0	1	2.6	2	5.1
NM	57	8	14.0	7	12.3	11	19.3	11	19.3
NY	161	8	5.0	9	5.6	12	7.5	12	7.5
NC	207	36	17.4	43	20.8	46	22.2	46	22.2
ND	29	3	10.3	5	17.2	7	24.1	7	24.1
OH	126	10	7.9	12	9.5	14	11.1	18	14.3
OK	68	5	7.4	14	20.6	13	19.1	22	32.4
OR	81	13	16.1	12	14.8	16	19.8	18	22.2
PA	177	11	6.2	10	5.6	9	5.1	16	9.0
RI	15	1	6.7	1	6.7	1	6.7	1	6.7
SC	104	13	12.5	12	11.5	12	11.5	22	21.2
SD	34	6	17.7	8	23.5	6	17.6	7	20.6
TN	154	28	18.2	34	22.1	45	29.2	50	32.5
TX	286	63	22.0	68	23.8	89	31.1	93	32.5
UT	30	5	16.7	6	20.0	8	26.7	7	23.3
VT	18	1	5.6	1	5.6	0	0.0	0	0.0
VA	134	22	16.4	23	17.2	28	20.9	34	25.4
WA	95	11	11.6	16	16.8	16	16.8	18	18.9
WV	60	7	11.7	3	5.0	9	15.0	12	20.0
WI	103	12	11.7	9	8.7	12	11.7	11	10.7
WY	27	4	14.8	3	11.1	6	22.2	4	14.8

1974 rank by percentage of all-country stations (top 12 states)

1.	MO	33.0		7.	LA	26.1
2.	TX	32.5		8.	VA	25.4
3.	TN	32.5		9.	GA	24.3
4.	OK	32.4		10.	ND	24.1
5.	AL	29.7		11.	AR	23.8
6.	MS	26.9		12.	KY	23.6

	1972	1973	1974
New stations opened	120	143	109
Stations closed	12	12	17
Net increase	108	131	92

Source: *Radio Station Growth Report* supplied by Jan Ray Garratt, Archives of C.M.A., Nashville, TN.

(29.2 percent), followed by Utah (26.7 percent), Kentucky (25.5 percent), Montana (25.0 percent), North Dakota (24.1 percent), Missouri (22.9 percent), Florida (22.7 percent), and Wyoming (22.2 percent). Utah's high percentage, as in the case of Nevada and South Dakota, reflects a situation in which a large number of small-wattage country-music stations compete for the market. In addition, the Mormon Church fosters various forms of folk dances, including the square dance, which have historically utilized traditional country music as background.[13]

By 1974 there were 856 all-country radio stations or 20.0 percent of all AM stations (Table 13.1). This represented a gain of 92 over the 1973 figure, an indication that adoption of all-country formats was leveling off. Also, the locus of adoption shifted. The most noticeable increases in the South, for example, were in Oklahoma (9), Missouri (11), South Carolina (10), Georgia (7), Virginia (6), Mississippi (6), and Tennessee (6), a shift in focus from states such as Texas and Alabama where most adoptions took place in previous years. Also emerging as a new pocket of all-country radio stations was the Ohio Valley, especially Pennsylvania (7), Indiana (5), Illinois (4), and Ohio (4) (Fig. 13-2). By 1974 eight states in the Southeast and South Central regions ranked highest in terms of the ratio of all-country to total AM stations. These included Missouri (33.0 percent), Texas and Tennessee (32.5 percent), Oklahoma (32.4 percent), Alabama (29.7 percent), Mississippi (26.9 percent), Louisiana (26.1 percent), and Virginia (25.4 percent).

All-country-music radio stations are largely concentrated in small towns (Table 13-1). Of the 856 all-country stations, 487 (56.9 percent) are located in cities of 250,000 or less, and 720 (84.1 percent) are in towns no larger than 100,000. These size differences are less distinct but still recognizable if the percentage of all-country to total AM stations in each category of city size is considered. Towns of 100,000 or less have had country-music formats adopted by approximately 23 percent of their AM stations, in contrast to approximately 9 percent in cities of 500,000 or more.

Once considered a small-town phenomenon, the all-country radio stations appears to be sliding up the urban hierarchy in opposition to the more common pattern in which an innovation originates in large cities and trickles down.[14] Although the early centers of country-music programming in the 1920s and 1930s were cities such as Chicago, Nashville, Fort Worth, and Shreveport, the formats were not exclusively country music, and among that early group only Chicago could be classified as a large city. Further, it was not until 1973 that stations in the two largest urban centers in the United States, WHN in New York and KMPC in Los Angeles, switched to the all-country sound. Reverse-order hierarchical diffusion is also illustrated by the late adoption (in 1973) of all-country programming in Phoenix, Indianapolis, Jacksonville, and Memphis.

Underlying Factors

Cultural historians, folklorists, and sociologists have agreed for some time that the hearth of country music is the South, including both upland Appalachia and the coastal lowlands.[15] Early pioneer migration from this area, directed toward areas with physiographic conditions similar to those left behind, shifted the southern frontier. Thus, migration from the Appalachian sections of the Upper South flowed toward the Ozarks, while migration from the Lower South flowed toward the potential cotton-producing regions of Arkansas, Louisiana, and Texas.[16] In this fashion the population of the hearth of country music pushed steadily westward in the nineteenth century, moving the southern music culture with it.

Available data are consistent with these observations. The states of the Upper and Lower South as well as Texas, Louisiana, Arkansas, Oklahoma, Kentucky, and Missouri provide the largest contiguous area where the highest proportion of all-country stations to the total number of AM stations is found. Within this area, however, the influence of the early centers of country-music programming, which likewise tended to be located in the South (Fig. 13-1), also is evident. Consider, for example, the cluster of all-country stations located near Fort Worth–Dallas and Shreveport, early centers of country-music programming (Fig. 13-2).

The location of all-country-music radio stations in the Central Valley of California and the Willamette Valley of Oregon can be attributed to later migration. The population of these areas consists primarily of Okies, Arkies, and Texans, who migrated during the 1930s, and their descendants.[17] The Dust Bowl refugees' affection for country music has remained strong, and their interests are reflected by the number of stations that serve them.

Migration from the South also played a role in the reverse-order hierarchical diffusion pattern, creating a demand for all-country-music radio stations in metropolitan areas such as Chicago, Detroit, Cleveland, and Cincinnati.[18] Additional factors in this "sliding up" diffusion include the changing musical tastes of urbanites who have become disenchanted with the quality of Tin Pan Alley music, the rejuvenation of interest among city people for the vanishing countryside and its rural folkways such as country music, and the organized effort of the country music industry to broaden its audience by personal appearances of performers outside of Nashville.[19] Thus, the all-country-music radio station has moved *uptown* from *down home*.

Since the demands for country music were not met simultaneously, we must consider the processes underlying the establishment of the all-country-music radio station to understand its diffusion fully. The first conversion to the all-country-music format was at station KDAV in Lubbock, Texas. This change was initiated by Dave Stone, then the new station manager, who had previously had a one-hour country music show on Lubbock's KSEL and found listener response overwhelming (two sacks of mail per day). Stone's communication of his experience to other Texas station managers was partly responsible for the spread of the all-country-music format during the 1950s. In addition, some of Stone's former employees carried the innovation to their new posts at other stations in the South Central states, and Stone himself was personally responsible for adoption of country broadcasts by KZIP in Amarillo, KPEP in San Angelo, and KPIK in Colorado Springs, Colorado.[20]

During the 1960s, however, the Country Music Association became the marshalling force in urging radio stations to convert to the all-country sound. Its efforts were encouraged by the heavy competition among stations that featured rock, Top 40, and easy-listening formats and the view in broadcasting circles that "too many were trying to cut the pie," particularly in urban areas. When stations with such formats began losing money, the Country Music Association encouraged them to change over to all-country. An instrument in this effort was the *Pulse* twenty-three-market survey of country music stations, which was promoted in broadcasting journals, trade magazines (such as *Billboard, Record World,* and *Cash Box*), and record company literature in order to reach potential adopters.[21] This survey revealed that the country music audience was stable, loyal, and had considerable buying power, and that stations converting to the all-country sound increased both their ratings and sales.

It thus appears that the establishment of all-country-music radio stations in the initial stages of diffusion during the 1950s was largely a contagion based upon personal contact. In the 1960s, however, the Country Music Association acted as a central propagator,[22] contacting station managers (particularly those losing money with rock and pop formats) and showing them that ratings and sales could be increased by adopting the all-country format.

Conclusions

Although country music programming originated in large cities such as Fort Worth, Chicago, and Nashville, the all-country-music radio station has been more common in small towns of 25,000 or less and for the most part has diffused up the urban hierarchy instead of down. The all-country-music radio station originated in the South and South Central states, where the majority are still found, and diffused outward from that hearth in all directions.

Several processes have affected these patterns. On a local level, evidence of a contagion based on personal communication can be found. Thus, we note a markedly higher incidence of country music programming. More interesting, however, is that all-country-music radio is an innovation reflecting southern music culture. While this culture originated in the southern highlands, migration is the mechanism by which it has been spread, first to other areas in the deep South and South Central states and later to western and northern areas. The result is a diffusion pattern from south to west and north, and from small towns to large cities. In a more general context, the diffusion of the all-country-music radio stations, an expansion process,[23] follows on the diffusion of its opportunity set[24] of persons imbued with the southern music culture, a migration or relocation process.[25] Also evident is the role of a central propagator, the Country Music Association, which promoted change to the all-country format by employing surveys indicating the economic advantages of such a shift and communicating through broadcast industry media. Thus, we are able to observe a polynuclear process lacking central propagator support initially, but giving way to one with central propagator support later.[26] This innovation provides a good example of how several different, seemingly disparate processes coalesce to bring about what on the surface appears to be simple diffusion.

Notes

1. Larry Ford, "Geographic Factors in the Origin, Evolution, and Diffusion of Rock and Roll Music," *Journal of Geography* 70 (1971): 445–64; George O. Carney, "Bluegrass Grows All Around: The Spatial Dimensions of a Country Music Style," *Journal of Geography* 73 (1974): 34–55; idem, "Country Music and the Radio: A Historical Geographic Assessment," *Rocky Mountain Social Science Journal* 11, No. 2 (April 1974): 19–32; William Bell, "The Diffusion of Radio and Television Broadcasting Stations in the United States" (Master's thesis, Pennsylvania State University, 1965); and Brian J. L. Berry, "Hierarchical Diffusion: The Basis of Developmental Filtering and Spread in the System of Growth Centers," in *Growth Centers in Regional Economic Development*, ed. Niles M. Hansen (New York: Free Press, 1972), pp. 108–38.

2. Bill C. Malone, *Country Music, U.S.A.* (Austin: University of Texas Press, 1968), p. 35.

3. See "All States Broadcast except Wyoming," *Literary Digest* 75 (1922): 29.

4. The Fort Worth *Star-Telegram* for 1922–23 contains a wealth of information concerning the early WBAP barn dance shows.

5. Boris Emmet and John Jeuck, *Catalogues and Counters: A History of Sears, Roebuck and Company* (Chicago: University of Chicago Press, 1950), p. 624.

6. Clarence B. Newman, "Homespun Harmony," *Wall Street Journal* 37 (1957): 6.

7. Malone, *Country Music, U.S.A.*, p. 195.

8. Linnell Gentry, ed., *A History and Encyclopedia of Country, Western and Gospel Music* (Nashville: McQuiddy Press, 1969), p. 354.

9. Interview with Jan Ray Garratt, Country Music Association Archives, Nashville, Tennessee, July 8, 1971.

10. The Country Music Association evolved from the Country Music Disc Jockeys' Association.

11. Telephone interview with Mel Ryan, vice president and general manager, radio station KRAM, Las Vegas, Nevada, February 16, 1976.

12. Telephone interview with Mike Murphy, program director, radio station KGFX, Pierre, South Dakota, February 16, 1976.

13. Telephone interview with Gene Guthrie, general manager, radio station KRGO, Salt Lake City, Utah, February 16, 1976; and C. R. and M. B. Jensen, *Square Dancing* (Provo, Utah: Brigham Young University Press, 1973).

14. Peter R. Gould, *Spatial Diffusion*, Association of American Geographers, Commission on College Geography, Resource Paper No. 4 (Washington, D.C., 1969), p. 508.

15. Malone, *Country Music, U.S.A.*, pp. 3–4; Alan Lomax, *The Folk Songs of North America* (Garden City, N.Y.: Doubleday and Company, 1960), p. 153; and A. P. Hudson, "Folk Songs of the Southern Whites" in *Culture in the South*, ed. W. T. Couch (Chapel Hill: University of North Carolina Press, 1934), p. 520.

16. Frank L. Owsley, "The Pattern of Migration and Settlement of the Southern Frontier," *Journal of Southern History* 19 (1945): 147–76.

17. Warren S. Thompson, *Growth and Changes in California's Population* (Los Angeles: Haynes Foundation, 1955), p. 68.

18. Lewis M. Killian, *White Southerners* (New York: Random House, 1970), pp. 104–12; Roscoe Griffin, "Appalachian Newcomers in Cincinnati," in *The Southern Appalachian Region: A Survey*, ed. Thomas R. Ford (Lexington: University of Kentucky Press, 1962), pp. 79–84; and Erdmann D. Beynon, "The Southern White Laborer Migrates to Michigan," *American Sociological Review* 3 (1938): 333–45.

19. Robert Shelton and Burt Goldblatt, *The Country Music Story* (Indianapolis: Bobbs-Merrill Company, 1966), pp. 20–22.

20. Telephone interview with Dave Stone, owner of radio stations KDAV in Lubbock, KZIP in Amarillo, KPEP in San Angelo, and KPIK in Colorado Springs, April 9, 1976.

21. See "The Growing Sound of Country Music," *Broadcasting* 18 (October 1965): 69–72.

22. Lawrence A. Brown, "The Market and Infrastructure Context of Adoption: A Spatial Perspective on the Diffusion of Innovation," *Economic Geography* 51 (1975): 185–216.

23. Lawrence A. Brown, *Diffusion Processes and Location: A Conceptual Framework and Bibliography* (Philadelphia: Regional Science Research Institute, 1968), p. 3.

24. E. G. Moore, "Some Spatial Properties of Urban Contact Fields," *Geographical Analysis* 2 (1970): 376–86.

25. Brown, *Diffusion Processes*, pp. 2–3.

26. Brown, "Market and Infrastructure Context," pp. 185–216.

The Spatial Impact of White Gospel Quartets in the United States

A. D. Horsley

The United States was just returning from World War I when gospel quartet music began to expand its singing region, its book publishing, and its influence as a musical form. From 1920 to 1978, gospel quartet singing grew to become one of America's entertainment and religious institutions as it contributed richly to the varied musical traditions and accomplishments of America. It grew each year in number of groups and concerts and was characterized by W. B. Nowlin, one major gospel entertainment entrepreneur in the United States, as "good entertainment . . . a spiritual lift . . . that's why it will survive. Gospel has a great future."[1] Nowlin is only one of the numerous national promoters who have capitalized on and aided the growing gospel music industry.

What is gospel quartet music? This author proposes a simple, broad but traditional definition of gospel quartet music based on interviews with Gospel Music Association members and many retired gospel quartet musicians. That is, that it is the popular music of American Christianity.[2] In addition, it is the most widely recognized and familiar form of popular religious music as measured by concert attendance and record sales since 1960. Gospel quartet music by tradition has four common elements: (1) four-part vocal harmony; (2) text derived directly, symbolically, or interpretatively from the Christian story of the Bible; (3) an entertaining mixture of several music forms; and (4)

Reprinted by permission from the *John Edwards Memorial Foundation Quarterly* 15 (1979): 91–98.

a dependency on the vocal form for proselytizing. Several similar definitions have been written or attributed to certain members of the gospel quartet music industry since it began. David Crawford, in his study of court decisions on gospel music copyrights in 1957, defines gospel music as "rural music . . . dealing with the issues of contemporary evil."[3] James C. Downey wrote that "gospel music was a descendant of the revival songs of the 1800s."[4] Some early songwriters viewed gospel music as music based on the four gospels of the New Testament.

The music played and sung by most of the early groups during the 1920s, 1930s, and 1940s, however, was not restricted only to material based on the four gospels.[5] Crawford's study quotes other definitions of gospel music. A gospel music publisher from Fayette, Alabama, during the 1957 court case defined gospel music as "songs that deal with the human experiences of life that are written in a folksy manner."[6] During the same court case Willard Rhodes, professor of ethnomusicology at Columbia University, described gospel music as that "with a verse and chorus pattern . . . and a fast tempo with a predominant rhythmic element like syncopation."[7] Finally, an official of SESAC, a major performance licensing agency for writers and song owners, characterized gospel music as music that "sounded like popular . . . with lyrics of a religious nature."[8] Homer Rodeheaver defined gospel music as "music addressed to the people presenting some phase of God's plan of salvation."[9]

J. D. Sumner, a charter member of the national Gospel Music Association, noticed one of the differences between nonreligious music and gospel quartet music when he wrote that

> there is only one difference in gospel music and that is the message. This is where our music is head and shoulders above it all. Our music brings a message to the soul, it tells of one who was the Son of God, who became man so that man might become the Son of God. It brings hope instead of despair, joy instead of sorrow, and peace instead of troubled mind.[10]

This difference of a special message has been the central theme found among the three thousand traveling gospel groups in the United States in 1979.[11] These three thousand groups have developed as a result of more than sixty years of organized gospel quartet music traveling across the United States, singing in churches and auditoriums, and promoting records, books, and other materials—the result a very particular American music.

Interested gospel singers in the late 1880s and 1890s were taught and influenced by shaped-note singing-school teachers who spread gospel music to many frontier counties.[12] By 1920 these singing-school teachers were climaxing their week-long schools with a Sunday program called a "singing convention." Since these conventions used available songbooks, and demanded more songbooks, several printing companies developed to supply the thousands of gospel music songbooks required. The companies circulated them among the county sing conventioneers by hiring trained quartet singers to travel to these conventions, sing from, and then sell the songbooks.[13] This development transformed a locally centered musical form (the singing school and convention) into a national network of touring white gospel quartets. This network marked the spatial movement of a cultural phenomenon due to a set of nonrandom forces.[14] These groups depended upon the combination of cooperating churches, printing companies, radio programs, and sponsors in maintaining and organizing monthly singing conventions, which by 1930 were a regular weekend event in 95 percent of the counties in the United States from western Texas and Oklahoma throughout the southern states, and Midwest to Pennsylvania and Maryland (Fig. 14-1A).

The traveling quartets and conventions were those hired by the printing companies and/or those who sprang from its initiation including the dozen or so Vaughan Quartets and the numerous Stamps and Stamps-Baxter Quartets, the Speer Family, the Le Fevres, and others.[15] Vaughan's first four-part quartet in 1912 grew with the advent of radio technology in the 1920s, as did many others. By the 1940s they had extended the original white gospel quartet area into California and the upper Midwest and by 1950 were singing in New England and southern Canada (Fig. 14-1A). As gospel-quartet-listening Americans moved into the industrial North and West, they took along their music. The white gospel quartet singing area was expanding also because of another new phenomenon—the one-night stand called "the all-nite sing." Popularized in the 1940s, the "all-nite sing" was extremely well received. *Collier's Magazine* in 1955 reported that "gospel music quartets can draw larger audiences more consistently than any other regularly scheduled paid admission music."[16] The "all-nite sing" opened white gospel music quartets to increasing numbers of listeners who continued the gospel tradition of purchasing the music sung. Though other music was sold in printed form during the 1800s, few could compare with the Stamps Printing Company's claim of over five million sold by the early 1950s.[17]

Those purchases were enlarged with the advent of long-play albums, another technological advance that again extended the influence of quartet music. Although gospel music recording had begun as early as 1924 by the Vaughan Quartet and 1927 by the Stamps All Star Quartet for Victor, it took twenty-five years for sales to support regally the singing groups.[18] By 1960 many groups had released 78-rpm records and long-play albums, and full-time gospel music radio stations began to collect quality gospel quartet music

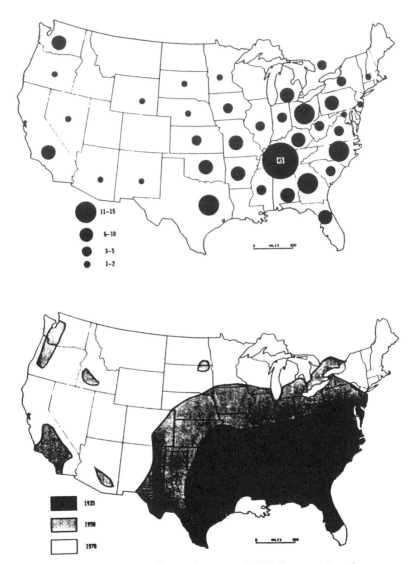

Fig. 14-1A. Top: Full-time professional quartets (1978). Bottom: Gospel quartet touring region.

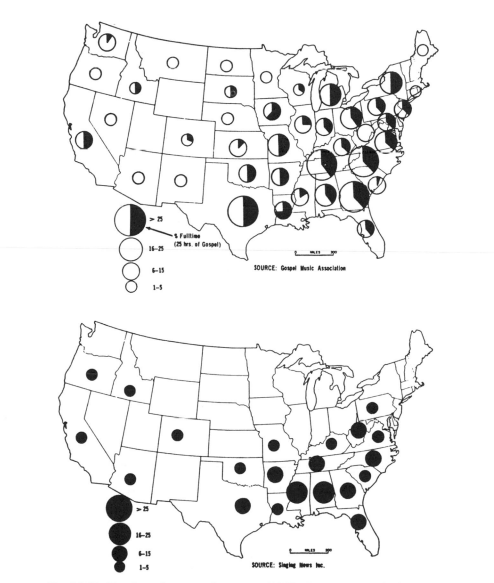

Fig. 14-1B. Top: Gospel music radio stations (1978). Bottom: J. G. Whitfield gospel quartet concert promotions.

libraries. Figure 14-1B displays the number of radio stations in 1978 that are full time or play more than twenty-five hours of gospel/religious music per week. The largest numbers of stations are found in the southern states, Michigan, California, Missouri, Indiana, Ohio, and New York. Spatially, gospel quartet music's impact reflects its origins in the southern states, although it has extended its influence internationally. Figure 14-2 depicts that southern core by displaying the home location of the 3,000 traveling professional and semiprofessional gospel quartets and singing troupes. The symbols represent quartets found in a contiguous region. For example, the dot of twenty or more groups on Atlanta, Georgia, includes those with addresses in the city and its surrounding suburbs. Several interesting regionally clustered patterns may be discerned from the map.

One cluster is the "Southern Mountain Region," which extends along the Appalachian Mountains from Birmingham, Alabama, northeastward through northern Georgia, eastern Tennessee, western South Carolina and western North Carolina, West Virginia, western Virginia, and southern Pennsylvania. This has to be the largest United States concentration of traveling gospel quartets, with about 800 groups headquartered there.

A second cluster centers on Nashville, Tennessee, which is considered by many gospel activists as the capital of gospel talent agencies, recording companies, musicians, and traveling groups. For instance, the National Quartet Convention held annually in Nashville attracts thousands of fans and singers to a seven-day-and-night series of meetings and singings.[19] The Gospel Music Association offices and the Gospel Music Hall of Fame are located in Nashville.

A third cluster that is less contiguous than the "Southern Mountain Region" is the "Midwestern Region," which extends from central Oklahoma northeastward through northeastern Arkansas, southern and eastern Missouri, St. Louis, southern Illinois, central Indiana, southern Michigan, and all of Ohio. This region is the home base of approximately 500 groups.

Another cluster, though smaller in number, is in Texas, which was one of the early centers of gospel music singing schools during the 1920s, 1930s, and 1940s. Today it is a strong gospel music promotional and publishing area, with more than 150 such organizations operating actively.

In addition to these four main regions, several outlying nodes of gospel quartet locations have spread from these older regional clusters. Included are the three West Coast states (California, Oregon, and Washington) that have created a regional gospel music association; New England; Ontario, Canada; and urban areas in the upper Midwest, Southwest, and Florida. Obviously, gospel quartet music's spatial clusters still reflect its earliest beginnings, but its diffusion is considerable.

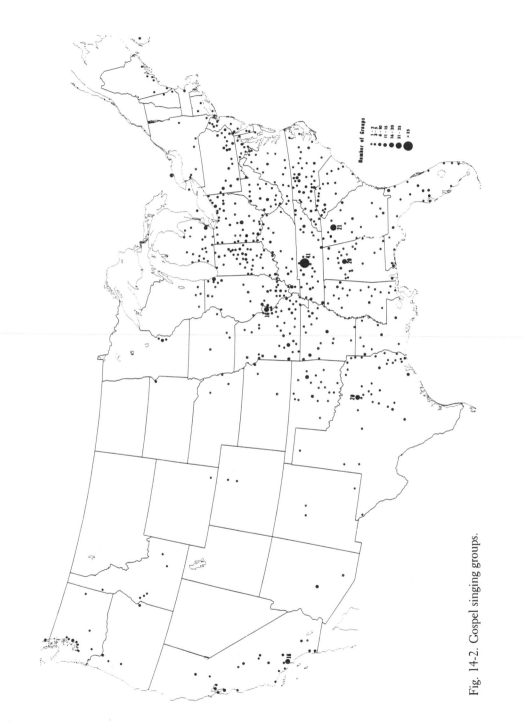

Fig. 14-2. Gospel singing groups.

Currently, 200 of the 3,000 known groups are full time. "Full time" is a label applied to those traveling groups that earn their livelihood solely on the income from gospel music concerts and related sales[20] (Fig. 14-1A). Most of these groups are in the southern states or have migrated into Nashville, Tennessee, for proximity to gospel studios, song writers, gospel publishing and printing facilities, other gospel groups, talent agencies, and musicians. Those full-time groups that are not headquartered in Nashville have developed complex retailing operations and recording studios in their local areas, exemplified by the Thrashers in Birmingham, the Dixie Echoes in Pensacola, the Blackwoods in Memphis, and the Couriers in Harrisburg, Pennsylvania.

Some of the most prominent full-time quartets exert regional, national, and international influence on the spread of gospel quartet music. They are the innovators in promotion, songwriting, stage performance, concert tours, and other trends of change. Their concert territories are international.

A series of maps has been designed by the author to illustrate the spatial impact of concert travel by the most-traveled quartets in the United States (Fig. 14-3).

One of the oldest continuous names in gospel quartet music is that of the Memphis-based Blackwood Brothers Quartet. Since 1934 this quartet has sung gospel music. Figure 14-3 reveals their 1977 concert distribution by states. Clearly the Blackwoods follow a nationally dispersed schedule, with the greatest number of concerts in Missouri, Illinois, Texas, and California, and fewer in the gospel music belt of the Southern states. Although they are southern-based, their 1977 tours were primarily midwestern. This pattern is a result of their espoused goal to tour large northern cities regularly.

The 1977 number-one gospel quartet as voted by the national industry-wide Gospel Music Association was the Cathedral Quartet of Stow, Ohio. Their concert pattern for 1977 shows how confined they were to their home region of the upper Midwest (Fig. 14-2). It reveals a lack of travel among the cities in the southern states, except within North Carolina. Their concert tours reflect closely the background of three of the group members, who began in North Carolina, Pennsylvania, and Michigan. Their appeal to home-state promoters in Ohio is overwhelming compared to other national groups.

The Inspirations of North Carolina are a very successful group rated among the top five groups in the United States for the last five years by annual fan polls. Their 1977 concert itinerary was totally based on southern-state support—a reflection partly of their singing style, which is very traditional; their personal choice of travel as expressed by their promoter and tour manager; and their fee schedule, which is one of the highest among all quartets (Fig. 14-3).

The Imperials Quartet has been voted the number one gospel quartet by the Gospel Music Association four times in the last eight years, including 1978, and has been among the finalists each of those eight years. Their contemporary music style leads them to numerous urban concerts, all of the "Jesus" gospel concerts, and into college tours.[21] Their tours throughout Canada extended gospel music's penetration considerably. (All of the Canadian concerts are displayed in the Ontario circle—Fig. 14-3.)

J. G. Whitfield of Florida is one of the many full-time promoters of gospel music whose multimillion dollar business maintains a half-million-dollar tour dominating urban concerts across the southern states and some midwestern states. His 150 or more concerts annually employ three or four nationally known quartets and involve fees of $3,000 to $4,000 for each concert (Fig. 14-1B). According to his data, average concert attendance is greater than two thousand.[22] His area of influence is tied closely to his personal convictions about the market area of gospel quartets and his past success with large urban concerts throughout the South. Whitfield also publishes the gospel quartet newspaper with the largest circulation. Table 14-1 displays that newspaper's regional circulation, with strong areas in the South and Midwest.

It has been over sixty years since the first traveling quartet began, but gospel quartet music is a successful musical tradition that has spread throughout the American states and overseas and is viewed as a major entertainment form. Although the full-time groups do not reach every city in the United States, they and the hundreds of local and part-time groups ply their tours weekly across the southern states, throughout the midwestern states and mid-Atlantic states and the Pacific coast. So the area of impact covered by gospel quartet music is nationwide, with valleys of less impact in the heavily populated regions in New England, the upper midwestern tier of states, and the less populated Great Plains and Mountain states. Even though regional quartets are based within these less impacted areas, few full-time groups hold concerts there.

Thus, in sixty years, gospel quartet music, which began within the Southern states, has diffused nationally and is now spreading into international areas. Even though the impact is national and international, the home hearth remains southern for many of the full-time professional gospel quartets, most of the part-time groups, and many of the major concert promoters.

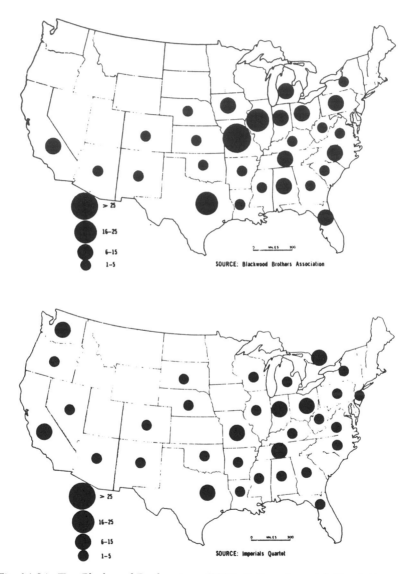

Fig. 14-3A. Top: Blackwood Brothers tours (1977). Bottom: Imperials Quartet tours (1977).

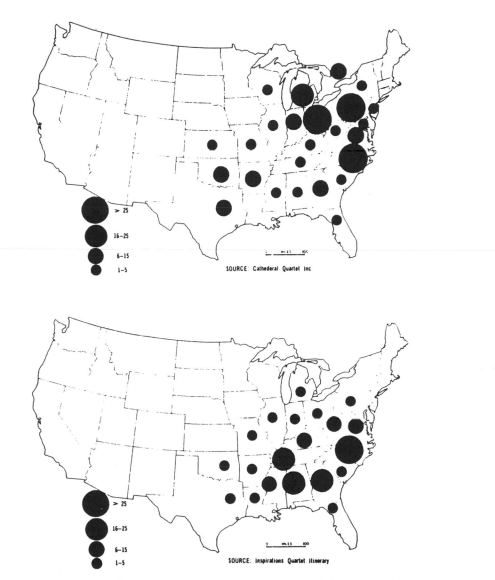

Fig. 14-3B. Top: Cathedral Quartet tours (1977). Bottom: Inspirations Quartet tours (1977).

Table 14.1.   *Singing News*—1978 Monthly Newspaper Circulation*

Region	Total
1. South Atlantic Region** (FL, GA, NC, SC, VA, WV, ME, DE)	82,000
2. East South Central Region (KY, TN, AL, MS)	50,000
3. East North Central Region (IL, IN, OH, MI, WI)	45,000
4. West South Central Region (TX, OK, AR, LA)	43,000
5. Mid-Atlantic Region (NY, PA, NJ)	25,000
6. West North Central Region (Great Plains)	20,000
7. Pacific Region (CA, OR, WA)	20,000
8. Mountain Region	8,000
9. New England Region	7,000

*Singing News Inc. 1978.
**Regional titles are newspaper's divisions.

Notes

1. W. B. Nowlin, president, Entertainment Promotion, Dallas, Texas. Personal communication, October 1975.

2. A.D. Horsley, "The Development and Diffusion of Gospel Quartet Music in the United States" in George O. Carney (ed.), *The Sounds of People and Places: Readings in the Geography of Music* (Washington, D.C.: University Press of America, 1978) pp. 174–75.

3. David Crawford, "Gospel Songs in Court: From Rural Music to Urban Industry in the 1950's," *Journal of Popular Culture* 11 (Winter 1977), p. 552.

4. James C. Downey, "Revivalism, the Gospel Songs and Social Reform," *Ethnomusicology* 9 (1965), pp. 115–16.

5. Lois Blackwell, *The Wings of a Dove: The Story of Gospel Music in America* (Norfolk, Va.: Donning Press, 1978).

6. David Crawford, op. cit., p. 554.

7. Ibid., p. 555.

8. Ibid., p. 557.

9. Homer Rodeheaver, *Hymnal Handbook for Standard Hymns and Gospel Songs* (Chicago: Moody Press, 1933), p. v.

10. James D. Sumner, "President's Comments" in *Gospel Music Association Yearbook* (Nashville: 1974), p. 2.

11. A. D. Horsley, op. cit., p. 194. Gospel quartet address data were collected by the author over a three-year span from many sources including talent agencies, recording companies, booking agencies, local concert promoters, the Gospel Music Association, over 300 radio stations, and gospel newspapers.

12. Robert Gay, singing school teacher 1925–55, personal communication, November 1971; and Lois Blackwell, op. cit., pp. 63–68.

13. A. D. Horsley, op. cit., pp. 176–77; and Lois Blackwell op. cit., pp. 63–68.

14. Peter R. Gould, *Spatial Diffusion*, Resource Paper #4, Commission on College Geography (Washington, D.C.: Association of American Geographers, 1969), pp. 3–5.

15. LeRoy Abernathy, personal communication during the National Quartet Convention, Nashville, October 5, 1975; Paula Becker, *Let the Song Go On: Speer Family Story* (Nashville, Tenn.: Impact, 1971); James Buckingham, *O Happy Day: The Happy Goodman Story* (Waco, Tex.: Word, Inc., 1973); William C. Martin, "At the Corner of Glory Avenue and Hallelujah Street," *Harper's Weekly*, January 1972, p. 98; and Kree Jack Racine, *Above All: The Story of the Blackwood Brothers Quartet* (Memphis: Jarodoc Publications, 1967).

16. Allen Rankin, "They're 'Singing All Nite' in Dixie," *Collier's*, August 19, 1955, pp. 26–27. In 1977 promoters in the GMA estimated that $10 million was paid in admissions nationally and millions more were given as offering to groups in church programs; and M. C. Bates, "The All-Nite Singing," *Billboard* 72, No. 12, June 1963.

17. David Crawford, op. cit., p. 561.

18. Jesse Burt, and Duane Allen, A *History of Gospel Music* (Nashville, Tenn.: K & S Press, 1971), p. 42; *Time Magazine*, November 7, 1949, p. 44; and Blackwell, Lois, op. cit., pp. 120–27.

19. Don Baldwin, "Gospel Music Growth," *Gospel Music Association Yearbook* (Nashville, Tenn.: 1974); and Marvin Norcross, president, Canaan Music, Word, Inc., Waco, Texas, personal communication at National Quartet Convention, October 7, 1976

20. A. D. Horsley, op. cit., pp. 183–84.

21. A. D. Horsley, "Trends in Gospel Music Stylings," *Gospel Banner Newspaper* (St. Louis, Mo., November 1975), p. 3.

22. J. G. Whitfield, *Singing News Newspaper*, Pensacola, Fla., Vol. 8, No. 8, 1977.

An Example of Spatial Diffusion: Jazz Music

Jon A. Glasgow

Diffusion and migration are important processes in the development of the cultural regions of the United States. Geographers and others have analyzed patterns of folk housing, political attitudes, place names, and other cultural elements to detect the boundaries of cultural regions. These boundaries appear to be related to flows of migration westward from three major cultural hearths on the east coast.[1] The north-south cultural zonation generated by these more or less distinct westward streams has been noticed as far west as California.[2] Another migratory stream, less studied for its impact on the cultural geography of the United States, is that of blacks from the rural South to the cities of the North. One especially important current in that stream was of jazz musicians from New Orleans to Chicago.

Students of its history generally agree that (1) jazz was local, black, and Creole folk music in New Orleans in the 1890s; (2) "the most far-reaching and positive contributions to jazz in the (nineteen) twenties were made in Chicago"; and (3) jazz was not generally accepted in New York until the 1930s.[3] An interesting aspect of this New Orleans to Chicago to New York sequence is that it contradicts the generalization that innovations tend to diffuse outward from nodes of relatively intense social and cultural interaction, usually from core areas where there is a concentration of power, wealth, and talent. Only in rare instances do new ideas or inventions seep back from periphery to nucleus.[4]

Reprinted by permission from *Geographical Survey* 8 (1979): 10–21.

Spatially as well as socially jazz diffused up the hierarchy rather than down. Neither Chicago in the 1920s nor New Orleans in the 1890s was a center of national culture. It might be argued that New Orleans was the focal point of an emerging Afro-American culture in 1890. Even so, the roots of jazz extended into the rural South and crucial, early innovations were made in places such as Sedalia, Missouri, a frontier town in many respects at that time.[5] The fact that jazz diffused up the social hierarchy from a generally despised black minority to acceptance by the white majority is well known and will be of only indirect concern here.[6] This paper provides empirical evidence that the spatial sequence was, in fact, from New Orleans to Chicago to New York, and it adds some details and refinements to the account of the spatial diffusion of jazz. The study also includes speculation about the reasons for the specific features of this particular cultural diffusion and some thoughts about the general role of diffusion in creating the national and regional cultures of the United States.

The primary data used in this study are the place and date of birth of 317 jazz musicians. Of these, 173 were obtained by using the first entry on each page in the biographical listings in Leonard Feather's *The Encyclopedia of Jazz in the Sixties*;[7] 64 more were chosen by using the last entry beginning on each page of Barry Ulanov's *A Handbook of Jazz*;[8] the obituaries from *Downbeat* magazine from January 1, 1971, through November 11, 1973, provided 54 more; finally, the 26 members of the *Downbeat* Reader's Poll Hall of Fame as of 1973 that were not included in the above lists were added. Using these data, maps were prepared showing the number of sampled musicians born, by county, in each census decade from the 1880s through the 1940s. That these maps show the diffusion of the acceptance of jazz is based on the conviction that most jazz musicians were influenced by exposure to the music at very early ages in localities where jazz had already been accepted. From the biographies of jazz musicians that were consulted,[9] it appears that with very few exceptions these crucial exposures occurred at or very near the nascent musician's place of birth.

Another series of maps was prepared showing the ratios of number of musicians born in each state in each decade to the number of children aged ten years or less at the end of the decade.[10] These ratios are approximations of the probability that a child born in a given state and decade would become a jazz musician. Only the maps for two crucial decades are reproduced here. The maps for the 1880s and 1890s were clearly dominated by New Orleans. The maps for the decade of the 1900s (Figs. 15-1 and 15-3) show that Chicago was the leading center (Fig. 15-1) and that the state of Illinois had a ratio of over six jazz musician births per million people aged less than ten years in 1910 (Fig. 15-3). The only other states in that decade with ratios

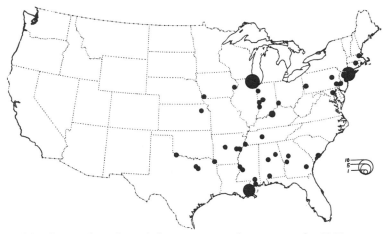

Fig. 15-1. The number of sampled jazz musicians by county in the 1900s.

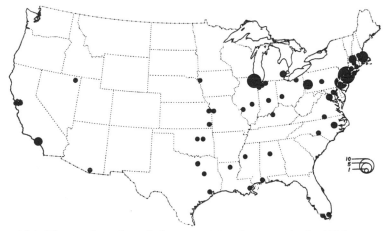

Fig. 15-2. The number of sampled jazz musicians by county in the 1920s.

over six per million were adjacent Indiana and the delta states of Louisiana, Arkansas, and Mississippi. The decade of the 1910s is possibly a transitional one as the leading center was neither New York, Chicago, nor New Orleans, but Pittsburgh, Pennsylvania. The subsequent decades, beginning with the 1920s (Figs. 15-2 and 15-4) show a definite shift to the Northeast. Using the data displayed on the maps like those in Figures 15-1 and 15-2, it was possible to calculate the median distances from New Orleans, Chicago, and New York to all the sample birth places in each decade. The results (Table 15-1) indicate that the majority of jazz musicians were born nearer to New Orleans than to

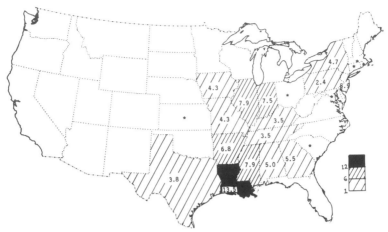

Fig. 15-3. The number of sampled jazz musicians born in the 1900s per million people 10 years old or younger in 1910 (by state).

Fig. 15-4. The number of sampled jazz musicians born in the 1900s per million people 10 years old or younger in 1930 (by state).

either Chicago or New York in the decades before 1900, nearer to Chicago than either of these other two centers in the decades between 1900 and 1920, but nearer to New York in the decades beginning in 1930.

The spatial patterns and time sequence implied·by the maps and the data in Table 15-1 are consistent with the jazz historians' view that Chicago replaced New Orleans as the dominant center during the 1920s, to be replaced by New York in the 1930s. Evidently the musicians born in and around Chicago in the 1900s were proselytized in the 1920s by musicians who had been born in New Orleans.[11] Enough Chicago-born musicians then went to New York in the 1930s to influence the musicians who had been born there in the 1920s to become jazz players.[12] Additional factual evidence for this sequence is provided by Figure 15-5, which shows the place of birth and place of death of a sample of jazz musicians who died in either New Orleans, Chicago, or New York. The lifetime migrational pattern of these

Table 15-1. Median Distance of Birthplaces of Jazz Artists from New Orleans, Chicago, and New York and Number of Births, by Decade

| Decade | Median distance from | | | Number Births |
	New Orleans	Chicago	New York	
1880	16	840	1176	8
1890	396	736	840	14
1900	712	616	720	67
1910	836	600	720	64
1920	980	704	352	90
1930	936	720	496	65
1940	936	584	496	9

Source: Computed by author.

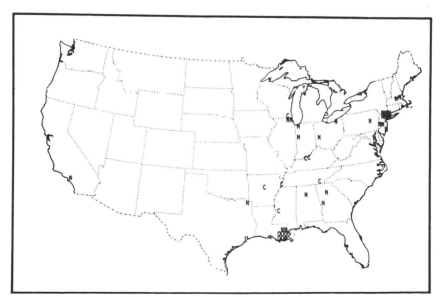

Fig. 15-5. The place of birth of a sample of jazz musicians that died in New Orleans (O), Chicago (C), or New York (N).

musicians was remarkably one-way. The migration field for New Orleans was limited to New Orleans itself; that of Chicago included New Orleans and the lower Mississippi Valley; and that of New York extended to the whole country.

Two interesting questions are raised by these data: (1) why did jazz diffuse to Chicago before New York? and (2) why did certain other midwestern centers stand out on the maps of jazz musician birth places? For example, Pittsburgh was the leading center in the decades of the 1910s, Detroit in the 1930s, and Louisville was the birthplace of more sampled jazz musicians than much larger cities such as Washington, D.C., or Los Angeles. An examination of available published sources indicates that the answer to these questions is related to the greater intensity and longer duration of interaction between the delta South and the Midwest compared to that between the delta South and the Northeast.

Evidently northerners, white and black, who lived in the cities and towns along the Mississippi River and its navigable tributaries were more willing to accept jazz than those in other cities. Well before the decade of the 1920s jazz musicians had performed in nearly all the large cities of the United States. For example, Freddie Keppard's band from New Orleans was a brief sensation in both New York and Los Angeles in 1913.[13] Although such performances drew large and enthusiastic crowds in other places, it was in Chicago that the enthusiasm first led to a coterie of northern white followers who became important jazz musicians.[14] Many of these first converts had come to Chicago from small towns in the Midwest. A history of intensive interaction with the South, especially during the riverboat era, in fostering a tradition of accepting blacks as entertainers may have been an important element here.

In describing steamboat activity on the Ohio River in the 1880s, Charles Ambler reports that "In the early eighties practically every important Ohio River packet carried a colored orchestra. . . . Leaders of such aggregates were rather privileged and some were very popular." He also notes that

> Along the upper Ohio . . . the average small farmer could not afford to remain idle during the whole winter season. . . . Therefore (he) got a berth on the river, where he sometimes spent the whole boating season . . . (and often) indulged in the use of intoxicants and gambling.

For the more sophisticated, steamboats towed barges that served as floating brothels "equipped with barrooms, dancing halls, dining rooms."[15] Lewis Atherton reports that the *Ladies Home Journal* of February 1922 "condemned Iowa and Illinois river town dance halls with their modern jazz and bootleg liquor."[16] The Chicago-era jazz scene was studded with young whites rebelling against the morality of their small midwestern hometowns. They were preconditioned to accept jazz by a long-standing association between the black music of the river towns and forbidden pleasure. Two of these white Chicago-era jazzmen from small towns in the Midwest were Bix Beiderbecke and Eddie Condon. Some quotations from the biographies of each are pertinent.

Bix Beiderbecke was first exposed to jazz by the music from the riverboats that he could hear in his neighborhood in Davenport, Iowa. One informant quoted in Beiderbecke's biography recalled

> the music was so clear that it could be heard like it was in your front parlor. Often Bixie, with two pieces of wood . . . would sit there on the playground grass tapping out the rhythm he was hearing from the river boats.[17]

Furthermore, it was a riverboat of the Steckfuss line that gave Bix his first opportunity to hear the music of Louis Armstrong in 1919, and another gave him one of his first opportunities to play in a jazz band in 1921.[18]

Eddie Condon's grandfather, who traveled from Ottawa, Illinois, in 1859 to work on the levees in New Orleans, wrote to his wife that "the city . . . had a great deal of music," and that "the Negroes . . . sang especially well, and had many songs and dances of their own."[19] Condon claims that the tradition of playing music in his family extends at least back to his grandmother, who "encouraged her children to play . . . combs, jews harps, accordions, violins, harmonicas, banjos." Condon also claims that his father "was the best fiddler in Benton County," Indiana; that his brother was a member of a racially integrated vocal quartet in 1913 or 1914 in Momence, Illinois; and that one of his sisters, by about 1915, was playing ragtime piano so well that a Chicago teacher conceded she was too far advanced for him.[20]

Three additional examples illustrate the wide temporal and spatial impact of the Mississippi River in the diffusion of black music from the delta South. The first involves Stephen Foster:

> In the four years (1846–1850) that Foster spent as a river-boat agency employee in Cincinnati, (he absorbed) the coonjine dancing and singing of the boatmen. Foster's best and most Negroid songs . . . derive from this experience.[21]

The next example, the obituary of Erroll Garner in the *New York Times*, refers to an event nearly one hundred years later, in Pittsburgh, Pennsylvania.

> When he was 11, (in 1934) he was sneaking out of the house . . . to play on a riverboat with a band led by Fate Marable, a legendary riverboat band leader whose bands had included Louis Armstrong.[22]

It was this Fate Marable band with Louis Armstrong that Bix Beiderbecke heard in Davenport, Iowa, in 1919. The third example involves Eddie Condon. While touring the small towns of the Midwest in 1922 with Peavey's Jazz Bandits, he encountered the Steckfuss excursion liner Capitol tied up to the wharf at Winona, Minnesota. The entertainment on the boat was provided by a jazz band called Tony's Iowans.

> . . . there were children and mothers and nurses and old folks and youngsters who stood by the band with their ears and mouths open. . . . We made another river boat at LaCrosse; this one was the J.S., named for Steckfuss himself.[23]

It is evident that the riverboats carried black musicians and jazz music from New Orleans to the furthest navigable reaches of the Mississippi River system. Apparently jazz spread from the river towns to their hinterlands and worked its way through the urban hierarchy to become concentrated in the primate center of the regional hierarchy— Chicago.

An additional reason for Chicago preceding New York as a jazz center is implied by some contemporary comments on the comparative degree of tolerance for the outcast social groups that nurtured jazz. Jelly Roll Morton suggests that Tony Jackson, one of the first New Orleans musicians to make an impact in Chicago, was homosexual and " . . . that was the cause of him going to Chicago about 1906. He liked the freedom there." With regard to racial tolerance, Morton, a Creole, has this to say:

> In Chicago . . . in 1912 you could go anywhere you wanted regardless of creed or color. So Chicago came to be one of the earliest places that jazz arrived, because of nice treatment.[24]

New Yorker Willie (the Lion) Smith is quoted as saying:

> . . . there was a lot more mixing of the races in Chicago at that time (1927) than there was in Harlem. I sure found that "toddlin town" to be real friendly.[25]

This is not to say that most or even many Chicagoans were paragons of racial brotherhood. But it does appear that there was sufficient appreciation of black music in Chicago so that black musicians were given more freedom there than in many other northern cities, including, very probably, New York City. Even though New Orleans musicians performed in New York as early as 1913 and even though some native northeasterners born before 1900 were important in the formative years of jazz, general acceptance of the music and jazz musicians did not occur in the northeast until the 1930s.

H. O. Brunn attributes the premature demise of jazz in New York after a brief period of acceptance before 1920 to the influence of Tin Pan Alley on popular tastes in music and to a 1922 city law that "outlawed all jazz and dancing on Broadway after midnight. This spelled the beginning of the end for jazz in New York City."[26] During this period, jazz musicians

> looked to Chicago as a place where mobs could keep the booze and good times flowing without interference from politicians, parents, or meddling newspapers.[27]

Although jazz was still played in New York's Harlem,

> violins and cellos returned to the pits of Broadway theatres, and no first-rate hotel or restaurant dared hire a jazz band . . . the whole phonograph industry steadfastly refusing to record any more jazz music.[28]

Brunn's comment may be true of the phonograph industry in New York City, but in Richmond, Indiana, the Gennett Record Company was playing

> a uniquely seminal role in early history of jazz on record. As the first label to operate something approaching a liberal policy toward jazzmen of *both races* (emphasis added), it managed to attract many of the most important artists of the early 1920s.[29]

Eddie Condon found New York in 1928 to be much as Brunn had described it in 1922: "We didn't realize then how little chance we had in New York. Violins and soft saxophones were the fashion."[30] Other comments pertinent to the situation in New York in the 1920s include the opinion that "New York was content with a desultory ragtime and the music of revues and operettas";[31] and that although "New Yorkers were high on technique and polish, their jazz seldom exceeded the limits prescribed by the public taste for 'novelty music.' "[32]

Although these comments refer mostly if not entirely to white New York jazz, Smith went so far as to say, "Many of the New York City colored folks, including . . . musicians, did not go for the blues music."[33] Jazz critics still note a distinction between New York jazz and midwestern jazz, as this quotation from a review of Cleveland saxophone player Frank Wright's recent New York performance demonstrates:

> Mr. Wright has remained faithful to the rowdy, celebratory essence of what might be called the Cleveland style . . . in the context of the cooler, more deliberate New York avant-garde of the 60s, the combination of maturity and power in his playing comes as something of a shock.[34]

In the 1920s then, jazz flourished in Chicago while it languished in New York. Evidently the entrenched commercial interests of Tin Pan Alley were too strong in New York; the influence of Broadway, European classical music, and perhaps European folk music as well were too immediate in New York. Schuller claims that "Keppard's New Orleans music . . . was too strange for 'sophisticated' New York ears."[35] Chicago, somewhat removed from these stifling influences, was more receptive to new cultural innovations, especially ones from the black culture of the delta South. Remoteness from the eastern establishment control of music and a long-standing tradition of accepting black entertainers based on the riverboat era made Chicagoans more willing than New Yorkers to accept jazz in the 1920s.

New York did eventually replace Chicago as the major center of jazz music. And it was in New York that the transition from local folk music (New Orleans jazz) to national popular music (the big-band swing of the 1930s) was completed. That this transition took place in New York reflects the unique role that New York plays in the creation and dissemination of our national popular culture. Innovators of new cultural forms are not born any more frequently per capita in New York than in any other place. But if the innovations are to become part of the national culture, they must be disseminated by the New York City monitors of that culture. In the case of jazz, hot New Orleans black jazz had to be sweetened or "whitened," largely in Chicago, before it could become acceptable to the Tin Pan Alley overseers of popular taste in music. It should be noted that although black jazz was driven from Broadway in the 1920s it continued to evolve in Harlem and emerged in the 1940s as a very sophisticated music known as bebop. Some commentators interpret bebop as being the result of black musicians' desire to create a music that white musicians could not play, in reaction to the white appropriation of earlier forms of jazz.[36]

Consideration of bebop and other, later developments in jazz lies beyond the scope of this paper. The primary purpose here is to seek quantitative evidence to test the notion that jazz received popular acclaim in Chicago and the Midwest before it was generally accepted in New York and the Northeast. This has been provided. Furthermore, secondary sources have been quoted to indicate that the reason for the earlier acceptance in the Midwest was that white society there was more willing than that in the Northeast to assimilate elements from the black culture of the delta South. Finally, the opinion has been presented that diffusion of cultural innovations from smaller to larger places in the urban hierarchy, or diffusion from the periphery to the core, may not be at all unusual. It is interesting to note that a study of the diffusion of country music found a similar pattern of reverse diffusion, and for reasons comparable to those suggested in this study. According to Carney:

Migration from the South also played a role in the reverse order hierarchical diffusion pattern, creating a demand for all country music radio stations in metropolitan areas such as Chicago, Detroit, Cleveland, and Cincinnati. . . . Additional factors . . . include the changing musical tastes of urbanites who have become disenchanted with the quality of Tin Pan Alley music. . . . [37]

It may be that certain kinds of innovations, exemplified by jazz and country music, tend to occur more often in places remote from the stultifying influences of the intense social and cultural interaction that cultural geographers view as promoting innovation in the nodes of core areas. In the core areas, continuous exposure to the existing forms may repress the creation of new forms. Obviously, much research remains to be done before any conclusions can be reached about these matters. It is hoped that this study has indicated some avenues that such research might follow.

Notes

1. Wilbur Zelinsky, *The Cultural Geography of the United States* (Englewood Cliffs, N.J.: Prentice-Hall, 1973), pp. 77–108.

2. Stanley D. Brunn, *Geography and Politics in America* (New York: Harper and Row, 1974), pp. 300–301.

3. Barry Ulanov, *A History of Jazz in America* (New York: Viking Press, 1952), p. 117; Gunther Schuller, *Early Jazz: Its Roots and Musical Development* (New York: Oxford University Press, 1968).

4. Zelinsky, p. 34.

5. R. Blesh and J. Harriet, *They All Played Ragtime: The True Story of an American Music* (New York: Alfred A. Knopf, 1950), pp. 14–34; Francis Newton, *The Jazz Scene* (New York: Da Capo Press, 1975), p. 46.

6. M. Berger, "Jazz: Resistance to the Diffusion of a Culture Pattern" in C. Nanry (ed.), *American Music: From Storyville to Woodstock* (New Brunswick, N.J.: Transaction Books, 1972).

7. Leonard Feather, *The Encyclopedia of Jazz in the Sixties* (New York: Horizon Press, 1966).

8. Barry Ulanov, *A Handbook of Jazz* (New York: Viking Press, 1960).

9. Sidney Bechet, *Treat It Gentle* (London: Cassell, 1960); Eddie Condon, *We Called It Music: A Generation of Jazz* (London: Peter Davies, 1948); Dan Morgenstern, "Bouquets for the Living," *Downbeat* 39 (1972), pp. 14–15; Nat Shapiro and Nat Hentoff (eds.), *The Jazz Makers* (New York: Peter Davies, 1958); Willie Smith, with George Hoefer, *Music on My Mind: The Memoirs of an American Pianist* (Garden City, N.Y.: Doubleday and Company, 1964); R. M. Sudhalter and P. R. Evans, with W. Dean-Myatt, *Bix: Man and Legend* (New Rochelle, N.Y.: Arlington House, 1974); and J. Tracey, "Ray Brown: Rhythm + Rosin = Royalty," *Downbeat* 43 (1976).

10. U.S. Bureau of the Census, *U.S. Census of Population 1890, 1900, 1910, 1920, 1930, 1940* (Washington, D.C.: Government Printing Office).

11. N. Leonard, *Jazz and the White Americans: The Acceptance of a New Art Form* (Chicago: University of Chicago Press, 1962), pp. 13, 14, 57.

12. Ibid., p. 105.

13. Alan Lomax, *Mister Jelly Roll: The Fortunes of Jelly Roll Morton, New Orleans Creole and "Inventor of Jazz"* (New York: Duell, Sloan, and Pearce, 1950), pp. 153–54.

14. Newton, pp. 52–53.

15. Charles H. Ambler, *A History of Transportation in the Ohio Valley, with Special Reference to Waterways, Trade, and Commerce from the Earliest Period to the Present Times* (Westport, Conn.: Greenwood Press, 1970), pp. 325, 328, 343.

16. Lewis Atherton, *Main Street on the Middle Border* (Bloomington: University of Indiana Press, 1954), p. 273.

17. Sudhalter and Evans, p. 328.

18. Ibid., pp. 39, 51.

19. Condon, p. 18.

20. Ibid., pp. 13, 14, 43, 47.

21. Blesh and Harriet, p. 107.

22. J. S. Wilson, "Erroll Garner, Jazz Pianist, 53; Composed 'Misty' and 'That's My Kick,' " *New York Times* (January 4, 1977), p. 30.

23. Condon, pp. 66–67.

24. Lomax, pp. 44, 150.

25. Smith, p. 127.

26. H. O. Brunn, *The Story of the Original Dixieland Jazz Band* (Baton Rouge: Louisiana State University Press, 1960), pp. 146, 175.

27. Sudhalter and Evans, p. 83.

28. H. O. Brunn, p. 181.

29. Sudhalter and Evans, p. 114.

30. Condon, p. 146.

31. Ulanov, *A History of Jazz in America*, p. 142.

32. Sudhalter and Evans, p. 114.

33. Smith, p. 101.

34. R. Palmer, "Frank Wright's Saxophone Warms Ali's Alley," *New York Times* (January 6, 1977), p. 24.

35. Schuller, p. 250.

36. O. Walton, *Music; Black, White and Blue: A Sociological Survey of the Use and Misuse of Afro-American Music* (New York: William Morrow and Company, 1972), p. 94.

37. George O. Carney, *Spatial Diffusion of the All-Country Music Radio Stations in the United States, 1971–74*, Studies in the Diffusion of Innovation, Discussion Paper No. 39 (Columbus, Ohio: Department of Geography, Ohio State University, 1976).

16

Geographic Factors in the Origin, Evolution and Diffusion of Rock and Roll Music

Larry R. Ford

Many interesting generalizations have been put forth in the field of cultural geography dealing with such things as culture hearth, diffusion patterns, culture contact, and migrations of peoples and ideas, but most of the examples used to illustrate these generalizations or concepts have been rather peripheral to the interests of most American students. Most available readings in the field of cultural geography deal with such things as ancient pottery, European housetypes, agricultural crops and practices, and dry, quantitative treatments of such things as the diffusion of radios in Sweden.[1] Cultural geography thus has an image among many students that is perhaps somewhat less than inspiring. Very little has been done with popular, observable elements of our culture even though many of these aspects lend themselves quite readily to a diffusionist point of view and can be used successfully to illustrate most of the important concepts in cultural geography. One such topic is popular music, including the various musical styles and instruments that influence the musical culture of an area.

There are several ways in which popular music can be geographically relevant. For example, since imagery is becoming an important part of geography and geographers are increasingly concerned with such things as cognitive maps, the image of San Francisco has been modified in the minds

Reprinted by permission from *The Journal of Geography* 70 (1971): 455–64.

of many radio listeners over the past decade as its song image changed from
"I Left My Heart in San Francisco" to the more hip "Warm San Franciscan
Nights." Music has certainly played a very big part in the images many people
have of such places as New Orleans and Liverpool, and it would be interesting
to know what impact the "California surf" sound of the early 1960s had on
the migration of young people to that state. In this paper, however, I am
going to deal mostly with the concept of cultural diffusion as illustrated by
the origin, evolution, and diffusion of a particular kind of American music,
rock and roll—later to become simply "rock." I will look at the roles that
various geographic centers have played in the development of what is probably
the nation's, if not the world's, most popular music as well as some of the
spatial relationships that were important in its rise to international popularity.
In addition, I will also discuss the topic of cultural resistance to rock and roll,
both within the United States and, briefly, on the international level.

Basically, rock and roll music emerged from a combining of black rhythm
and blues and white country and western into a type of music that was
acceptable to the adherents of both styles. Its formation also represented a
geographically based revolt by "the provinces" against an old cultural capital
(New York City) that was not fulfilling the needs of a great many people in
the country. Due to the importance of these two cultural streams (black blues
and white country) in the formation of early rock and roll, I will briefly
outline some geographic and social factors associated with them. I will relate
this discussion, if only indirectly, to such important geographic concepts as
the culture hearth, processes of diffusion, and patterns of acceptance and
rejection.

The culture hearth concept in geography concerns aspects of the culture
of a particular place as they relate to the origin of certain new culture traits
in that place. In other words, why did a particular cultural trait or group of
cultural traits originate where it did? What special characteristics did the
hearth area have that led to the origin of new behavioral or material cultural
baggage? In this paper, such areas as the Appalachian Mountains, the
Mississippi Delta, and various cities will serve to illustrate the idea of a
culture hearth.

Diffusion processes involve the ways in which the new culture traits are
spread. Since a new musical style is basically a new idea, it is relevant to look
to such articles as Fritz Redlich's "Ideas, Their Migration in Space and Over
Time" in order to identify some of the different processes by which new
musical traits may diffuse.[2] Redlich talks of three processes by which ideas
spread: (1) Personal contact—senders and receivers are neighbors or are able
to congregate someplace for face-to-face communication; a nightclub in the
case of music, for example; (2) Actual human migration occurs—people

move to new environments taking their ideas with them; (3) Objectification—putting the ideas down in the form of books, records, and music sheets, which can be diffused by retailers or by mass media. All of these processes are well illustrated by the study of American rock and roll.

The study of rock and roll also illustrates nicely the idea of geographic variation in patterns of acceptance and rejection. For example, although the American South gave rise to most of the components of rock and roll, it was the last region to fully accept it. This was probably due to the fact that the South was satisfied with blues and country music while rock and roll took the relatively amusical North by storm. There are many other relevant factors here, such as the degree of urbanization, level of racial integration, size of black population, and existing musical talent, which affected the regional variation in the success of early rock and roll. To fully cover all of these factors would require a much larger study, but some generalizations can be made.

Since American music is a vast subject, I will concentrate on the verbal, or at least vocal, aspects of the evolution of rock and roll and will probably slight some very important developments such as jazz.

White Country and Western

There is an old Irish saying that the Celtic people were happy in war and sad in song, and it was this Celtic heritage, along with a strong English ballad influence, that the Scots-Irish frontiersmen took with them into the Appalachian Mountains of Tennessee and Kentucky. The most popular instrument at that time was the fiddle, which was replacing the more expensive pipes in Britain, and it was not until much later than guitars and banjos became common. Many old songs remained intact or only moderately changed in this region until the twentieth century, due to extreme isolation. As the area opened up and new instruments were developed and introduced, especially the banjo, dobro, and electric guitar, country music evolved. The emergence and popularization of any new kind of music needs a patron and a center so that ideas may be exchanged and songs can be written and performed—in short, a place to facilitate personal contact.

In this case the "Grand Ole Opry" radio show became the focal point and Nashville became the center. The "Opry" began in 1925 and is the oldest regularly scheduled radio program in the United States. At first, most performers dropped in from the nearby Tennessee hills, so that country music became sort of a commercialization of Appalachian folk music. Gradually the popularity of this music spread, at least in the white, rural South; soon

Nashville became known as "Hillbilly Heaven" and aspiring young musicians from all over the rural South began to wander into town hoping to make it big.[3] Country music became increasingly eclectic as it was combined with the plaintive wails of white Texas cowboy songs and yodels to form country-and-western music (complete with fringe and cowboy hats—many new types of music have associated clothing styles). In spite of this broadening, country music was still almost totally ignored in the North or else was looked down upon as "hillbilly trash."

Black Music

There are two streams of black music that can be identified here—gospel and blues. Although religious music was also important in white country music, it was perhaps more important and more distinctive in black music for several reasons. During slavery, the blacks of the South were allowed to be "Christianized" only by very fundamentalist religions that emphasized singing and praying and "pie in the sky" attitudes. Thus during the Great Awakening of the late 1700s and early 1800s, most plantation blacks became inculcated with the highly emotional Baptist and Methodist religions of the era. Religious singing was very much a part of this heritage, and Negro spirituals began to evolve. Although Negro spirituals were sung around the old plantations before the Civil War, it was only after the end of the war that the music became fully formed. As the Methodist and Baptist churches split over slavery and as the blacks were emancipated, separate black churches were formed, and black composers and black gospel choirs began to perform regularly. By the 1870s, black gospel choirs were touring the country. Meanwhile, the northern churches (especially the Methodists) had begun to abandon their revivalistic fervor and to become solidly middle class—looking down upon any kind of emotional display during a church service. Most white Americans thus lost touch with their religious musical heritage while blacks took that heritage and combined it with their own musical tradition.

The other major stream of black music came from the field hollers and chants of cotton pickers and other field hands—usually including such things as falsetto breaks and vocal twists and snaps. The African musical tradition is not simply one of a drum beat but also consists of a great deal of melody and, perhaps most importantly, the use of a statement by an individual and restatement by a chorus, or call and response. This style is still very popular in black musical groups today (i.e., three or four people behind the lead singer). Field hollers and songs also included a strange blue note, or the flatted third and seventh notes of the scale in any key—perhaps an attempt to adjust the European scale to African music.

The field holler–work song tradition was most pronounced in the Mississippi Delta cotton fields—perhaps due to the very high concentration of blacks in that area and the fact that the river provided a communication link that helped standardize certain styles as black workers visited many docks. In areas where the black population was small and scattered, there was a greater probability of a shared black-white musical culture.[4] In the very early 1900s, an Alabama black named W. C. Handy moved to Mississippi and noticed the prevalence of the blue-note work songs and began to compose new ones and, more importantly, to write them down in a definite twelve-bar style that became the standard blues form.[5]

Memphis, already the cotton center of the delta, became the blues center as blacks from Mississippi congregated there to load cotton, find work, and exchange songs. Beale Street in Memphis became the black musical equivalent of the "Opry" as far as personal contact and the exchange of ideas were concerned. The first blues song, "Memphis Blues," was published in 1912, and in 1920 the first black blues record was made. New Orleans jazzmen such as Jelly Roll Morton looked down upon the blues as crude, and, although the two traditions were never completely separate, I feel that the more sophisticated urban, creole tradition of New Orleans jazz is, to some degree, a different story.[6] Unlike jazz, which was immediately picked up by white musicians (The Original Dixieland Band, for example) and spread north to Chicago, the blues with their crude, gutsy sound and often vulgar lyrics were largely ignored by white America. Although there was some blues influence in jazz and swing, especially bouncy blues like "St. Louis Blues," this represented a great modification of the original style.

During the 1920s, most record companies had both white and "race" labels, and most "race records" were available only in black communities. Gradually the blues spread out of the delta area and became popular throughout the black South. The blues were spread west to Texas by people like Huddie Ledbetter (Leadbelly) and Blind Lemon Jefferson, where they became known as the Texas country blues. The blues also spread to the East to places like Georgia where a new type of music evolved—a mixture of gospel and blues. Most blues singers were "down and out" and did not mix socially with churchy gospel people, but in Georgia, a fellow called Georgia Tom started writing gospel tunes in a blues form, and it was in Georgia that Ray Charles was later able to blend the two perfectly (Fig. 16-1).[7]

Meanwhile, although occasional blues singers like Bessie Smith were able to make breakthroughs (the fact that only female blues singers gained white

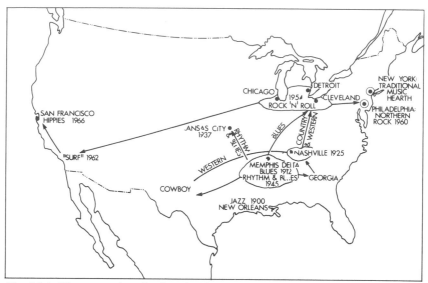

Fig. 16-1. The geography of rock and roll music.

popularity is interesting), most black blues singers did not make a dent in the white music market.

The Establishment—Tin Pan Alley

Although Broadway had toyed with black musical comedy in the 1920s and many black musicians were important in New York City, black music was still not important there; nor was white country music. Composers and performers in New York City were mostly New Yorkers (black and white) writing and performing sophisticated songs for a very staid, conservative, and small middle-class national market. A record was a hit in the 1930s if it sold only 20,000 copies. What black performers there were either conformed to the shuffling black stereotype or sang basically white songs. White composers were usually immigrant or second-generation immigrant—often Jewish but sometimes Italian or Irish—trying to be American but at the same time urbane and sophisticated (some say many songs of the 1920s and 1930s carry minor strains of the cantorial tradition) lyrics such as

> *Thanks for the memory*
> *Of your lips next to mine*
> *Castles on the Rhine*

The Parthenon, and moonlight on
The Hudson River line

were typical. Many songs required a smattering of knowledge of art history and Russian literature to be fully appreciated. New York City ran the pop show while blues and country became more ingrained in much of Depression America.

The Turning Point—The 1940s

Two big events during the 1940s began to change the American music scene. First, the virtual monopoly of the American Society of Composers, Authors and Publishers (ASCAP), which had protected New York's ascendancy in the music market since 1914, was broken by a legal judgment. This opened broadcasting and recording channels to non-ASCAP composers and publishers, many of them unknowns outside the conventional music establishment of Tin Pan Alley, who catered to newly affluent blacks and whites working in war-related industries.[8] After the war, New York found itself with competition. Nashville began recording songs like "Your Cheatin' Heart" and "Tennessee Waltz," which were able to break out of the limited country market and make it big nationally. Black record companies also boomed.

Second, the mass migration of white and black Southerners to the large urban centers of the North and the entrance of these newly "affluent" people into the music market meant that the middle class lost its monopoly on national taste. Country and western bands were formed in nearly every northern city to play for the white migrants; and in the black parts of town, rhythm and blues was coming on strong. Rhythm and blues perhaps first began in the 1930s in the Kansas City area as blues "shouters" with swing bands had to shout to be heard over the new electric guitars. After the war, however, blues singers once more congregated in Memphis and what Keil calls the "Memphis synthesis" gave rise to modern urban blues or rhythm and blues.[9] Rhythm and blues quickly became popular in such urban centers in the Midwest as Detroit, Cleveland, and Chicago since those cities were the destinations of most migrating blacks from the Mississippi Delta (Fig. 16-1).

Tin Pan Alley disdained these "new" types of music as lower class, as to some extent they were, but more importantly, new geographic centers were now playing an ever-increasing role in the national music market. Park Avenue Fantasies and Penthouse Serenades were on their way out. American "folk" music was coming out into the open.

Rock and Roll Is Born

In about 1950, Alan Freed took a job as a disc jockey in Cleveland, played typical pop tunes, and got an increasingly apathetic reaction to his radio show. One day while in a black neighborhood record store he noticed that many young white customers were buying rhythm and blues records (still called "race" records by the recording industry) and so he decided to play some on his show. In order to avoid the old racial connotations as much as possible, he borrowed a term used in many R&B hits (such as "my baby rocks me with a steady roll") and called his music "rock and roll." Freed was one of the first white commercial disc jockeys to play rhythm and blues and this, together with his new phrase and his dynamic promotion efforts, increased its popularity among young whites.

In 1951 and 1952, huge rhythm and blues concerts were held in the Cleveland area, and on one occasion 30,000 people showed up for 10,000 seats.[10] Television was still off-limits for most black music and so the movement remained rather local, or at least midwestern-urban for a while. Soon, however, white country and western bands began to notice the appeal of rhythm and blues and started to play it—notably Bill Haley and the Comets in Detroit. With the recording of "Rock Around the Clock" and "Shake, Rattle, and Roll" in 1954, rock and roll was born. The meeting of rhythm and blues and country and western in the big cities of the Midwest brought about a new style of music that would become popular throughout the world (Fig. 16-1).

Rock and roll brought about a boom of sorts in both of the historic centers of American music. In Memphis, Sun Records attracted people like Jerry Lee Lewis and Elvis Presley (both from the Memphis area) and had them listen to blues and rhythm and blues in order to combine those sounds with their own white country backgrounds. Bo Diddley was a big influence on Elvis's style, and because Elvis was white, many doors were open to him in television and magazine coverage that were locked for black performers. Meanwhile, in Nashville, people like the Everly Brothers were discarding their fringe and cowboy hats and adding country harmony to rhythm and blues hits like "Lucille." Most of the songs sung by these early white rock and rollers were already hits in the black R&B market, but "Hound Dog" still took middle-class America by surprise.

The reaction to the new sound was often not favorable. New Yorkers like Frank Sinatra called rock and roll "the martial music of juvenile delinquents" while the white music establishment searched frantically for clean-cut singers to cover the hits of the original artists, especially the black ones. Pat Boone gained fame redoing hits by black and boisterous Little Richard, and even

Perry Como's sleepy version of "Kokomo" was an attempt to hold back the tide. The television show *Hit Parade* was a chaotic mess, and it finally folded.

By 1957 Elvis and Bill Haley had paved the way for black stars to gain national attention, and Chuck Berry, Bo Diddley, Little Richard, and Lavern Baker became known to white audiences as well as black. The practice of covering songs died as young people began to demand the originals. The Georgia center mentioned earlier was especially important in the introduction of black talent—Little Richard, Ray Charles, James Brown, and Otis Redding all were from Georgia. Perhaps Memphis blacks were still a bit too basic for national tastes.

Radio also played a very important part in the popularization of the new sound in the mid-1950s. Top-40 radio shows (begun in Kansas City and Omaha in 1954) gained in importance as television took away old radio dramas and comedies. Mass media also played an important part in the popularization of rock and roll in England, where Chuck Berry records had a tremendous influence on young people like John Lennon and Paul McCartney.

The middle-class reaction, however, was strong. Elvis was arrested in Florida on a morals charge and made to stand still in a tuxedo on the Ed Sullivan show. Rock and roll was banned on radio stations from Houston to New Haven, and one Chicago disc jockey broke rock and roll records over the air. Southern ministers declared rock and roll to be a plot by the NAACP to mongrelize the races, and some scholars began to investigate possible ties to communism and to prophesy the decline of the West. No dancing to rock and roll was allowed in Atlanta without parental consent, and Alan Freed was arrested in Boston on charges of inciting a riot. There was also a growing concern over the effect of earthy black lyrics on middle-class youngsters—"I Got a Woman," "Empty Bed Blues," "Annie Had a Baby," etc.

The Decline of Southern Rock

Southern Rock was Hard Rock,
Northern Rock was High School.[11]

In the face of the middle-class reaction, the southern rural whites and ghetto blacks who made up the list of most of the early rock and roll stars were too inflexible and perhaps too naive in the ways of show business to survive. Elvis was drafted, Chuck Berry was in and out of jail, Jerry Lee Lewis was censored for his marriage to a thirteen-year-old, Little Richard decided to give up rock and become a preacher, Buddy Holly was killed in a plane crash, Fats Domino retired, and Alan Freed was fired over payola scandals and died shortly thereafter. Philadelphia (home of Dick Clark's *American Bandstand*) emerged as the center for clean, wholesome, and almost exclusively white rock and roll. With the help of a national television show and countless fan magazines, several Philadelphia neighborhood kids were paraded out as stars—among them Fabian and Frankie Avalon, which led to a clean, well-controlled type of music that I call "Disney rock." "Long Tall Sally Jumped Back into the Alley" was replaced by Mouseketeer Annette's "Tall Paul":

> Tall Paul is my love
> Tall Paul is my dream
> He's the captain of
> The high school football team,

and long hair and sideburns disappeared. Novelty songs by the Chipmunks and endless "high school" songs filled in the gaps as the white North was not quite ready to produce its own true rock and roll. Many of the old rock and roll stars toured England, and the Kingston Trio arose as a possible folk alternative to commercial rock and roll. By 1962, however, Philadelphia was dying as a rock and roll center, and two new geographic centers were gaining prominence—Los Angeles and Detroit (Fig. 16-1).

Rock and Roll Comes Back as Rock

In Detroit, the gospel-blues combination emerged in a highly polished, smooth, but definitely black sound known as Motown. Again local talent provided the sound as the auto-city ghetto housed Diana Ross and the Supremes, Smokey Robinson and the Miracles, the Temptations, Aretha Franklin, Little Stevie Wonder, and Martha and the Vandellas.

Meanwhile, a new folk culture was growing up on the West Coast based on youth, hot rods, and surfing, and a new style of music evolved to reflect this life-style. The Beach Boys, Jan and Dean, and the Suns all produced song after song about beaches, waves, and camshafts. Although a far cry from the Memphis blues, this music was generally good and succeeded in presenting a vivid image of some aspects of teenage life in southern California.

Both of these types of music were smooth and commercial but the music of Los Angeles and Detroit was much better, and more real, than that of Philadelphia, and the Annette-Fabian style began to disappear.

Enter the Beatles

An analysis of the role of place in British rock would also be relevant here since the Irish–North Country city of Liverpool gave rise to many of the early groups and was, in a sense, peripheral to the musical culture hearth at London, just as Memphis and Nashville were to New York. However, suffice it to say here that the Beatles and, especially, the Rolling Stones, reimported black sounds and black lyrics to the United States, and for the first time such things gained wide and open appeal in this country. "I Can't Get No Satisfaction" and "Let's Spend the Night Together" are phrases right out of Memphis 1920, but as Muddy Waters said of the 1964 rock boom, "They had to go all the way to England to get it and here it was right in their own backyard all the time." This time the tremendous popularity of white singers singing black lyrics with English accents opened the floodgates for black talent. The roots were exposed.

Memphis has been revived as a recording center for soul music, which is generally less polished than Motown. Local talent again has played an important part as Booker T. and the M.G.'s, Carla Thomas, Rufus Thomas, and B. B. King are all from the Memphis area. Nashville is also stronger than ever, with forty recording studios, 400 music publishing houses, twenty-nine talent agencies, and 1,500 union musicians.[12] "Music City, U.S.A." has also become the home of nationally televised country TV shows.

Rock Comes of Age

Today, rock is part of the establishment. It is no longer a "lower class" type of music associated with ghettos and greasy-haired hubcap stealers. The Broadway show "Hair" is popular throughout the world, and musicians of all kinds are playing songs originally produced by rock groups. The roots of rock have also been exposed, and rhythm and blues and country and western are now more popular than ever in all parts of the nation. Rock and roll brought real American music into the spotlight. It was here all the time, but its rise was a long time coming, geographically as well as historically.

Rock Music and Cultural Convergence

Rock music is now popular throughout the world, but there is some controversy about what the result of this will be. Many nations view the spread of American music as a sort of "cultural imperialism," and loud objections have been raised, from Europe to Asia and Africa. In Africa, where "The James Brown Show" is fantastically popular, Tanzania announced it had outlawed soul music and that it would take immediate action against soul nightclubs that continued to ignore the decree.[13] Even North Vietnam is worried about what it terms "imperialistic records" that "clandestinely popularize musical pieces fraught with profane, romantic feelings, stimulating the bestiality of men."[14] Ireland has ruled that dance halls in its extremely rural Gaelic West may have only traditional bands rather than the otherwise dominant rock showbands.

Some see this increasing cultural homogeneity as bad in that the worldwide diffusion of American popular culture is dulling regional variations and destroying ancient musical traditions. On the other hand, while this is probably true, there may be some benefits for the cause of world brotherhood as well. For example, I arrived in Peru during the height of the "tuna boat tension" fully expecting to meet with at least a few cold stares. Instead, I was nearly mobbed on a main street by a group of teenagers who wished to know what I thought of a certain American and English rock group. As Chuck Berry so aptly sang in the mid-1950s, "C'est la vie, say the old folks, it goes to show you never can tell."

Notes

1. See, for example, Phillip Wagner and Marvin Mikesell (eds.), *Readings in Cultural Geography* (Chicago: University of Chicago Press, 1962).

2. Fritz Redlich, "Ideas, Their Migration in Space and Transmittal Over Time," *Kyklos* 6 (March 1954).

3. Paul Hemphill, *The Nashville Sound* (New York: Simon and Schuster, 1970), p. 84.

4. Tony Russell, *Blacks, Whites, and Blues* (New York: Stein and Day, 1970), p. 32.

5. Phyl Garland, *The Sound of Soul* (Chicago: Henry Regnery Company, 1969), p. 87.

6. Ibid., p. 82.

7. Ibid., p. 94.

8. Jonathan Eisen, *The Age of Rock* (New York: Vintage Books, 1969), p. 15.

9. Charles Keil, *Urban Blues* (Chicago: University of Chicago Press, 1966), p. 61.

10. Paul Dickson, "Eye's Rock Crammer," *Eye* (October 1968), p. 51.

11. Nik Cohn, *Rock, From the Very Beginning* (New York: Stein and Day, 1969), p. 51.

12. Hemphill, op. cit., p. 30.

13. J. K. Obatala, "Soul Music in Africa," *The Black Scholar* (February 1971), p. 8.

14. "Hanoi Youth Become Hip; Adults Irate," *Los Angeles Times* (January 1, 1971).

17

The Geography of Rock: 1954–1970

Richard W. Butler

Few cultural innovations in the last half-century have resulted in impacts as far-reaching as those of modern popular music, or rock and roll. Despite the profound influences of this music and its related phenomena, including dress, behavior, language, and economics, the subject has received less than may be expected by way of serious academic research. As Ray Browne notes: "Academics with a few notable exceptions [are] largely indifferent to the role of popular music in their culture."[1] Musicologists have tended either to disregard popular music, thinking it technically inferior to other types of music and therefore not worthy of serious academic consideration, or have placed, in this author's opinion, ludicrous levels of interpretation on much of what were intended to be purely commercial and unpretentious sounds. Not surprisingly, geographers too have been conspicuous by their relative absence in the analysis and examination of rock and roll. With the notable exceptions of a few authors, such as George O. Carney, Larry Ford, and Richard Francaviglia, geographers have avoided the examination of the subject. This is unfortunate because, as with most social and cultural phenomena, there are innumerable ways in which the topic could be examined from a spatial perspective.

There can be little doubt that spatial elements play some role in the development of music. While one may be reluctant to go as far as Sister Violita[2] who states that "geography determines the type and character of music," it is clear that regional variations and preferences exist in music.

Reprinted by permission from *Ontario Geography* 24 (1984): 1–33.

Ford and Floyd Henderson,[3] in discussing the image of place in popular music, hypothesized that "songs both reflect and influence the images people have of places and . . . these songs and images have changed significantly over time." While Ford and Henderson examined the lyrics and titles of songs over eight decades to determine shifts in images, Ron Murray[4] and Francaviglia[5] have examined the diffusion and subsequent modification of popular music in the United States. Carney[6] has also documented spatial patterns of diffusion and acceptance of both bluegrass and country and western music, and in the first edition of *The Sounds of People and Places* Carney[7] assembled a most useful collection of papers relating to the geography of music, including several essays on rock and roll.[8]

The study of rock and roll, particularly its early years, reveals a great deal about the way that society in the 1950s and 1960s operated and was manipulated. This paper focuses on the spatial aspects of the evolution of rock and roll from 1954 to 1970 in its two principal source areas—the United States from 1954 and the United Kingdom from 1962. The influence of spatial factors in the development of the music and the acceptance and dispersion of the music are noted and discussed, and comparisons and contrasts between the United States and the United Kingdom during this period are drawn.

A major problem in research in popular music, as in many other fields of enquiry, is the dubious reliability of many of the statistics, where such exist at all. Charts of best-selling records are often based on limited and in some cases suspect samples of record stores sales, or even orders, and often depend on voluntary returns. *Billboard's* relative ranking is based on "a weighted sample of 65 retail record stores and ten record distributors in 21 major record markets selected randomly each week from a list of 2,000 possible replacement firms."[9] In Britain for many years no charts were produced for the week including Christmas, and again in the United Kingdom certain years have as few as forty-nine or as many as fifty-five weeks, depending on the days on which the charts were released. Inconsistencies abound. One source, for example *Billboard*, may show a particular record as topping its chart on a certain date while another, such as *Cashbox*, may have a different record at the top of its chart. In general, in an effort to reduce inconsistency, the data used here are gathered from *Billboard* for the United States, and the *New Musical Express* for the United Kingdom. Other discrepancies emerge, including the length of time a record is at the top of the charts, the date of release, and first and last appearance in charts.

Classifying artists and groups is also difficult. A decision has to be made for example, whether artists should be classified by where their recordings are made, or by place of birth, a difficult process for groups, especially when members are born in different parts of a country or even different countries. In this paper, where a group began in a particular location and where that coincides with the origin of at least some of the group members, then that location has been used. In the earlier period of popular music this is less of a problem, firstly because there were more single artists, and secondly because in the absence of the so-called "supergroups," most of the members of groups tended to come from the same general geographical area, if not the same community. In this paper the birthplaces of the artists have been used, although qualifications have to be made in a few cases, such as Chuck Berry, who was born in St. Louis, recorded in Chicago, and spent a great deal of time in Los Angeles. Carney[10] suggests that "place of birth is not only the most widely available information but also the best single indicator of a performer's heritage."

In agreement with Carney's statement, and because the basic purpose of this paper is to discuss the spatial origins of rock and roll, the birthplace of an artist is considered more important than a location to which an artist may have moved after achieving success or where the artist's records were produced. Although the Beatles recorded many of their records in London, they will clearly be forever identified with Liverpool, and their influence upon the breaking of the London dominance of the British popular music scene, discussed below, is clear proof of that. The origins of artists in shaping the type of music they produced was clearly of major significance in the early days of rock and roll, and much less so later with access to national charts, rock and roll radio and television shows, portable radios and records, and traveling pop circuses.

The accessibility of clubs featuring live artists, and of small independent recording studios, were of critical importance in the development of the careers of artists such as Chuck Berry, Elvis Presley, Buddy Holly, and Jerry Lee Lewis in the mid-1950s. Lewis noted:

> I used to hang around Haney's Big House, that was a colored establishment where they had dances and such. . . . We was just kids, we wasn't allowed in. So we'd sneak in whenever we could. I saw a lot of 'em there, all those blues players. . . .[11]

Southern black gospel music and rhythm and blues influenced other white performers known primarily as country and western singers. Carl Perkins, whose work with Presley and authorship of "Blue Suede Shoes" made him a notable figure of the first years of rock and roll, explained:

> I was raised on a plantation in Tennessee, and we were about the only white people in it. . . . Working in the cotton fields in the sun, music was the only

escape. The colored people would sing and I'd join in . . . and that was colored rhythm and blues, got named rock and roll, got named that in 1956, but the same music was there years before, and that was my music.[12]

However, despite the tremendous publicity given to popular music, precise and reliable information on its history is scarce. Pareles and Romanowski noted:

> how poorly that history has been preserved. It is simply a mess. From its inception nearly three decades ago, rock 'n' roll has been only rarely and sporadically documented . . . literally hundreds of record labels have come and gone . . . and files either stored, lost or destroyed.[13]

They go on to comment:

> it's easy to see why most books on the subject present information that is often contradictory and sometimes wrong. . . . With very few exceptions, once a performer or group leaves a record company, all press releases and other sources of information simply disappear . . . and the issue of a performer's public image frequently serves to restrict and sometimes distort the information.[14]

As a further illustration of this problem, in undertaking the research for this paper, it was not possible to discover the existence of, let alone gain access to, a complete set of *Billboard* "Buyer's Directories," which provide information on recording studios, producers, companies and other services, even from *Billboard* itself. As a result, while the data used in this paper have been verified from more than one source where possible, inconsistencies and omissions are almost inevitable.

The Emergence of Rock and Roll in the United States—1950–1959

The emergence of rock and roll has been discussed by a number of authors, such as Ford,[15] Murray,[16] and Francaviglia,[17] and there is general agreement over the basic origins of the music and its spatial linkages. Rock and roll is accepted as being the combination of two streams of black music in the southern United States, gospel and rhythm and blues, with an equally strong form of white music, namely country and western. While gospel music had no clear-cut single focus in terms of area but was widespread throughout the South and Southwest,[18] rhythm and blues was most associated with Memphis, Tennessee, through the works of artists such as Muddy Waters and B. B. King. Country and western music had an equally strong spatial focus in

Nashville, Tennessee, accentuated by the presence there of the radio show and theater, the Grand Ole Opry. While racially and culturally the two basic music forms may have appealed to totally different populations, the subject matter of much of the music (love, religion, and survival), coupled with the fact that all three types of music are concentrated in the South and Southwest of the United States, meant that eventual links between the forms were not too surprising. Ray Charles, one of the major black rhythm and blues artists, commented:

> Although I was bred in and around blues, I always did have interest in other music, and I felt the closest music, really, to the blues was country and western. They'd make them steel guitars cry and whine, and it really attracted me. [19]

It is appropriate to point out that certain forces operating within the music industry in the United States (which has dominated the nonclassical music scene in the world in the twentieth century) had undergone major changes in the decade following World War II. One of the most profound of these was the removal by a legal judgment of the previous dominance by the American Society of Composers and Publishers (ASCAP) of song publication, which had resulted in a concentration of composers, publishers, and recording people in New York. The effect of the legal judgment was to change the pattern of music production and publication, including recording, by allowing dispersal out of New York. Nashville, Chicago, Los Angeles, and Memphis in particular began to emerge as centers of contemporary music production and composition. Over 400 new record companies appeared in the 1940s, and over 100 lasted into the next decade. [20] It was these companies, such as Sun in Memphis and Chess in Chicago, that would produce the first real rock and roll records.

The postwar period saw major technological innovations in the production of different types of radios, record players, and records, and later still the appearance of prerecorded tapes. The popularization of automobile radios and small, almost unbreakable 45-rpm records, in particular revolutionized the listening patterns of the American and later the European markets. Third, social and economic change was prevalent in the United States following the recovery after World War II and the Korean War, with growing attention being paid to civil rights issues, especially in the southern United States; and a major migration of blacks from the South to northern cities such as Detroit, bringing with them their taste for a different form of music.

The early years of the 1950s saw a slow acceptance of black rhythm and blues records, which were almost all produced at independent studios (i.e., not owned by one of the five "major" companies that dominated the record business at that time). A major catalyst in the popularization of this music among white youth was a disc jockey in Cleveland named Alan Freed. Freed is credited with popularizing the phrase "rock and roll," and making it more respectable than previously, when it had blatant sexual connotations in songs like "Roll with Me Henry" and "Rock Me Baby." Freed played black rhythm and blues music on his radio show in Cleveland and later in New York and staged live shows of black artists to mixed audiences in the North with spectacular if notorious success. The music was still not widely accepted, however. The major companies ignored it, and few black artists made the popular music charts. "Crying in the Chapel" by the Orioles, a country and western song sung by a black rhythm and blues group on an independent record label, was unique in reaching number 3 in the charts in 1953 but was clearly indicative of what was to come.[21]

The charts were still dominated in the United States, as in the United Kingdom, by records produced by the major companies, featuring white artists such as Perry Como, Vic Damone, Johnny Ray (who by his actions on stage was a foretaste of the future), or sophisticated blacks like Nat King Cole and the Platters, who produced gentle music for a white audience. The five major companies (Decca, Columbia, and RCA Victor in New York; Capitol, MGM and later ABC-Paramount in Los Angeles; and Mercury in Chicago) produced over 80 percent of popular music recordings in the United States in the early 1950s. The independent companies such as Sun Records in Memphis concentrated on black rhythm and blues, jazz, or other regional and limited variations of music.

Ironically the record that was destined to become the largest selling and most successful rock and roll record in terms of longevity was produced by a major company, Decca. The record was "Rock Around the Clock," the singer Bill Haley. One of Haley's earlier records, "Crazy Man Crazy," is generally credited with being the first rock and roll record to enter the *Billboard* pop charts.[22] Haley had begun his music career as a country and western artist, but by 1952 he had begun to sing rhythm and blues with more commercial success. The appearance of Haley and the Comets singing "Rock Around the Clock" in an otherwise forgettable movie, "Blackboard Jungle," provided additional publicity. While black rhythm and blues records had never sold well in the United Kingdom, the popularity of Haley's white rhythm and blues was as great or greater in the United Kingdom than in the United States. "Rock Around the Clock" entered and reentered the United Kingdom charts seven times, the last time as late as 1974, twenty years after its year of issue.

At least a part of Haley's success was undoubtedly because he was white. A white artist singing about rocking around the clock did not have the same sexual undertones as a black blues performer singing "Rock Me Baby." Even then, rock and roll was banned in Boston and other cities, banned on several radio stations, rock and roll records were broken on the air, and teenagers needed parental permission to attend rock and roll dances in places such as Atlanta.[23] Haley and his group, while dramatically different from anything that had hit the music stage previously, were not highly charismatic, and neither were they a group with which the young audience could truly relate, because they were clearly older than most of their fans. Knowledgeable individuals in the rock and roll field knew what was needed: "a white man with the Negro sound and the Negro feel."[24]

It was eminently appropriate, if not almost inevitable, that the individual who best fitted this description should appear in Memphis. Memphis and the surrounding area provided the opportunity for an intermixing of music styles and for black and white performers not only to hear each other but also to work with each other. Murray notes:

> It was this regional origin and isolation in the early 1950s that gave rock and roll its driving force . . . rock and roll was probably the first music with regional origins to be commercially successful on a nationwide scale.[25]

The role of the independent record producers, such as Sam Phillips in Memphis and Leonard Chess in Chicago, was critical.

> Phillips tapped into the first generation of white singers that had been influenced by black blues and hillbilly music. Haley, who was not from the South, had put the styles together to a certain extent, but never managed the feeling that the Sun artists were to bring to rock and roll.[26]

The first and most successful of these artists was Elvis Presley. Described as "a white Southerner singing blues laced with country and country tinged with gospel,"[27] Presley's first commercial recordings were a black number, "That's Alright," and a country song, "Blue Moon of Kentucky." In his first year he was still considered a country act, appearing at the Grand Ole Opry and on the "Louisiana Hayride" radio program. His move to RCA Records late in 1955 marked the transformation to international stardom and a shift from country to rockabilly songs, such as "Don't Be Cruel" and "All Shook Up." His other early releases however, such as "Hound Dog," reveal the major influence of black blues singers on his style. Presley, along with other classic rock and roll artists from Sun Records such as Carl Perkins and Jerry Lee Lewis:

all came out of Southern backgrounds that mixed black and white cultures and music in ways not possible before the fifties . . . they were able to relate to white teen culture, black r & b and country western music.[28]

Along with these artists who were recording in Memphis, two other southern performers with similar backgrounds were major contributors to the development of rock and roll. Little Richard, from Macon, Georgia, personifying the black gospel singing tradition, gave visually dramatic performances and produced orally unique records, which remain classic early rock and roll and were almost all covered by white artists. The other and much more significant black performer of the early 1950s was Chuck Berry, whose compositions and guitar style have influenced rock and roll as much as any other single artist, and have served as models for groups as varied as the Beach Boys, the Beatles, and the Rolling Stones. Berry, recording with another independent studio, Chess Records in Chicago, was one of the few black artists to achieve chart success playing his own music in an unadulterated style in the mid-1950s.

At the same time, a second stream of artists, all white and almost all established country and western performers, began to feature in the charts with records, mostly recording in Nashville. They included the Everly Brothers, Conway Twitty, and Marty Robbins. While the songs are distinct and very different in sound, their messages, as noted earlier have a great similarity. "Maybelline," "Lucille," "Heartbreak Hotel" and "A White Sport Coat," all have enough in common to satisfy the most demanding analyst. Two major country and western artists also recorded at Sun Records in Memphis— Johnny Cash and later, Roy Orbison, although the latter's major hits in the 1960s were recorded by Decca in Nashville. One other artist, also of southern origin, deserves mention in this section, both for the profound and permanent impact he has had on rock and roll in terms of innovation and composition and for the addition of what has become known as the Tex-Mex sound. Buddy Holly, from Lubbock, Texas, is credited with establishing the basic format for the rock group of the 1950s and 1960s, with writing some of the best and most influential music, and like Chuck Berry, with being a mentor to the Beatles and the Rolling Stones. He also introduced the violin and the aspirated glottal stop[29] to rock and roll. His untimely death in 1959 undoubtedly cut short one stream of rock and roll innovation.[30]

Sun Records in many ways typifies the evolution of rock and roll, beginning in 1950 as a black rhythm and blues studio. By 1954 its records were predominantly by white rockabilly and country artists, many of whom had achieved fame by drawing heavily upon their familiarity with black artists. By 1957 rock and roll was well established, and the independent companies were producing more pop singles than the majors. The cultural hearth, as Murray[31] indicates, was clearly Memphis, with secondary foci in Nashville and Chicago. The fusion of musically different but spatially close musical forms had been achieved with spectacular success. Within three years, however, the spatial pattern of rock and roll was destined to change radically.

Shifts in Spatial Patterns in the United States—1958–1970

The origins of rock and roll artists in North America in the period 1954–59 are shown in Figure 17-1. As noted above, the southern and southwestern states dominate. The pattern changes dramatically, however, during the next decade (Fig. 17-2).[32]

While the South and Southwest still produced a noticeable number of performers, several new centers of origin are clearly visible. Almost 20 percent come from the Detroit area and a similar proportion from New York, while over 20 percent come from California, with the majority from Los Angeles. Only Nashville, Chicago, and San Francisco emerge as other centers of note. The reasons behind this spatial transformation are reasonably clear and generally accepted.

The major record companies decided that involvement in rock and roll was essential for their survival, and took two major steps to regain control of the popular music field. One step was to sign the major performers, such as Presley, which had no effect on the spatial pattern; and the second, of more

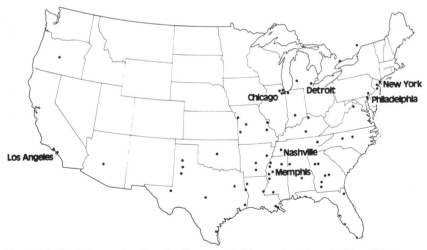

Fig. 17-1. Birthplaces of rock and roll artists (U.S.) recording from 1954 to 1959.

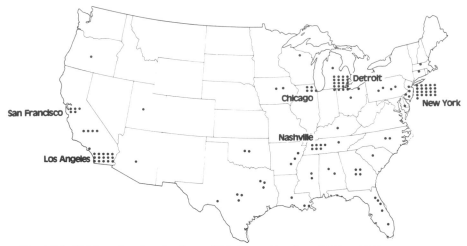

Fig. 17-2. Origins of rock and roll acts (U.S.) recording from 1960 to 1970.

significance in the spatial sense, was to attempt to reproduce the rock and roll sound by copying and diluting it, hoping to reach both the new young audience and their established white audience. The results can be seen in the appearance of copies of black rhythm and blues songs by "respectable" white artists such as Pat Boone and Tab Hunter. This strategy was successful for a period of time, and as Jonathan Kamin[33] shows, during 1955 the cover versions outsold the original recordings, and received more air time. By 1956, however, the situation had changed. Original recordings, even by black artists, were outselling cover versions, and cover versions were not produced in any numbers.

In the United Kingdom, the rock and roll audience had additional problems in listening to original rock and roll or rhythm and blues. All radio was under the control of the ultraconservative BBC; and it took a number of years before the music was played on the air, and then only in extremely limited quantities (partly because of agreements with musicians' unions to limit the amount of recorded music played).[34] The music was further adulterated in the British situation, by British artists, almost all white, covering versions of the original music.[35] To the real enthusiast, only Radio Luxembourg on a Sunday evening offered an alternative and access to authentic rock and roll. It says a lot for the appeal of the music that its acceptance in Britain was if anything more rapid and complete than it was in the United States. Alternatively it may say something about the abysmal competition that the music faced in the United Kingdom.

The spatial pattern was also changed radically by the efforts of other individuals and companies to gain access to the increasingly lucrative rock and roll market by creating new performers. Philadelphia, primarily through the efforts of Dick Clark, emerged as a new center for rock and roll. Based on market research undertaken to determine the public's image of the ideal rock and roll performers, Clark and his affiliated record companies, primarily through "American Bandstand," his extremely popular rock and roll TV show, succeeded in foisting on the American, and to a lesser extent the European, public a succession of look-alike and often sound-alike performers, including Fabian, Bobby Rydell, Frankie Avalon, and Dion. A few could sing; most looked presentable; and all were white, often of Italian origin, which matched the Sinatra-Martin-Como image. The success of "Philadelphia Scholck Rock" was partly due to the success of "Bandstand" and Dick Clark's business enterprises and partly due to other events outside his control.

Clark's "Bandstand" was aired from 3 p.m. to 5 p.m. every weekday to an enthusiastic and enormous national market. Artists appearing on the show were almost assured of their record appearing in the charts. Clark had many artists who recorded for his Philadelphia-based record companies: Cameo-Parkway (Chubby Checker, Bobby Rydell), Swan (Freddy Cannon, Deedee Clark), and Chancellor (Fabian, Frankie Avalon) were all represented on his TV show. The other events alluded to saw the major early artists inactive at the same time as Clark's efforts began to achieve success. Buddy Holly was killed in a plane crash, Elvis Presley was drafted into the Army, Jerry Lee Lewis was disgraced by revelations of a thirteen-year-old wife, and Chuck Berry was jailed on a morals charge. In addition, the payola scandals had resulted in Alan Freed being fired as a disc jockey. Rock and roll had lost its major creators, and the end of the 1950s and the early 1960s is widely regarded as a nadir in rock and roll. George Lucas encapsulated it succinctly in his movie "American Graffiti," when his hard-driving, macho character John Milner remarks, "I don't like that surfing s—, rock and roll's gone downhill since Buddy Holly died," a comment echoed more lyrically in Don Maclean's epic "American Pie."

Two other major innovations appeared in the early 1960s, however, to counter the effects of the adulteration of rock and roll by northeastern companies. One was the development by Berry Gordy, Jr., of the Motown recording company in Detroit in 1959.[36] A successful songwriter, Gordy saw a potential market for black artists groomed in a specific format. Beginning with two record labels, Tamla and Motown, Gordy began what was by 1977 the largest black-owned conglomerate in the United States.[37] Gordy produced a string of artists and hits that has kept Detroit and his company at the forefront of popular music for a quarter of a century; and while many of the artists have since left his company, no other individual in rock and roll has introduced so many successful artists, including Marvin Gaye, Stevie Wonder, Diana Ross and the Supremes, the Temptations, Martha and the Vandellas, Smokey Robinson, and ultimately the most lucrative artist in popular music, Michael Jackson.

The effect of the creation of the Motown label can be seen in Graph 17-1. Black artists prior to 1955 had less than 10 percent of the top fifty single records in the United States, and none of these were rhythm and blues or soul performers. The situation changed with the success of southern artists such as Chuck Berry and Little Richard, and by 1959, with the appearance of the Motown artists, well over 20 percent of the top fifty records were made by black artists. Gordy's efforts succeeded not only in changing the spatial pattern of rock and roll by providing a new culture hearth but also in changing the music, both racially and stylistically.

The second major innovation and final major spatial shift in the United States' music picture began in 1961 with the formation of the Beach Boys, and the appearance in 1962 of "Surfin' Safari." Of all the musical forms of rock and roll, the surfing sound has the strongest and most obvious spatial connotations. The images in the songs extolled the virtues of southern California—sun, sand, surf, cars, and girls. "Surfin' USA" was a note-for-note copy of Chuck Berry's "Sweet Little Sixteen," with new lyrics, but most of the Beach Boys' records were original and in a class and style of their own. Records about cars ("Little Deuce Coupe," "Little Old Lady from Pasadena"), surfing ("Surfin' Safari," "Surfin' USA") and girls ("Barbara Ann," "Surfer Girl," and the classic "California Girls") resulted in a flood of imitations by groups such as Jan and Dean. As well as producing some of the best rock and roll records ("Good Vibrations" was voted best "summer record" of all time on the "Solid Gold" television show in August 1984) and a unique sound, the Beach Boys created and confirmed an image of southern California that

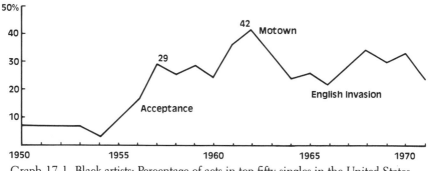

Graph 17-1. Black artists: Percentage of acts in top fifty singles in the United States (1950–1970).

still endures, and the crowds that attend their Memorial Day concerts attest to their continued popularity. Steve Chapple and Reebee Garofalo argue that:

> surfing music represented an authentic West Coast rock 'n' roll culture that differed in one important way from earlier rock and roll produced by urban blacks and southern rockabillies; it was made by middle class whites.[38]

The attention drawn to southern California by the Beach Boys and their imitators was accentuated by the records produced in Los Angeles by Phil Spector. Already a successful songwriter and producer, Spector began producing records in Los Angeles in 1962 and in the next three years had twenty consecutive smash hits. Spector's major contribution to rock and roll was his "Wall of Sound," which "changed the course of pop record producing."[39] Created by filling the recording studio and adjoining rooms and corridors with musicians and breaking many of the basic rules of recording up to that time, Spector emerged as a major force on the West Coast and played a significant role in Los Angeles's rise as a rock and roll center. Ever the perfectionist, he once spent twelve hours producing the first chord of a record.[40]

By the end of the period under examination the map of rock and roll had changed markedly from that of 1955. By the late 1960s the focus on the West Coast had shifted northward to some degree. While "bubblegum rock," as produced by TV rock stars such as the Monkees and the Archies, was being produced in Los Angeles, San Francisco had emerged, following the Monterey Pop Festival in 1967, as the "in" place for rock and roll fans. The Haight-Ashbury area, famed for hippies and flower people, received national attention, and songs like "San Francisco" (the John Phillips composition) received gold records.

> What is different about most of the white groups after 1967 is not their basic musical structure, which is still largely blues R and B derived, but rather the lyrics and the lifestyle that the groups represented. . . . The new groups represented an authentic white subculture that had been produced by the economic and social conditions of the sixties.[41]

At no time since 1970 has the rock and roll scene in the United States revealed such clear spatial patterns as it did in the first decade or so of its evolution. Improvements in technology, increased availability of facilities, and the dispersal of artists had destroyed the unique advantages that locations such as Memphis or Los Angeles had. Of the music centers in 1984, only Nashville holds sway as a true culture hearth, and that for country and western music as it has been for over half a century.

Rock and Roll in the United Kingdom—1955–1970

Before 1963, rock and roll in Britain was dominated entirely by the American music and artists. Almost without exception the only non-American rock and roll artists in the British charts were those covering American records. Thus Figure 17-3 shows the overwhelming dominance of London, not as a culture hearth, but as a recording, or rather rerecording and broadcasting, center. There was no regional rock and roll in the United Kingdom before 1962, and indeed little or no original rock and roll. Richard Mabey notes: "British songs were almost all early American; not one group to my knowledge, ever wrote or sang about contemporary Britain."[42] While there was a wealth of authentic folk music (especially Scottish and Irish) in Britain, there was also no real equivalent of country and western music, although a pale imitation, skiffle, appeared briefly in the late 1950s.

British rock and roll, as noted earlier, saw cover versions of cover versions, and artists imitating American artists. Cliff Richard began as an Elvis Presley clone, and a veritable stable of London-based artists mirrored the Philadelphia group, with names like Marty Wild, Vince Eager, Johnny Gentle, Duffy Power, and Billy Fury. Only a few—Richard, Fury, Wild, and Adam Faith—survived more than one or two years. This death of original music and artists may go some way toward explaining the incredible loyalty British fans developed for the early American artists. Bill Haley's popularity continued in Britain much longer than in America; posthumous adulation of stars such as Buddy Holly, Jim Reeves, and Eddy Cochrane still continues; and it was not by accident that the Everly Brothers chose London for their reunion concert in 1984. Other artists such as Roy Orbison, Gene Pitney, and Duane Eddy were still major attractions when their American popularity was minimal.

The spatial pattern of rock and roll in the United Kingdom remained static until 1963, with over half of the rock and roll artists coming from the London area and no other center existing. Songs written and recorded in Britain rarely owed anything to rhythm and blues or country and western music, which is hardly surprising considering the absence of a tradition in these fields in Britain. Rather they resembled diluted rockabilly sounds, similar to the songs sung by Ricky Nelson, or on the more negative side, by the Philadelphia group of artists. Not until December 1962 did a new, original form of homegrown music appear on the British scene, when "Love Me Do" by the Beatles entered the *New Musical Express* top-20 chart.[43]

The influence of the Beatles in musical terms has been explored in great detail by many writers, and the sections devoted to them in encyclopedias and anthologies of rock and roll[44] do justice to their creativity and impact. In terms of their impact on the spatial patterns of rock and roll in Britain the

Fig. 17-3. Origins of British rock and roll acts, 1955–1962.

Beatles were unique. It is no exaggeration to state that they alone were responsible for the changes between Figure 17-3 and Figure 17-4. Their major impact was to make respectable, and indeed desirable, acts from outside the London area. The predominant position of London as a source of recording artists was destroyed in less than a year. (Little immediate change

Fig. 17-4. Origins of British rock and roll acts, 1963–1969.

occurred in the pattern of record production or the location of companies. Even the Beatles located their Apple company headquarters in London.) Because of the spectacular success of the Beatles in Britain, in the United States, and elsewhere, record companies frantically sought out other groups that bore any passing resemblance to the Beatles. As almost no other group did in terms of talent and charisma, the companies selected the next best alternative, groups from the same location as the Beatles, and/or with non-London origins and accents.

Whereas a bland accent and a London address were major assets to a British pop performer from 1950 to 1962, in 1963 they were real handicaps. Mabey's comment that "the pop music scene has become an arena in which the old lodestar divisions of class, age, sex, status and geography have been challenged and uprooted"[45] was particularly true as far as geography was concerned. Three new foci emerged in the British pop scene in the decade ending in 1969: Liverpool, origin of the Beatles, Gerry and the Pacemakers, the Merseybeats and the Searchers; Manchester, the source of the Hollies, Herman's Hermits, and Billy J. Kramer's Dakotas; and Birmingham, source of the Moody Blues, the Honeycombs, and the Spencer Davis Group, who in Stevie Winwood had the closet thing to a black rhythm and blues artist that a white Englishman could hope to become. For the first time in Britain regional preferences and favorite artists began to emerge, such as the Animals in northeastern England, and later, in 1967, the Bay City Rollers in Scotland.

The early Beatles performances, both in the Cavern in Liverpool and in Hamburg, featured a large number of black rhythm and blues songs such as "Money," "Please Mr. Postman," "Kansas City," and "Boys"; two classic early rock songs, Little Richard's "Long Tall Sally" and Chuck Berry's "Roll Over Beethoven"; and Buddy Holly numbers such as "Rave On." Their musical origins and the influences upon their early years were clearly similar to those of Presley, Lewis, and the early white American rock singers. Because of the British situation, however, the influences were somewhat diluted and secondhand. The real influence of the Beatles was felt once they wrote and recorded their own lyrics and music, breaking the myth that pop music had to be American to be good. The result of this revelation encouraged many other British groups to write and produce their own songs, including the Rolling Stones, the Kinks, and the Who.

The Rolling Stones, like the Beatles, began by performing rhythm and blues songs such as Rufus Thomas's "Walking the Dog," Arthur Alexander's "You'd Better Move On," Chuck Berry's "Come On" (their first single release), and several Buddy Holly songs, including "Not Fade Away," (which reached number 3 in Britain and was their first record to hit the American charts). The Stones, more than any white group in popular music, have retained the black rhythm and blues influences, and perhaps as a result of that, have arguably remained the best rock and roll group for the last two decades. Their own compositions have belied Mabey's earlier comment concerning the lack of songs about contemporary Britain. The Stones' subject matter dealt heavily with urban deprivation and degradation and other contemporary issues. In terms of social commentary on and description of the British cultural scene, however, the Kinks emerged as the most perceptive group. Ray Davies's compositions, such as "Waterloo Sunset," "Dead End Street," "Dedicated Follower of Fashion," and "Sunny Afternoon," captured images of Britain as strongly as the Beach Boys' songs mirrored southern California.

The last years of the 1960s saw the continuation of the diffusion of origins of artists in the United Kingdom; for example, Donovan, Britain's answer to Bob Dylan, came from Scotland. The appearance of the Beatles' *Sgt. Pepper's Lonely Hearts Club Band* album in 1967 marked a new trend toward psychedelic and drug-related pop music both in Britain and elsewhere, and the same year saw Elvis Presley without a hit record in the British charts for the first time since 1956. To paraphrase Bob Dylan, "the times they were a changing," and the changes manifested themselves in primarily musical and social rather than geographical forms. The interchange of personalities among groups and a much more rapid formation and disbanding of groups in the late 1960s served to confuse and obliterate any clear spatial pattern.

The Success of Rock and Roll in the United States and the United Kingdom

In the popular music business, success is measured in record sales, and the best though not perfect indicator of record sales is the pop chart. Several publications—*Billboard, Cashbox, Record Mirror,* and *New Musical Express,* for example—publish charts of best-selling records. In the early years these charts showed only total sales, but now there are separate charts for different types of popular music such as country and rhythm and blues. In this section the focus is upon the national pop singles sales charts for the United States and the United Kingdom, using the charts from *Billboard* and *New Musical Express* respectively, to explore similarities and differences between the two areas. Four sets of data are used: the numbers of records topping the charts, the proportion of the charts topped by rock and roll records, the origin of artists topping the charts, and the origin of the artists topping the charts as a proportion of time at the top of the charts.

One of the major features of rock and roll in the 1950s was the speed with which it was accepted by the record-buying public. Graph 17-2 shows the proportion (numbers of weeks of the year) that the charts in the United States and the United Kingdom were topped by rock and roll records. (The definition of rock and roll record and artist is a personal definition, by the author, based primarily on the background of the artist and the nature of the

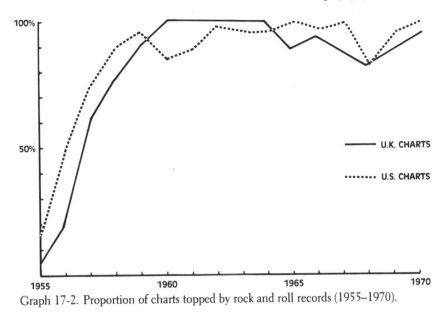

Graph 17-2. Proportion of charts topped by rock and roll records (1955–1970).

record jointly. In most cases there is little difficulty. In a case such as Pat Boone singing "Tutti Frutti" a problem may have arisen; fortunately this record and others like it rarely topped the charts.)[46]

The predominant feature of Graph 17-2 is the rapid rise of rock and roll in both charts, from 6 percent in 1955 (represented by Bill Haley's "Rock Around the Clock") to 62 percent in 1957 and 100 percent in 1960 in the case of the British charts; and from 16 percent in 1955 (again, "Rock Around the Clock") to 75 percent in 1957 and 95 percent in 1959 in the case of the American charts. It is interesting to note that while the United Kingdom was behind the United States in terms of initial acceptance of rock and roll in 1955, it surpassed the U.S. figure in 1959, and remained at 100 percent for the period 1960 to 1964. The figure for the U.S. charts on the other hand did not reach 100 percent until 1965. The records of Percy Faith in the United States in 1960 and Englebert Humperdinck and Frank Sinatra in the late 1960s in Britain made the only significant non-rock and roll impacts during this period.

Graph 17-3, which shows the numbers of records topping the single charts, reveals several features. First, both in the United States and the United Kingdom, the number of records topping the charts each year increased overall until 1965–66. In both cases for the first three years of the period there were fourteen to sixteen chart toppers each year, giving each record an average of slightly under four weeks at the top of the charts. In the United

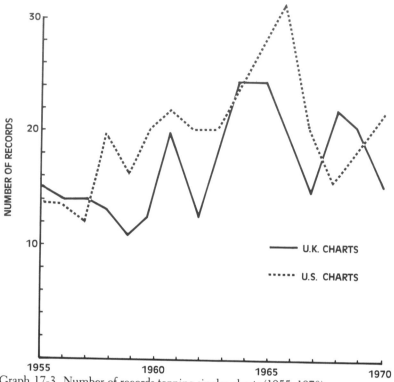

Graph 17-3. Number of records topping singles charts (1955–1970).

States from 1957, however, the number of records involved increased fairly steadily to 1963, at 22, and reached 31 by 1966. This rise mirrored the actual number of records released during that period. A rapid decline to 16 in 1968 was followed by an almost equally rapid rise in numbers to 22 in 1970. The spectacular rise in numbers from 1963 to 1966 was caused in part by the Beatles and other British groups. Demand for their records was so great that in April 1964 the Beatles held the top five places in the American charts, with the Dave Clark Five also in the top ten. Thus the Beatles had six chart toppers in America in 1964, along with three other British groups with single chart toppers. By 1968 however, the Beatles were the only British group to top the American charts, and they did it only once.

In the United Kingdom the pattern is more confused, and while the overall numbers of chart toppers increased to a plateau in 1964 and 1965 at 25, there are several major rises and falls in intervening years. In part the mid-1960s peak was caused, as in America, by the Beatles and others of that ilk, with nine chart toppers from Liverpool groups in 1963, ten by northern groups in 1964, but only four in 1965 and two in 1966. While the number of records hitting the top of the charts determines the average number of weeks a record will top the charts, there are frequent exceptions to the average. In the early years of the British charts each year produced one or two records that topped the charts for more than double the average period. In the earlier years, however, the length of time these particular records topped the charts was slightly longer than was the case for their counterparts in the American charts (an average of 7.5 weeks in the period 1955–62, compared to 6.4 weeks in the United States), while for the latter period, 1962–70, the length of time was almost identical (6.0 and 5.7 weeks respectively).

In the United Kingdom nineteen artists made twenty-six records with double the average time at the top of the charts, and in the United States twenty-seven artists made thirty-three such records. Only Elvis Presley and the Beatles were featured more than once in both charts. In the United Kingdom charts five artists in the first period and two in the second cannot be classified as pop artists; in the United States the comparable figures are four and none. In both cases the artist having the longest stay at the top was not a rock artist—Slim Whitman in the United Kingdom and Perez Prado in America.

The final data sets used here deal with the spatial origin of artists who had records topping the charts in the United Kingdom and the United States. Unlike the patterns shown in Graphs 17-2 and 17-3, which showed considerable similarities between the United States and the United Kingdom, Graphs 17-4 and 17-5 show marked differences between the two sets of charts. Whereas Graphs 17-2 and 17-3 dealt with rock and roll as a music form irrespective of the origins of the artist, Graphs 17-4 and 17-5 add this spatial dimension. Graph 17-4 illustrates the origin of artists who had chart topping records in the United States and the United Kingdom, and the length of the bars in the graph represent the numbers of artists from each origin involved as a proportion of the total numbers of artists who topped the charts. Graph 17-5 is only slightly different; it shows the proportion of time the respective charts were topped by artists from different locations. In both figures the origins of artists are grouped into American, British, and "other," with the third category comprising the rest of the world.

Perhaps the most revealing feature of both figures is the very low proportion of artists in the "other" category, making up only 3 percent of both the American and British charts in Graph 17-4, and 3 percent and 2 percent respectively in Graph 17-5. In comparative terms Canadian artists have a reasonably high share of this future through the efforts of Paul Anka, the Diamonds, and Lorne Greene in the pre-Beatle era, and the Guess Who and

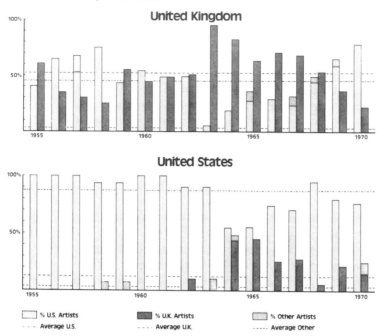

Graph 17-4. Origin of artists with chart toppers (1955–1970).

Neil Young in the late 1960s. Only Australia, initially with comic acts such as Slim Dusty ("Pub With No Beer") and Rolf Harris ("Tie Me Kangaroo Down, Sport") and more lately with the Seekers, the Bee Gees, and Olivia Newton-John, has approached the Canadian share of the "other" category total.

The U.S. charts in Graphs 17-4 and 17-5 show clearly the overwhelming dominance of American artists in topping those charts. Between 1955 and 1962, American artists provided all of the records topping the charts, and only Domenico Modugno ("Volare") and Paul Anka ("Lonely Boy") broke this domination. In the United Kingdom, partly because rock and roll was accepted slightly later, and more importantly because of British versions of American records (e.g., Tommy Steele's cover of Guy Mitchell's "Singing the Blues"), American artists did not achieve the same dominance that rock and roll records in general did. The proportion of non-British records declined from 60 percent to 23 percent from 1955 to 1959, while the American proportion rose to 77 percent, as American rock and roll reached what many regard as its best years in terms of music produced.

From 1959 to 1962, however, the British proportion more than doubled from the 1958 figure, and indeed not until 1970 would it fall below 30

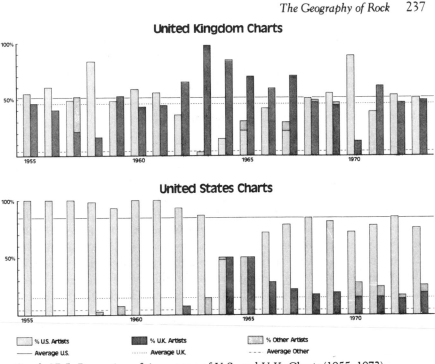

Graph 17-5. Proportion of time at top of U.S. and U.K. Charts (1955–1973).

percent again. The principal reason for the rise was the success of British acts covering American records (e.g., the Shadows' version of "Apache" or Craig Douglas's "Only Sixteen"), and more importantly the growing popularity of Cliff Richard, Adam Faith, and other mild rockers. Cliff Richard topped the charts for nineteen weeks between 1959 and 1962, while traditional jazz saw a resurgence in Britain with Acker Bilk topping both the British and American charts in 1961 and 1962 respectively and remaining in the British charts for thirty-nine weeks.

The most dramatic change in the charts, of course, took place in 1963 in Britain and 1964 in the United States with the appearance of the Beatles, although as noted above, British artists achieved considerable success in Britain from 1959 onward, with some very minor success in the United States in 1961 and 1962. In Britain the effect of the Beatles and the artists who followed them was to push the British proportion of chart topping records to 94 percent in 1963 and 83 percent in 1964, and around the 60–70 percent level until 1967. Indeed, from the beginning of 1963 until June 1964 when Roy Orbison topped the British charts for two weeks, only Elvis Presley of non-British artists managed to top the charts, and then only for one week.

The British dominance continued to February 1965, apart from two other weeks when Roy Orbison again topped the charts. During this period the Beatles topped the charts for twenty-nine weeks and other Liverpool groups for an additional thirty-three weeks. One group, Gerry and the Pacemakers, achieved the unique distinction of being the only group in pop history to have their first three records reach the number one position in a national chart.

In the United States, prior to 1964, most foreign records topping the charts or becoming major hits were novelty records or "one-off" records with a peculiar and unique appeal, such as Kyu Sakamota's "Sukiyaki" in 1963, the Tornados' "Telstar" in 1962, or the Singing Nun's "Dominique" in 1963. This pattern was broken permanently by the Beatles in 1964, and while the proportion of British records only reached 45 percent at its highest in 1965 (and 50 percent of the time at the top of the charts in 1964 and 1965), in relative terms it was a much greater increase than had taken place in Britain. The "British Invasion" of the mid-1960s declined in significance in 1966 and 1967, almost disappeared in 1968, and reappeared in 1969. Only the Beatles topped the American charts in 1968, although "Hey Jude" remained at the top for nine weeks—the longest stay since Percy Faith's "Theme from a Summer Place" in 1960, and only one week less than the record-breaking "Cherry Pink and Apple Blossom White" in 1955. Artists from other countries had no success in topping the U.S. charts after Lorne Greene in 1964, until 1970 when the Guess Who achieved this feat.

In Britain, the proportion of British acts declined steadily from 1963's high of 94 percent and was mirrored by a rise in the proportion of American acts to 79 percent in 1970. There was an increase in the mid-1960s of acts in the "other" category, which included acts such as the Bee Gees and Rolf Harris.

One of the problems with dealing only with records topping the charts is that they do not represent the complete picture. Several other differences emerged between the British and American rock and roll scene in the period under discussion. While there was universal acceptance of rock and roll, the styles that were popular varied between the two major areas. In Britain, which, as mentioned earlier, had no equivalent tradition of black blues music, there was much less acceptance of black artists' records, especially noticeable in the early years of the Motown developments. Thus Chuck Berry had almost twice as many hits in America as Britain (9 to 5), as did Fats Domino (15 to 8), while other major black artists such as Aretha Franklin (23 to 4) and Marvin Gaye (23 to 6) had proportionally even fewer hits in Britain, and James Brown only managed 1 in Britain compared to 15 in America. Only Diana Ross and the Supremes (24 to 28) and Little Richard (4 to 9) reversed this pattern. Indeed it was not until 1959 with Emile Ford that British charts had a black male with the top record, and then it was not a rhythm and blues record.

On the other hand, despite a similar absence of a tradition of country and western music, many country artists did as well or better in Britain than America, for example, Jim Reeves (2 to 13), Roy Orbison (10 to 16), and Frankie Laine (1 to 11). In addition, very few of the novelty or comedy records that were hits in America (for example, those of David Seville and the Chipmunks, Ray Stevens, or the Hollywood Argyles) were successful in Britain, and the reverse was also true. Bernard Cribbins, Rolf Harris, and Benny Hill did not reach the American charts. "Answer" records, while quite popular in America, did not sell well in Britain, even when the original record, for example, Jim Reeves's "He'll Have to Go," was a hit. Perhaps the most distinctive group of records that sold well in America but did not do so in Britain were "death" records, such as "Teen Angel," "Last Kiss," and "Tell Laura I Love Her" (answered by "Tell Tommy I Miss Him"). This was not so much due to a difference in taste but more a reflection of exposure, because death records were not played by the BBC for many years, thus depriving the record-buying public of its major opportunity to hear them.

There are a large number of artists who had hit records on one side of the Atlantic and not the other. The most spectacular being Cliff Richard, who had 48 hits in Britain from 1957 onward, and waited until 1976 for his first American hit, followed by Lonnie Donnegan (2 hits in America, 26 in Britain), Billy Fury (0 and 19), Frankie Vaughan (0 and 18), and Adam Faith (0 and 16). On the reverse side, Brook Benton (16 and 0), Jackie Wilson (13 and 3), Bobby Vinton (14 and 1), and the Temptations (24 and 9) figure highly. In the case of the British artists this is in part because they recorded cover versions of American songs which were never released in America (e.g., Donnegan's "Battle of New Orleans") or because their appeal was not considered appropriate to the American market in the pre-Beatle era. Most of the American artists fall into the black rhythm and blues style mentioned earlier, except for a few such as Vinton and Paul Revere (11 and 0), and in most of these cases one assumes taste was the determining factor.

The major artists with very few exceptions produced hits on both sides of the Atlantic: Presley (56 to 69), the Beatles (37 to 23), Connie Francis (22 to 19), the Beach Boys (20 to 12 despite the California image,), the Everly Brothers (17 to 19), the Four Tops (17 to 15), and the Rolling Stones (17 to 17). To put these figures into perspective, in the period 1955 to 1973, out of a total of 1,558 artists who had hit records, 894 artists (57.4 percent) had only one hit, 75 (4.8 percent) had from 10 to 19 hit records, and only 22 (1.4 percent) had 20 or more hits.

Conclusions

This paper has attempted to demonstrate the geographical aspects of rock and roll music during its evolution and acceptance in the period 1955 to 1970. It has been suggested that by the end of that period both the music and particularly its spatial elements had become more confused, and for these reasons the discussion does not extend beyond 1970. (To many rock and roll fans the real rock and roll began to disappear a decade earlier, as it began to be divided and diluted into a number of different forms from 1959 onward.) While rock and roll has changed drastically over the thirty years since its emergence, it has not lost its popularity. To many who grew up with the music during their adolescence in the 1950s it represents more than a sound, as H. Kandy Rhode comments: "we can read the list and hear every song . . . our memories are stored in our music."[47] So too are images of places as well as time, as Ford and Henderson illustrated.[48]

The audience for rock and roll has grown vastly as at least a proportion of each new generation has been attracted to the music, and there is clear evidence that fans from the 1950s have not ceased to listen to the music, even if they prefer "oldie goldies" to new records. The use of parodies of songs from the 1950s and 1960s to sell products in the 1980s is widespread. Commercials for beer ("Sea Cruise," "Dance to the Music," "Blue Moon"), for cheese ("Great Balls of Fire"), and for hamburgers ("Only You") are representative of this trend. The success of television spectaculars featuring artists from twenty to thirty years ago, and the continued personal popularity of artists such as the Beach Boys, Chuck Berry, Jerry Lee Lewis, and following their spectacularly successful reunion concert, the Everly Brothers, are other indications. So, too, are the emergence of artists copying the 1950s sounds, such as Sha Na Na, and copies of earlier records; for example, Linda Ronstadt's copy of Roy Orbison's "Blue Bayou," or the four subsequent versions of the Rolling Stones' "Satisfaction," each version being a hit. Finally, perhaps as a comment both on the standard of the early records, and of the lack of quality of some recent pop music, there is continued success in reissuing records that were hits earlier, a practice begun by Jonathan King in 1969 with the rerelease of the Righteous Brothers' "You've Lost That Loving Feeling." While the cultural hearth of rock and roll in Memphis has long disappeared, to be partially and temporarily replaced by Philadelphia, Detroit, Los Angeles, and Liverpool, its influence, like the melody, lingers on.

Notes

1. R. B. Browne, "Foreword," *Popular Music and Society* 1 (1971), pp. 1–3.
2. Sister Violita, "The Geography of Music" in R. B. Mandal and V.N.P. Sinha

(eds.), *Recent Trends and Concepts in Geography* (New Delhi: Concept Publishing Company, 1980), p. 333.

3. L. R. Ford and F. M. Henderson, "The Image of Place in American Popular Music: 1890–1970," *Places* 1 (1974), p. 31.

4. R. S. Murray, "From Memphis to Motown: Some Geographical Implications of the Origin and Diffusion of Rock 'n' Roll Music," in G. O. Carney (ed.), *The Sounds of People and Places* (Washington, D.C.: University Press of America, 1979), pp. 233–47.

5. R. V. Francaviglia, "Diffusion and Popular Culture: Comments on the Spatial Aspects of Rock Music," in D. A. Lanegran and R. Palm (eds.), *An Invitation to Geography* (New York: McGraw-Hill, 1973), pp. 87–96.

6. G. O. Carney, "Bluegrass Grows All Around: The Spatial Dimensions of a Country Music Style," *Journal of Geography* 73 (1974), pp. 34–55, and G. O. Carney "T for Texas, T for Tennessee: The Origins of American Country Music Notables," *Journal of Geography* 78 (1979), pp. 218–25.

7. G. O. Carney (ed.), *The Sounds of People and Places: Readings in the Geography of Music* (Washington, D.C.: University Press of America, 1979).

8. See also B. L. Cooper, "Popular Music in the Classroom: A Bibliography of Teaching Techniques and Instructional Resources," *International Journal of Instructional Media* 10 (1982), pp. 71–87, and P. H. Nash, "Music and Environment: An Investigation of Some of the Spatial Aspects of Production, Diffusion, and Consumption of Music," *Canadian Association of University Schools of Music Journal* 5 (1975), pp. 42–71.

9. P. Hirsch, J. Robinson, E. K. Taylor, and S. B. Wilkey, "The Changing Popular Song: An Historical Overview," *Popular Music and Society* 1 (1971), pp. 81–89.

10. Carney, "T for Texas, T for Tennessee," p. 219.

11. S. Chapple and R. Garofalo, *Rock 'N' Roll Is Here To Pay* (Chicago: Nelson-Hall, 1977), p. 245.

12. Ibid.

13. J. Pareles and P. Romanowski, *The Rolling Stone Encyclopedia of Rock and Roll* (New York: Rolling Stone Press/Summit Books, 1983), xi.

14. Ibid., xii.

15. L. Ford, "Geographic Factors in the Origin, Evolution and Diffusion of Rock and Roll Music," *Journal of Geography* 70 (1971), pp. 455–64.

16. Murray, "From Memphis to Motown."

17. Francaviglia, "Diffusion and Popular Culture."

18. Carney, *The Sounds of People and Places*.

19. Ray Charles quoted in Chapple and Garofalo, p. 243.

20. Ibid., p. 29.

21. Murray, "From Memphis to Motown."

22. Pareles and Romanowski, p. 235.

23. Ford, "Geographic Factors in the Origin, Evolution and Diffusion of Rock and Roll."

24. Sam Phillips, Sun Records, Memphis, in Pareles and Romanowski, p. 438.

25. Murray, p. 234.

26. Chapple and Garofalo, p. 41.

27. Ibid., p. 438.

28. Ibid., p. 39.

29. Described as a "series of hiccups and burps," Holly's distinctive break in voice and multisyllabic stretching of words was a distinctive feature of his records and was copied by several artists, such as Adam Faith in Britain and Bobby Vee in America.

30. M. Dean, "Who-Uh-Ho Peggy Sue: Exploring a Teenage Queen Linguistically," *Popular Music and Society* 2 (1973), pp. 244–54.

31. Murray, "From Memphis to Motown."

32. The data for the figures were taken from P. Hardy and D. Laing, *Encyclopedia of Rock 1965–1975* (London: Aquarius Books, 1977); N. Logan and R. Woffinden, *The Illustrated New Musical Express Encyclopedia of Rock* (London: Salamander Books, 1977); L. Vinson, *Encyclopedia of Rock* (New York: Drake Publishers, 1976); J. Pareles and P. Romanowski, *The Rolling Stone Encyclopedia of Rock and Roll* (New York: Rolling Stone Press/Summit Books, 1983); S. Nugent and C. Gillett, *Rock Almanac* (Garden City, N.Y.: Anchor Books, 1978); I. Stambler, *Encyclopedia of Pop, Rock and Soul* (New York: St. Martin's Press, 1974); and L. Roxon, *Rock Encyclopedia* (New York: Workman, 1971).

33. J. Kamin, "Taking the Roll out of Rock 'N' Roll," *Popular Music and Society* 2 (1972), pp. 1–17.

34. R. Mabey, *The Pop Process* (London: Hutchinson Educational, 1969).

35. N. Cohn, *Pop from the Beginning* (London: Weidenfeld and Nicolson, 1969).

36. For a comprehensive history of the Motown developments, see P. Benjamin, *The Story of Motown* (New York: Grove Press, 1979).

37. Pareles and Romanowski, p. 223.

38. Chapple and Garofalo, p. 52.

39. Pareles and Romanowski, p. 517.

40. The Ramones, quoted in "Rockin' and Rollin' with Phil Spector," Public Broadcasting System, Los Angeles, 1984.

41. Chapple and Garofalo, p. 73.

42. Mabey, p. 54.

43. A. Jasper (ed.), *20 Years of British Record Charts 1955–1975* (London: Queen Anne Press, 1975).

44. Stambler, *Encyclopedia of Pop, Rock and Soul*; Roxon, *Rock* Encyclopedia; Logan and Wiffinden, *The Illustrated New Musical Express Encyclopedia of Rock*; and Vinson, *Encyclopedia of Rock*.

45. Mabey, p. 33.

46. J. Whitburn, *Pop Annual 1955–1977* (Menomonee Falls, Wis.: Record Research Inc., 1978).

47. H. K. Rohde, *The Gold of Rock and Roll, 1955–1967* (New York: Arbor House, 1970).

48. Ford and Henderson, "The Image of Place in American Popular Music: 1890–1970."

Back issues of *Billboard*, *Cashbox*, and *New Musical Express* for various years between 1954 and 1970 were also examined to verify data used in this paper.

18

Selected Reading and Listening III

Chapter 11

Bane, Michael. *The Outlaws: Revolution in Country Music*. Garden City, N.Y.: Doubleday, 1978.

Carney, George O. "The Southwest in American Country Music: Regional Innovators and Stylistic Contributions." *Southwest Cultural Heritage Festival 1981: Selected Faculty Papers*. Edited by W. David Baird et al. Stillwater: Oklahoma State University Press, 1982, pp. 13–28.

Denisoff, R. Serge. *Waylon*. Knoxville: University of Tennessee Press, 1983.

Horstman, Dorothy. *Sing Your Heart Out, Country Boy*. New York: E. P. Dutton, 1975 (Revised edition by Country Music Foundation Press, 1986).

Malone, Bill C. " 'Honky Tonk': The Music of the Southern Working Class." *Folk Music and Modern Sound*. Edited by William Ferris and Mary Hart. Jackson: University Press of Mississippi, 1982, pp. 119–29.

Morthland, John. *The Best of Country Music*. Garden City, N.Y.: Doubleday, 1984.

Reid, Jan. *The Improbable Rise of Redneck Rock*. Austin, Tex.: Heidelberg, 1974.

White, John. *Git Along, Little Dogies: Songs and Songmakers of the American West*. Urbana: University of Illinois Press, 1975.

Authentic Cowboys and Their Western Folksongs (RCA Victor Vintage Series LPV-522).

Country Music in the Modern Era: 1940s–1970s (New World-207).

Country Music South and West (New World-287).

Nashville: The Early String Bands, Vols. 1–2 (County 541/542).

Ragged But Right: Great Country String Bands of the 1930s (RCA 8416-2-R).

Time-Life Collection of Country Music (14-LP set edited by Charles K. Wolfe).

Western Swing (Old Timey 105/116–117/119–123).

Chapter 12

Artis, Bob. *Bluegrass*. New York: Hawthorn, 1975.

Cantwell, Robert. *Bluegrass Breakdown*. Urbana: University of Illinois Press, 1984.

Rosenberg, Neil V. "From Sound to Style: The Emergence of Bluegrass," *Journal of American Folklore* 80 (1967): 143–50.

———. *Bluegrass: A History*. Urbana: University of Illinois Press, 1987.

Smith, L. Mayne. "An Introduction to Bluegrass," *Journal of American Folklore* 78 (1965): 245–56.

Bill Monroe's Country Music Hall of Fame (Decca DL 75281).

Early Bluegrass (RCA LPV-569).

Early Days of Bluegrass (Rounder 1013-17/1019-20).

Flatt and Scruggs at Carnegie Hall (Columbia 2045).

Hills & Home: Thirty Years of Bluegrass (New World-225).

Lester Flatt and Earl Scruggs: The Mercury Sessions (Rounder Special Series 18/19).

Mountain Music: Bluegrass Style (Folkways 2318)

Chapter 13

Barnouw, Erik. *A Tower in Babel: A History of Broadcasting in the United States*. New York: Oxford University Press, 1966.

Hurst, Jack. *Nashville's Grand Ole Opry*. New York: Abrams, 1975.

Patterson, Timothy A. "Hillbilly Music among the Flatlanders: Early Midwestern Radio Barn Dances," *Journal of Country Music* 6 (1975): 12–18.

Smyth, Willie J. "Early Knoxville Radio (1921–1941): WNOX and 'Midday Merry Go-Round,' " *J.E.M.F. Quarterly* 18 (1982): 109–16.

Tucker, Stephen Ray. "The Louisiana Hayride, 1948–1954," *North Louisiana Historical Journal* 8 (1977): 187–201.

Wolfe, Charles K. *The Grand Ole Opry: The Early Years, 1925–1935*. London: Old-Time Music, 1975.

Grand Ole Opry Spectacular (Starday 242).

Saturday Night at the Grand Ole Opry, Vols. 1-2 (Decca 4303/4539).

Sixty Years at the Grand Ole Opry (2-LP set 1928/1985 RCA CPL 2-9507).

Chapter 14

Fleming, Jo Lee. "James D. Vaughan, Music Publisher." (unpublished Ph.D. dissertation, Union Theological Seminary, 1972).

Jackson, George Pullen. *White Spirituals in the Southern Uplands*. Chapel Hill: University of North Carolina Press, 1933 (Paperback reprint, New York: Dover, 1965).

Stevenson, Robert. *Protestant Church Music in America*. New York: W. W. Norton, 1966 (Paperback reprint, 1970).

Warrick, Mancel et al. *The Progress of Gospel Music: From Spirituals to Contemporary Gospel*. New York: Vantage, 1977.

A Cappella Gospel Singing (Folklyric 9045/ Arhoolie C-223).

Favorite Gospel Songs (Folkways 2357).

Sacred Harp Singing (Archive of American Folk Song L-11).

The Golden Age of Gospel Singing (Folklyric 9046/Arhoolie C-223)

The Gospel Ship: Baptist Hymns and White Spirituals from the Southern Mountains (New World-294).

Chapter 15

Collier, James Lincoln. *The Making of Jazz*. Boston: Houghton Mifflin, 1978.

Giddins, Gary. *Rhythm-a-ning: Jazz Tradition and Innovation in the 80's*. New York: Oxford University Press, 1985.

Gitler, Ira. *Swing to Bop*. New York: Oxford University Press, 1985.

Kernfeld, Barry (ed.). *The Blackwell Guide to Recorded Jazz*. Cambridge, Mass.: Basil Blackwell, 1991.

Schuller, Gunther. *Early Jazz: Its Roots and Musical Development*. New York: Oxford University Press, 1968.

———. *The Swing Era: The Development of Jazz 1933–1945*. New York: Oxford University Press, 1989.

Stearns, Marshall. *The Story of Jazz*. New York: Oxford University Press, 1956 (Reprint, 1974).

Williams, Martin. *Jazz in Its Time*. New York: Oxford University Press, 1989.

————. *Jazz Changes*. New York: Oxford University Press, 1992.

Atlantic Jazz (15-LP set covering styles from Dixieland to Fusion—Atlantic 81700-11).

Blue Note's Three Decades of Jazz (United Artists BN LA 158/160).

Encyclopedia of Jazz on Records (3 sets of 2 LPs each covering 1920s through 1960s—MCA 406/4063).

The Folkways History of Jazz Series (FJ 280/2811).

The Smithsonian Collection of Classic Jazz (Revised—CBS Special Products-R C 033 P5T-19477).

Chapters 16 and 17

Belz, Carl. *The Story of Rock*. New York: Oxford University Press, 1972 (2nd ed.).

Bergman, Billy. *Recombinant do re mi: Frontiers of the Rock Era*. New York: Quill, 1985.

DeCurtis, Anthony (ed.). *Present Tense: Rock & Roll and Culture*. Durham: Duke University Press, 1992.

Eisen, Jonathan (ed.). *The Age of Rock: Sounds of the American Cultural Revolution*. New York: Vintage Books, 1969.

————. *The Age of Rock-2: Sights and Sounds of the American Cultural Revolution*. New York: Vintage Books, 1970.

Frith, Simon. *Sound Effects: Youth, Leisure, and the Politics of Rock 'n' Roll*. New York: Pantheon, 1981.

Hendler, Herb. *Year by Year in the Rock Era: Events and Conditions Shaping the Rock Generations That Reshaped America*. Westport, Conn.: Greenwood Press, 1983.

Marcus, Greil. *Mystery Train: Images of America in Rock 'n' Roll Music*. New York: E. P. Dutton, 1982.

Martin, Linda, and Kerry Segrave. *Anti-Rock: The Opposition to Rock 'n' Roll*. Hamden, Conn.: Archon Books, 1988.

Miller, Jim (ed.). *The Rolling Stone Illustrated History of Rock & Roll*. New York: Rolling Stone Press, 1980 (Rev. ed.).

Pielke, Robert G. *You Say You Want a Revolution: Rock Music in American Culture.* Chicago: Nelson-Hall, 1986.

Pollock, Bruce. *When the Music Mattered: Rock in the 1960s.* New York: Holt, Rinehart, and Winston, 1983.

Shaw, Arnold. *The Rockin' 50s: The Decade That Transformed the Rock Music Scene.* New York: Hawthorn Books, 1974.

Szatmary, David P. *Rockin' in Time: A Social History of Rock and Roll.* Englewood Cliffs, N.J.: Prentice Hall, 1987.

Ward, Ed, et al. *Rock of Ages: The Rolling Stone History of Rock and Roll.* New York: Rolling Stone Press, 1986.

American Graffiti (MCA 2-8001).

American Graffiti—Volume III (MCA 2-8008).

American Hot Wax (A&M SP 6500).

Atlantic Rhythm & Blues: 1947–1974 (A 14-LP set—Atlantic 81299-1).

Let the Good Times Roll (Bell 9002).

Motowns's Preferred Stock (A 3-volume set—Motown 6-881/882/883 S1).

More American Graffiti: A Collection of Rock Classics from the 60s (MCA 2-8007).

Shake, Rattle & Roll: Rock 'n' Roll in the 1950s (New World-249).

The History of British Rock (3-volume set—SASH 3702/3705/3712).

Part IV

The Role of Place in American Folk and Popular Music

19

Woody Guthrie and the Dust Bowl

James R. Curtis

Epic events in human history, be they magnificent triumphs or staggering disasters, have all had their chroniclers. Whether writing Homer-like prose, poetic verse, or lyrics to a revealing ballad, these chroniclers have left legacies often filled with personal and insightful perspectives on the historic dramas of their concern. One such saga was the Dust Bowl disaster of the 1930s. It too has its chroniclers.

Although geographers have occasionally written about the Dust Bowl, it has been couched largely in terms of rainfall regime, rainfall discontinuities, frequency ratios, marginal farming, absentee land ownership, and so on. The hapless plight and flight of the Dust Bowl migrants have conversely been left in the minds of most to the bitter pages of John Steinbeck's *The Grapes of Wrath*. Steinbeck as a literate, descriptive author is impeccable, and the picture he paints of the Dust Bowl folk is unforgettable. But there are other chroniclers who have spoken clearly and written and sung intensely on the human element involved in the Dust Bowl. One such person, largely ignored by the academic community, was folksinger, composer, and poet Woodrow Wilson (Woody) Guthrie. The purpose of this paper, therefore, is to examine the credentials of Woody Guthrie as a folk chronicler and to survey some of the more prevalent themes of the Dust Bowl as revealed in the lyrics of his songs.

But why should geographers, or any member of the academy for that matter, look beyond *The Grapes of Wrath* for comment on the tragedy of the

Reprinted by permission from *Places* 3 (1976): 12–18.

Dust Bowl migrants? An answer to that question is at once as simple as it is complex. It appears that all too often in academic pursuits our understanding of certain segments of society and ways of life are confined to analysis and description by nonparticipant observers of the group being studied. For an insight into the more mundane aspects of the life of a farmer, for example, we might turn to the writings of Thoreau while at Walden Pond. But while Thoreau or Steinbeck may have moved in the pseudocapacity of a farmer or Okie migrant, despite their lucid and sympathetic descriptions, they are not truly functioning members of those respective groups.

In certain instances, observations and analyses of nonparticipant observers are looked to in the absence of resident literati. In other cases, spokespeople of many groups are not recognized or either censored by more "literate" and powerful segments of society. This lack of recognition or censorship may either be a reaction to a perceived threat, misunderstanding or misinterpretation of the dominant theme of their message, or mere lack of knowledge concerning their existence.

The relative value of their contribution is often overlooked solely on the basis of their mode of expression; be it through folk songs or other means, or because of their unconventional writing style, often due to the pervasiveness of folk idiomatic expressions. Looking beyond the often less than sophisticated literary style, their contribution constitutes the most authentic, primary, and humanistic testament available. To ignore their work on the basis of their mode of presentation or their failure to conform to "accepted" academic or literary standards is, or should be, unacceptable. In other words, the modus operandi for those concerned with understanding events with humanistic components should entail not only efforts to define objective causality but should as well include subjective views of the actual participants. It is not being contended, however, that their contribution represents an end unto itself. For the geographer, a synergistic approach combining elements of both literary and folk sources should be followed whenever possible.

Woody Guthrie: Dust Bowl Chronicler

Most people have probably heard or even sung some of the better-known Guthrie songs, such as "This Land Is Your Land," "So Long It's Been Good to Know You," "Roll on Columbia," and "Pastures of Plenty." Indeed, "This Land Is Your Land" has been advanced by many as a more relevant national anthem and one that is certainly easier to sing. But Woody Guthrie, the man, remains an unknown figure to most. Even among those who claim to have known him, his life was enigmatic, mysterious, and controversial. Perhaps Steinbeck said it best:

> Woody is just Woody. Thousands of people do not know he has any other name. He is just a voice and a guitar. He sings the songs of a people and I suspect that he is, in a way, that people. Harsh voiced and nasal, his guitar hanging like a tire iron on a rusty rim, there is nothing sweet about Woody, and there is nothing sweet about the songs he sings. There is the will of a people to endure and fight oppression. I think we call this the American spirit.[1]

He has been characterized by others as "a rusty-voiced Homer"[2] and "our best contemporary ballad composer."[3] In the estimation of anthropologist John Greenway, Guthrie's reputation, based on his Dust Bowl ballads and Bonneville songs, "will—in my opinion—grow to a high rank even among sophisticated American poets."[4] To Richard A. Reuss, perhaps Guthrie's most able biographer, "his talents made him by far the greatest spokesman produced by the Okie migrant community," due to "his ability to communicate the life, feelings, attitudes, and culture of his people from the inside . . . using their terms, concepts, and modes of expression."[5]

Guthrie was born in 1912 in Okemah, Oklahoma, and died in 1967 in Brooklyn, New York. During the course of an often nomadic life he traversed the country many times from "California to the New York Island." Reuss has noted that he spent a better part of his life "simultaneously moving in three cultures: hobo, migratory, and labor-radical."[6] He held many jobs in his life, ranging from sign painter to radio performer to government employee hired for one month to compose songs about the government's Bonneville Dam project in the Pacific Northwest. During that twenty-eight-day period of government employment, he composed twenty-six songs, some of which rank among his very best. For that effort, on April 6, 1966, then Secretary of the Interior Stewart Udall presented Guthrie with the Department of the Interior's Conservation Service Award and named a substation in the Bonneville Power Administration in his honor. In his tribute to Guthrie, Udall noted: "Yours was not a passing comment on the beauties of nature, but a living, breathing, singing force in our struggle to use our land and save it, too."[7]

Regardless of the nature of his job at any point in time, he was almost continuously composing songs. In 1955 he told Greenway that he had composed at least 1,400 songs.[8] Stylistically, Alan Lomax, who in 1940 recorded Guthrie for the Folk Song Archives of the Library of Congress, commented that "like all folk poets, he uses familiar tunes, rewords old songs, adding new lines and phrases out of the folk-say of the situation that demands the new song."[9] For example, "Pastures of Plenty" was based on one of the numerous versions of "Pretty Polly," and "Roll on Columbia" was adapted from "Goodnight Irene." In this regard, Pete Seeger has noted that: "He was often not exactly conscious of where he got the tune, until it was pointed out to him."[10] Lomax concluded that Guthrie "feels that his function is to sum up and crystallize popular sentiment, to act as the voice of the common man.[11]

The lyrics of his songs are all basically straightforward, uncomplicated, and rather commonsensical. Seeger notes that: "His songs are deceptively simple. Only after they have become part of your life do you realize how great they are. Any damn fool can get complicated. It takes genius to attain simplicity."[12] In his own words, Guthrie said: "Let me be known as the man who told you something you already know."[13]

The Chronicle: Dust Bowl Themes

It is generally agreed that considered in toto, the Dust Bowl ballads rank among Guthrie's best work. Indeed, despite his association with the labor-radical movement of the 1940s and the songs that were born of that affiliation, he is perhaps best remembered as a spokesperson for the Dust Bowl migrants. He once wrote:

> I've lived in these dust storms just about all my life. (I mean, I tried to live.) I met millions of good folk trying to hang on and to stay alive with the dust cutting down every hope. I am made out of this dust and out of this fast wind.[14]

His position as the foremost Dust Bowl balladeer was perhaps solidified during the filming of the movie *The Grapes of Wrath*, when director John Ford consulted with the Okies and other Dust Bowl migrants recruited as character extras for the movie to determine what song would be best known by virtually all Dust Bowl folk. They chose, "without hesitation," Guthrie's "Goin' Down That Road Feeling Bad."[15]

A majority of the Dust Bowl songs were written while Guthrie was in California employed for the better part of 1937–39 as a performer on radio station KFVD, Los Angeles. Somewhat later, largely through the efforts of Lomax, a number of the more popular Dust Bowl ballads were recorded by Victor Records on 78s; of which twelve were reissued on long-playing albums under the title *Dust Bowl Ballads* by Folkways Records and fourteen under the same title by Victor Records. From these sources as well as other printed material, it is possible to isolate a number of recurring themes characterizing Guthrie's Dust Bowl ballads. For the purpose of overall continuity, these themes will be dealt with in chronological sequence rather than on an individual-song basis. Lastly, it should be cautioned, as Reuss points out, that "Woody's lyrics, in most cases, were written as songs, to be sung and performed in a dynamic atmosphere. Reduced to two dimensions on the printed page, they frequently suffer."[16] The strong message of the songs, nevertheless, is retained regardless of their mode of presentation.

The Dust Bowl themes to be discussed include the pre–Dust Bowl period, description of the storms and subsequent destruction, elements of migration, and California. Although the pre-Dust Bowl period received only minor attention in most of Guthrie's Dust Bowl-related songs, the image projected is one of rural simplicity, contentment, and relative prosperity based on favorable rainfall and agricultural success. The following stanza from "Talking Dust Bowl" is illustrative of this theme.

> *Back in nineteen twenty-seven,*
> *Had a little farm and I called*
> *   that heaven,*
> *Prices up, the rain came down,*
> *Hauled my crops, all into town,*
> *   Got the money . . . bought clothes*
> *   and groceries.*
> *Fed the kids . . . raised a big*
> *   family.*

Whereas academic accounts of the Dust Bowl have tended to concentrate on the causes, affects, and resulting efforts at conservation, we are still left wanting in such studies when it comes to actual description of the storms and the personal reactions, meanings, and interpretation of them. Guthrie is of particular value in filling this void. The blackness of the storms and strength and coldness of the wind are characteristics mentioned throughout many of the ballads.

> *But the rain quit and the wind got high,*
> *Black old dust storm filled the sky.*
> *   —Talking Dust Bowl*
> *You could see that dust storm coming, it looked so awful black,*
> *It fell across our city like a curtain of black rolled down.*
> *   —The Great Dust Storm*
> *I seen the dust so black that I couldn't see a thing,*
> *And the wind so cold it nearly shut your water off.*
> *   —Dust Bowl Blues*
> *A dust storm hit and it hit like thunder,*

> *It dusted us over, it dusted us under,*
> *It blocked out the traffic, it blocked out the sun.*
> *—So Long, It's Been Good to Know You*

The "dusters" were often interpreted as ominous warnings signaling the end of the world and the second coming of God.

> *They thought the Lord was a-coming.*
> *We thought it was our judgment,*
> *We thought it was our doom.*
> *—The Great Dust Storm*
> *We talked of the end of the world and then*
> *We'd sing a song and then sing it again.*
> *—So Long It's Been Good to Know You*

The destruction caused by the wind and dust is concisely yet descriptively stated in the following verses.

> *We saw outside our windows where wheat field once had grown*
> *Was now a rippling ocean of dust the wind had blown.*
> *It covered up our fences, it covered up our barns,*
> *It covered up our tractors in this wild and windy storm.*
> *—The Great Dust Storm*
> *Well, it turned my farm into a pile of sand.*
> *—Dust Bowl Blues*

Despite the despair and suffering at the loss of crops, property, equipment, and even lives, a determination to overcome and to persist and to survive is evident.

> *That old dust might kill my wheat, boys,*
> *Can't kill me, Lord, can't kill me.*
> *That old dust storm got my family,*
> *Can't get me, Lord, can't get me.*
> *—Dust Can't Kill Me*

Although geographers have studied the Dust Bowl disaster as being a classic example of the inevitable result of the culmination of maladaptive humid climatic farming techniques, archaic patterns of farm ownership, and inefficient modes of cultivation, of equal concern is that the Dust Bowl epitomizes many migrational elements of interest to geographers. Guthrie nicely articulates in a number of songs various examples of these elements, such as the inertia that must be overcome in a decision to migrate and the function of myth as a catalyst to the migration process. Perhaps the best example of apparent inertia to migrate is the verse from "Tom Joad" where Grandpa Joad

> *He took up a handful of land in his hand,*
> *Said, I'am sticking with the farm till I die.*
> *I'am a-sticking with the farm till I die.*

"Tom Joad" is the song adapted from *The Grapes of Wrath*. To those curious as to why "Tom Joad" was written when *The Grapes of Wrath* was available in movie as well as book form, Guthrie once explained: "because the people back in Oklahoma haven't got two bucks to buy the book, or even thirty-five cents to see the movie, but the song will get back to them and tell them what Preacher Casey said."[1/]

Important in the ultimate decision to migrate was the influence of the myth of California. The distribution of seductive handbills proclaiming the need for agricultural workers in California is a well-known story. But the myth entailed much more than employment opportunities. This fact is amply illustrated in a number of Guthrie's songs by selected passages referring to California. California was variously described as "the peach bowl," "the sugar bowl," "a garden of Eden," "a paradise to live in or see," "where the water tastes like cherry wine," "where the weather suits my clothes," and "where these dust storms never blow."

Despite the fact that geographers have historically included chronicles of travel within the eclectic realms of geographic interest, surprisingly little has been written on the actual migrational trek of the Dust Bowl refugees. The sight of makeshift "trucks" rolling down U.S. 66 loaded to the hilt with adults and children and family pets too dear to leave behind, and the precious, fundamental remnants of a family's life of accumulation, is a graphic image easily conjured up. Guthrie adds to this image by reference to some of the mundane problems encountered on the flight.

> *Way up yonder on a mountain road*
> *Had a hot motor and a heavy load*
> *Goin' purty fast, wasn't even stopping,*
> *Bouncing up and down like popcorn a-poppin'.*
> *Had a breakdown . . . nervous bust down.*
> *Mechanic feller there said it was engine trouble.*
> —*Talking Dust Bowl*

In "Tom Joad" Guthrie handled the Joad's exodus from Oklahoma to California with the terse statement:

> *They buried Grandpa Joad on the Oklahoma Road,*
> *Grandma on the California side,*
> *Grandma on the California side.*

For perhaps a majority of the thousands of Dust Bowl migrants to California (an estimated 100,000 from Oklahoma alone)[18] the hardships of the road were but a harbinger of things to come. Usually arriving in California broke, broken, and hungry, disillusionment began almost at once. Guthrie, in half-satirical manner, notes that the realities of California often began at the very port of entry.

> *Cross the desert sands they roll,*
> *Gittin' out of the old dust bowl,*
> *They think they're goin' to a sugar bowl,*
> *Here's what they find:*
> *The police at the port of entry say,*
> *'You're number fourteen thousand for today',*
> *If you ain't got the Do Re Mi, boys,*
> *If you ain't got the Do Re Mi.*
> *—Do Re Mi*

Upon entering California they continued ever west, then north across the Tehachapis and into the fertile San Joaquin and Sacramento Valleys, often in search of a Delano, Weedpatch, Arvin, or other small town where they knew friends or relatives had settled. They came not as single men to make a quick profit and return home but as families seeking a new, permanent home. That they became migratory farm laborers was not their intent either. Yet, as a combined result of the depression and the program of voluntary repatriation for Mexicans desirous of returning to Mexico, California agriculture was and still is one that requires heavy labor input only at harvest. Thus, in the failure to find more stable jobs, the migrants followed the harvesting of crops in the endless and often elusive search for work. In "Pastures of Plenty" Guthrie is at his very poetic best in describing this situation.

> *California, Arizona, I make all your crops,*
> *Well, it's north to Oregon to gather your hops,*
> *Dig the beets from your ground, cut the grapes from your vine . . .*
> *On the edge of the city you'll see us and then,*
> *We come with the dust and we go with the wind.*

The squalor of the ditch-bank camps and shantytowns that proliferated wherever crops were being harvested were but a part of the hardships that had to be endured. Paradoxically, even the exotic crops that had fascinated and enticed the migrants presented their own special problems. Not only did excessive consumption of these fruits often cause dysentery and other ailments, the very harvesting of these crops presented unfamiliar hazards. Guthrie laments:

> *From the dust bowl to the peach bowl,*
> *But that peach fuzz is killin' me.*
> *—Dust Bowl Refugee*

The Dust Bowl refugees encountered greater danger than just peach fuzz, however. Discrimination and injustice were found on all sides, and fear of local residents and vigilante crews permeated their very thoughts and lives.

> *I rambled around from town to town.*
> *And they drove us out like a wild herd of cattle.*
> *'Was that the vigilante man?'*
> *—Vigilante Man*

The transient community of the Dust Bowl migrants is generally considered to have persisted in California and the rest of the Far West until increased employment opportunities associated with World War II helped pave their transition into the mainstream.

Conclusion

Music, as an item in the cultural baggage of a people, has all too often been thought of as a literary marginalia and hence neglected by geographers. But lessons of history, tradition, and culture are all contained in the music that people write and sing and listen to and carry with them.

As a source of geographic or historic evidence, lyrics of songs, like poetry and other forms of literature, may present the researcher with a multitude of problems. But the value is there for an individual with the patience and perhaps predilections to pursue it. As Woody Guthrie often said: "Take it easy . . . but take it."

Notes

1. John Steinbeck, Foreword to *Hard Hitting Songs for Hard-Hit People*, by Alan Lomax, Woody Guthrie, and Pete Seeger (New York: Oak Publications, 1967), p. 9.

2. Olin Downs and Elie Siegmeister, A *Treasury of American Songs* (New York: Alfred A. Knopf, 1940), p. 395.

3. Alan Lomax, Prefatory Notes to Guthrie's recording of "The Gypsy Davy," Archive of American Folk Song, Album I.

4. John Greenway, "Woody Guthrie: The Man, the Land, the Understanding," *American West* 3 (Fall 1966), p. 28.

5. Richard A. Reuss, "Woody Guthrie and His Folk Tradition," *Journal of American Folklore* 83 (July–September 1970), pp. 274, 278.

6. Ibid., 277.

7. Stewart Udall, "A Tribute to Woody Guthrie," reprinted in *Bound for Glory*, by Woody Guthrie (New York: New York American Library edition, 1970).

8. Greenway, op. cit.

9. Alan Lomax, *The Folk Songs of North America* (Garden City, N.Y.: Doubleday and Co., 1960), p. 431.

10. Pete Seeger, Prefatory Remarks to *Woody Guthrie Sings Folk Songs*. Folkways Records, FA 2483.

11. Lomax, op. cit.

12. Pete Seeger, Foreword to *Bound for Glory*, op. cit.

13. Quoted in John Greenway, *American Folksongs of Protest* (Philadelphia: University of Pennsylvania Press, 1953), p. 289.

14. Woody Guthrie, Prefatory Remarks to *Dust Bowl Ballads*, Folkways Records, FH 5212.

15. Greenway, 1953, op. cit., p. 206.

16. Reuss, op. cit., p. 289.

17. Quoted in Greenway, 1966, op. cit., p. 30.

18. Walter J. Stein, *California and the Dust Bowl Migration* (Westport, Conn.: Greenwood Press, 1973), p. 6.

"The Miami Sound": A Contemporary Latin Form of Place-Specific Music

James R. Curtis and Richard F. Rose

Since the mid-1970s a distinctive style of Latin commercial music has emerged in southern Florida.[1] Known locally and increasingly in the music industry as the "Miami Sound," it represents a complex and still-evolving fusion of traditional and contemporary Latin, especially Cuban, musical influences with North American popular music formats and elements.[2] Recently Miami Sound groups, most notably the Miami Sound Machine, have gained considerable recognition and commercial success beyond the airways and discos of Miami. Their songs—some of which have topped the Latin Hit Parade—are now broadcast regularly on radio stations in other major Latin cities of this country, and record sales nationwide of Miami Sound groups have increased significantly.[3] This success has led to its diffusion abroad, especially to the Spanish-speaking countries of Latin America and to Spain. The move overseas has been achieved largely through the promotional and distributional efforts of major recording companies, such as CBS International, which have contracts with some of the more popular groups. It appears likely that further recognition and diffusion of the Miami Sound will continue both nationally and internationally.

The Miami Sound is a creative musical expression born of the Cuban-American experience in south Florida, particularly younger Cubans who have been thoroughly exposed to and who appreciate both Latin and North American musical idioms. The characteristic elements and fusions involved

Reprinted by permission from the *Journal of Cultural Geography* 4 (1983): 110–18.

in this Latin pop sound, the factors responsible for its emergence and growth in Miami, and its geomusical context are analyzed and described in this study.

Although geographers have published over twenty articles since the early 1970s on the spatial elements of music, the foci and methodologies employed have been extremely limited.[4] A majority of these studies has dealt primarily with the origin, distribution, and especially diffusion of selected musical forms, elements, and musicians. A few articles have been concerned with the popular images of people and places revealed through music.[5] In general, other geographical themes have received comparatively minor attention.[6] Moreover, the body of geographical literature on music is clearly dominated by studies utilizing country music, and to a lesser extent rock and roll, as their data base.

Beyond the paucity of studies dealing with the music of other countries and regions, as well as international forms including classical, the relative lack of investigation into the musical expression of American ethnic groups is particularly apparent.[7] In this respect, George Carney has concluded that "Our knowledge of North American ethnic music and dance is practically nil."[8] This is regrettable since music is often an important source of subcultural identity for many ethnic groups in the United States. The unbalanced treatment is further compounded by the fact that analyses of the music itself have largely been restricted to lyrics and titles of songs; the musical structure, format, patterns of instrumentation, and style of vocal presentation have been virtually ignored. In light of these trends this study will help contribute to the growing body of geographical literature on music by introducing the concept of place-specific music, focusing on a contemporary form of ethnic commercial music in the United States and analyzing musical components other than lyrics.

Place-Specific Music

The Miami Sound is a type of music that can be classified as a distinctive musical style or sound, or even a general category of music, that has come to be identified with a specific place, typically a city. Because of its spatial focus it is not necessarily the same as "regional" music, though it may be a variation of a regional style and clearly is of regional musical significance. Contemporary examples of place-specific music in America include Nashville and country music (which has become a metonym for the form), New Orleans and Dixieland jazz, Detroit and the "Motown" sound, Chicago and urban blues, New York and "hot" jazz, and more recently Austin and progressive country and western music.[9] Place-specific music is often ephemeral, meaning that a location may blossom as the center of a particular sound that is relatively short-lived in popularity. Both Los Angeles and "surfer" rock and roll in the early 1960s and San Francisco and the "acid" rock sound of the late 1960s are examples of this phenomenon.[10]

The reasons why place-specific music develops typically involve a combination of factors. To the extent that music is an expression of society, a host of social considerations particular to the places concerned contribute to its evolution. These factors include, but certainly are not limited to, past and present patterns of migration and settlement; ethnicity; social group values, institutions, and traditions, including musical heritage; socioeconomic conditions; rates of culture persistence, change, and adaptation; and the role played by community institutions such as the church, schools, and government. The development of Dixieland jazz in New Orleans is of course the classic American example of the relationship between social conditions and musical innovations. There a special set of social and geographical circumstances gave rise to a unique musical form. In respect to New Orleans, David Ewen states: "The receptivity of the city to the febrile rhythms of jazz music had long been prepared through its contact with the African bamboula. Besides this, the emotional climate was favorable to music as sensual and undisciplined as jazz in the only city in America in which prostitution was licensed."[11]

In addition, Ewen notes that the city was tolerant of black street musicians, that wind instruments were plentiful and inexpensive since New Orleans was a manufacturing center for such instruments, and that employment opportunities for jazz musicians were abundant. Yet, to a greater or lesser degree, all place-specific music evolves out of a permissive, or at least nonrestrictive, set of social realities.

More specifically, the presence of influential personalities (i.e., performers, musicians, groups, teachers) may be the single critical factor in the emergence of place-specific music. The growing recognition of Austin as the hub of progressive country and western music, for example, is inextricably linked to one person, Willie Nelson, who lives near the city.[12] This situation also characterizes Bakersfield, California, the so-called "Nashville West" that is based on the presence of Buck Owens and Merle Haggard.[13] In south Florida, Carlos Oliva, a Cuban-American musician and recording company executive, was instrumental in the early formation and dissemination of the Miami Sound. It should be stressed that once established, place-specific music may persist even after the originators have died or departed the area.

Although there are many distinctive "local" musical styles, few assume significance beyond a limited, surrounding area. The wider recognition and articulation of that sound, and the degree to which it is diffused elsewhere, is now most frequently based on the location and decisions of the recording industry and media exposure.[14] Many contemporary examples of place-specific music are found in association with the location of recording studios. Traditionally, recording studios have located near musical source areas. Nashville, for example, was the heart of country music long before it became a recording center, not vice versa.[15] Yet the presence of studios tends to assume an attractive force, a force that often becomes self-perpetuating and may help define the music of that location.

This is true even if the creative elements that gave rise to the music are no longer present. Regardless of whether the studios move to the music or the music moves to the studios, the critical point remains that at the present time place-specific music must be recorded if it is to exert an influence beyond a local market. The role of radio and television broadcasting is clearly the paramount factor in this concern. Crucial in the establishment of some of the contemporary examples of place-specific music cited above was the influence of radio and television programs that linked the sound with the place and that were disseminated to a regional or national audience. The "Grand Ole Opry" on WSM from Nashville and the "Austin City Limits" television show are representative examples.[16]

Place-specific music is charged with real and symbolic meanings that may hold significance for both residents and nonresidents of these cities. Viewed externally this spatio-musical association may serve as an important component in shaping the perceptions and images that "outsiders" have of the places in question, regardless of whether they have actually been there or not. Among residents this association between their city and a particular music can function as a source of geographical and perhaps even subcultural identity. It also may help foster a sense of community pride and a feeling of attachment to place. The emergence of the Miami Sound provides an excellent example of the operative processes and formative dynamics of place-specific music.

Miami: The Setting

That Miami is the hearth, the inspiration, the namesake, and the major market for this sound is based fundamentally on the phenomenal growth of the Cuban population in the metropolitan area and the attendant blending of Cuban and American culture elements. It further is related to the presence in Miami of a number of recording studios and Spanish-language radio stations that aided its dissemination immeasurably.

In just over twenty years—beginning in 1959 in the wake of the Castro revolution that sent waves of Cuban refugees fleeing to the United States— the Cuban population of Dade County has grown from about 20,000 to nearly 600,000.[17] Almost six out of every ten Cubans in the United States live in Dade County, and Cubans now account for approximately 35 percent of the total county population, compared to less than 5 percent in 1960 (Fig. 20-1). In the city of Miami, Cubans represent a clear majority. The growth of the Cuban population has functioned as a magnet that has attracted over 100,000 other Hispanics to the county in the past two decades.[18] This rapid process of Latinization has had profound consequences on both material and nonmaterial elements of the culture in the region.[19] In addition, it has created a burgeoning and relatively affluent Latin market, and Cubans have helped revitalize if not restructure the economy of the area.[20] During this period of cultural and economic transformation, most Cubans have zealously sought to maintain the integrity of traditional Cuban values and institutions while simultaneously adopting American ways. In the process of acculturation many elements of Cuban and American culture have fused, rendering culture traits and complexes that are new, unique, and particular to Miami. Younger Cuban-Americans have been especially instrumental in forging these new culture blends. In language, for example, English and Spanish (i.e., "Spanglish") words are frequently mixed in the same sentence, as a sign on a store window might announce "*Gran* Sale."[21] It was this process that gave rise to the Miami Sound.

Against this background, the establishment, evolution, and diffusion of the Miami Sound is further related to the fact that since the mid-1970s Miami has become an extremely important music recording center, ranking third nationally behind Los Angeles and New York in number of studios. Many of the sixty-plus studios in the county are Cuban-owned and cater to Latin music and musicians, both from the United States and abroad. This situation afforded local Cuban groups an opportunity to record their material on local independent labels that were highly supportive and relatively inexpensive. Its dissemination and exposure locally were greatly facilitated by the existence in Miami of six Spanish-language radio stations, the most of any city in the country.[22] Additionally, a local Spanish-language television show, "The Miami Sound," featured Miami Latin groups, and it, too, aided in the further recognition and growth of the sound.

The Miami Sound

Viewed historically the Miami Sound is the latest example of the merger of Cuban, and to a lesser degree other Latin influences, with North American

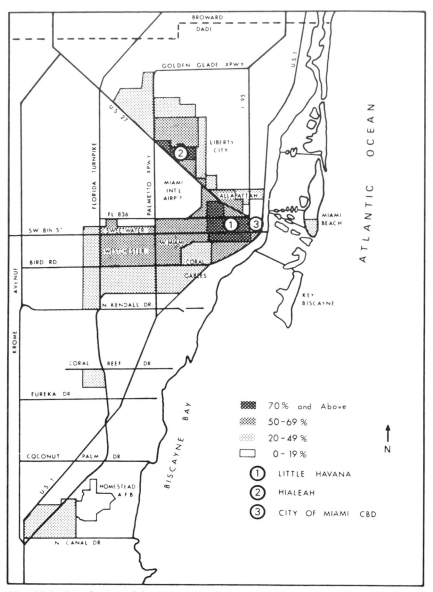

Fig. 20-1. Distribution of the Cuban-American population in Dade County, Florida, in 1980.

musical elements to form a commercially popular sound in the United States. These fusions have frequently been short-lived and often diluted or Anglicized to enhance their market appeal. The most important, readily identifiable, phases were typically followed by a retreat back to Cuban, or at least Latin, musical roots.[23] The progression began with the *rumba* craze of the 1930s and was followed by the *mambo* in the late 1940s and early 1950s, the *chachacha* in the mid-1950s, the Latin *bugalu* in the 1960s, and *salsa* (which is not a distinctive style per se) in the 1970s.[24] Though certainly less commercial, there also has been a continuing musical fusion with jazz. With the exception of Latin *bugalu*, which was closely associated with New York City, these styles were not centered on a specific place.

The Miami Sound is perhaps best described as a form of Latin pop, a mellow version of *salsa* mixed with elements of American rock and jazz. The music of the Miami Sound Machine was recently characterized in *Billboard* as a fusion of "disco, samba, salsa, pop and rock."[25] Clearly it is an eclectic fusion, though these influences vary from one song to another.

Typical of commercial music styles, the basic structure of the Miami Sound includes only two or three large musical sections, usually a verse and a bridge, each repeated several times. Additionally, most songs rely on a "hook"—a simple, catchy musical idea used throughout a song—to catch the ear of the listener.[26] This musical structure is in sharp contrast to traditional Latin forms, which most frequently include a *montuno* section, a two-, three-, or four-chord pattern that serves as a vehicle for either instrumental or vocal improvisation. A male voice in Latin music generally sings in a rough, angular manner, except on ballads, but singers in most of the Miami Sound groups tend to use a more open, less nasal tone. The *coro* (chorus) element of the music is usually sung by females. Their voices are blended in a Brazilian style of singing, which is characterized by soft, light unison singing.[27] This style, popularized in the United States by Sergio Mendez and Brazil 66, also is used by Miami Sound groups for lead vocals as well. Although lyrics are most often sung in Spanish, some songs have been recorded in English.[28]

The rhythm section forms the foundation and is the driving force of Latin music, and the Miami Sound is no exception. Most rhythms are based on the traditional Latin *clave*, which is an African-derived, off-beat 3/2 or occasionally 2/3 rhythmic structure played over a two-bar phase that is treated as one measure. This infectious, infinitely variable rhythmic pattern is produced by Latin and commercial rhythm sections that include piano, guitar, bass, and percussion. Miami Sound groups most commonly employ two percussionists. One plays the traditional Latin percussion instruments, especially *conga* and *bongo* drums, and outlines the rhythmic subdivision and meter of the music while the second plays a trap drum set in a commercial pop style that is generally "busier" sounding than rock music. Drum fills at the end of musical phrases are definitely Latin in nature. The piano generally is used to punctuate rhythmic elements. It is played in a "comping" fashion (an aspect of jazz) and tends to vary its rhythms more than in traditional Latin music.[26] The guitar is utilized for solo breaks, usually in rock timbre and style, and to sustain rhythmic and chordal patterns. The bass alternates between a syncopated, "off-beat" Latin bass line and a symmetrical pop bass part. These fundamentally different styles may even appear in contrasting sections of the same composition.

Other instruments and musical effects are added to "sweeten" a song after the rhythm section has been recorded. String lines, often synthesized, are identical to those found in commercial rock as well as in rhythm and blues songs. They add flowing counter melodies and serve to smooth and unify a song. Horn lines, by contrast, are most often rhythmic and brassy in keeping with the Latin tradition.

"The Miami Sound" as performed by a band in the Little Havana section of Miami (photo courtesy of Jim Curtis).

Conclusion

The Miami Sound continues to evolve. It is influenced by advances in musical technology, other musical fusions, and the demand of the market. Recently, for instance, the Latin influence on the Miami Sound has grown while the disco sound has diminished. This appears to be more a function of the market than of the place. The process of change, however, is the nature of commercial music. Changes notwithstanding, as one Latin recording executive in Miami said, "This sound could only happen here."[30]

The concept of place-specific music needs to be developed further and applied to other locales. The examples cited in this study provide excellent opportunities for additional research. Likewise, the spatial aspects of ethnic music in the United States, both traditional and contemporary, are important and existing topics that merit the attention of cultural geographers. Although a foundation has been laid, the geography of music calls for new methodologies, approaches, and concepts. The range of subject matter is limitless and the field warrants further investigation.

Notes

1. Loyd Grossman, *A Social History of Rock Music* (New York: David McKay, 1976), pp. 11–15.

2. John Rublowsky, *Popular Music* (New York: Basic Books, 1967), pp. 113, 128.

3. The Miami Sound Machine's latest album, *Otra Vez*, topped the Latin Hit Parade in 1982.

4. George O. Carney, "Geography of Music: A Bibliography," *Journal of Cultural Geography* 1 (Fall–Winter 1980), pp. 185–86.

5. Larry Ford and Floyd Henderson, "The Image of Place in American Popular Music: 1890–1970," *Places* 1 (March 1974), pp. 31–37; Floyd Henderson, "The Image of New York City in American Popular Music: 1890–1970," *New York Folklore Quarterly* 11 (Spring 1978), pp. 267–79, and Ben Marsh, "A Rose-Colored Map," *Harper's* 225 (July 1977), pp. 80–82.

6. Two exceptions: James R. Curtis, "Woody Guthrie and the Dust Bowl," *Places* 3 (July 1976), pp. 12–18, and Eric Weiland, "Woody Guthrie: An Informant of Geographic Themes," *The Mississippi Geographer* 6 (Spring 1978), pp. 32–37.

7. Peter H. Nash has contributed two articles that deal with these themes, including "Music and Environment: An Investigation of Some of the Spatial Aspects of Production, Diffusion and Consumption of Music," *Canadian Association of University Schools of Music Journal* 5 (Spring 1975), pp. 42–71, and "Music Regions and Regional Music," *The Deccan Geographer* 6 (July–December 1968), pp. 1–23.

8. George O. Carney, "Music and Dance," in John F. Rooney, Jr., Wilbur Zelinsky and Dean R. Louder, (eds.), *This Remarkable Continent: An Atlas of United*

States and Canadian Societies and Cultures (College Station: Texas A&M University Press, 1982), p. 237.

9. Fred Dellar, Roy Thompson, and Douglas Green, *The Illustrated Encyclopedia of Country Music* (New York: Harmony Books, 1977), pp. 16, 160–61; David Ewen, *Panorama of American Popular Music in Our Culture* (Kent, Ohio: Kent State University, 1970), p. 49; and Samuel Charters and Leonard Kunstadt, *A Jazz History of the New York Scene* (Garden City, N.Y.: Doubleday, 1962).

10. Grossman, pp. 32, 68, and Burton H. Wolfe, "New Music and the New Music Scene," in *The Age of Rock: Sounds of the American Cultural Revolution* ed. by Jonathan Eisen (New York: Vintage Books, 1969), pp. 30–41.

11. Ewen, p. 139.

12. Dellar, Thompson, and Green, p. 163.

13. Ibid., pp. 20, 103–4, 171.

14. Barbara Kuroff, (ed.), *1981 Song Writers Market* (Cincinnati: Writer's Digest Books, 1980), pp. 4–6.

15. Dellar, Thompson, and Green, p. 20.

16. Ibid., pp. 160–61.

17. The 1980 census data on the Cuban population of Dade County are misleading because the Mariel boatlift, which began one month after the census enumeration, contributed approximately 100,000 Cubans to the population of the county.

18. Thomas D. Boswell and James R. Curtis, *The Cuban-American Experience: Culture, Images and Perspectives* (Totowa, N.J.: Littlefield, Adams, 1984).

19. James R. Curtis, "Miami's Little Havana: Yard Shrines, Cult Religion and Landscape," *Journal of Cultural Geography* 1 (Fall–Winter 1980), pp. 1–15, and University of Miami, *The Cuban Immigration, 1959–1966, and Its Impact on Miami-Dade County, Florida* (Coral Gables, Fla.: Center for Advanced International Studies, University of Miami, 1967).

20. Antonio Jorge and Raul Moncarz, *The Failure of the Hispanic Market: The Cuban Entrepreneur and the Economic Development of the Miami Standard Metropolitan Statistical Area* (Miami: Discussion Paper No. 6, International Banking Center and Department of Economics, Florida International University, June 1982; Strategy Research Corporation, "Latin Market Survey," Miami, Florida, 1981, and Antonio Jorge and Raul Moncarz, *International Factor Movement and Complementary: Growth and Entrepreneurship Under Conditions of Cultural Variation* (The Hague, Netherlands: Research Group for European Migration Problems, R.E.M.P. Bulletin, supplement 14, 1981).

21. John Dorschner, "Growing Up Spanglish in Miami," *The Miami Herald* (September 11, 1977), Tropic section, pp. 6–13.

22. Mimi Whitefield, "Miami's Spanish Radio Stations: Sedate They're Not," *The Miami Herald* (February 2, 1981), Business Week section, pp. 20–21.

23. John S. Roberts, "Salsa: The Latin Dimension in Popular Music," *BMI, The Many Worlds of Music*, Issue 3, 1976, pp. 1–39.

24. John S. Roberts, *The Latin Tinge: The Impact of Latin American Music on the United States* (New York: Oxford University Press, 1979).

25. Enrique Fernandez, " 'Tropical Night' Promos Put Focus on Latin Beat," *Billboard* (April 10, 1982), p. 44.

26. Kuroff, p. 13.

27. Roberts, "Salsa: The Latin Dimension in Popular Music," p. 17.

28. The Miami Sound Machine in particular has recorded a number of songs in English.

29. Bernard Harding, *Key to the Jazz World* (Miami: Maple Leaf Publications, 1978), pp. 108–9.

30. Personal communication, Carlos Oliva, president of Crossover and Common Cause Records, Miami, Florida, April 8, 1982.

Texas (When I Die): National Identity and Images of Place in Canadian Country Music Broadcasts

John C. Lehr

As a nation linguistically and regionally fragmented, Canada faces unique problems of national unity and identity. The truth of Northrop Frye's observation that "Canada has passed from a pre-national to a post-national phase without ever having become a nation" is illustrated by the trauma of partially sloughing the trappings of colonial status in 1982, 115 years after attaining de facto independence in 1867.[1] National identity in Canada rests precariously on the shoulders of its peoples, for the fabric of national consciousness spun from myths and images is still being woven by its literati, bureaucrats, and politicians.

Not only does Canada have a small population and, as Mackenzie King put it, "too much geography," but the country is bordered by a culturally aggressive and dynamic English-speaking nation outnumbering it by more than ten to one.[2] If English Canadians are to formulate a distinctive cultural identity, to create their own images and myths of place, to come imaginatively into contact with the country, and to answer the fundamental question of "Where is Here?" they must do so on their own terms, not in a cultural vacuum but in a milieu protected in some measure from the onrush of values, attitudes, and beliefs emanating from beyond the borders of Canada.

Reprinted by permission from the *Canadian Geographer* 27 (1983): 361–70.

National Identity

In 1970, in an attempt to create an environment conducive to the development of a distinctive Canadian identity and to foster cultural nationalism by encouraging the development of the fledgling Canadian entertainment industry and associated artistic communities, the government of Canada acted to limit the amount of non-Canadian material broadcast on Canadian television and radio stations.

Two years earlier, in 1968, the government had laid the groundwork for its control of Canadian broadcasting when it obtained passage of the Broadcasting Act, in which it was stated (in section 1) that "the Canadian broadcasting system (public and private) should be effectively owned and controlled by Canadians so as to safeguard, enrich, and strengthen the cultural, political, social and economic fabric of Canada." The act established the Canadian Radio-Television Commission (CRTC) as a watchdog agency, with authority to regulate on a daily basis the amount of non-Canadian material broadcast by any radio or television station. This power is exercised through the control of licenses to broadcast, and since 1970 the CRTC has made the renewal or granting of licenses dependent upon the attainment of Canadian content goals that it established. In 1971, when the rules were last revised, the Canadian content requirement for AM radio stations was fixed at 30 percent of all material broadcast; for FM stations, each of which is treated individually, the percentage is higher.[3]

Although the Canadian content regulations have most often been justified on the economic ground of stimulating employment for Canadians within the Canadian entertainment industry, it is clear that the thrust of the CRTC initiatives was culturally inspired:

> Our mandate and our purpose is to ensure that Canadian broadcasting develops as a system for us to communicate with one another about our problems and the problems of the world; about our ideas and our views of the world; about our past and our hopes for the future, about our environment, about the quality of our lives, about our role in this area of the universe. . . . There should be wide and free expression through song and drama . . . of our feelings, of our joys and sorrows, of our worries, and our enthusiasms of our angers and our generosities, of our hopes and our dreams.[4]

But Alan W. Johnson, when president of the Canadian Broadcasting Corporation, put it more bluntly:

> We are in a fight for our soul, for our cultural heritage and for our nationhood. Without a culture there is no political survival and we are not a nation. It is

impossible to calculate, or even describe, the devastating, cumulative effects of the self-invited cultural invasion of Canada by American(s). . . . We simply are different from Americans in our history, traditions, institutions and values. . . . The timeless objective of surviving has been given a new imperative by the sudden awakening of the contemporary version of our Canadian crises of identity and nationhood.[5]

To aid this struggle for national identity, the CRTC has required that 30 percent of all the recorded music broadcast by AM radio stations meet the definition of "Canadian" by satisfying any two of the following criteria: a) the instrumentation or lyrics were principally performed by a Canadian; b) the music was composed by a Canadian; c) the lyrics were written by a Canadian; d) the live performance was wholly recorded in Canada and broadcast live in Canada. It is also required that either the music or the lyrics of at least 5 percent of the music broadcast by a station between 6 a.m. and midnight must have been composed by a Canadian. To ensure compliance, the CRTC spotchecks tapes of radio broadcasts that every Canadian radio station must furnish for this purpose.[6]

Country Music Radio

The purpose of this paper is to examine the success of the CRTC Canadian content regulations in the quest to stimulate the growth of national self-awareness by influencing the nature of music broadcast by Canadian AM radio stations. To determine whether the Canadian content regulations were effective in directing the attention of Canadians to Canadian places, in developing images of Canada and its regions, and building a sense of national identity, the lyrical content of the music broadcast by two Manitoba AM country music stations was examined, using the procedures of content analysis.

This inquiry was restricted to country music broadcasts because the country music genre is rich in environmental and spatial images. Moreover, its strong folk and regional roots are still clearly reflected in modern commercial country music aimed at the mass market of North America; and country music, more than any other genre, reflects the life style of the common people.[7] It has been argued that folk music offers clear insights into the environmental attitudes of the common illiterate folk of past times and other societies.[8] It is a premise of this study that modern commercial country music—and, for that matter, "pop" or rock music—through its lyrics similarly reflects the social and environmental attitudes of the functionally but not actively literate common people of present society.[9]

Country music, furthermore, is a popular musical form throughout Canada. According to the Country Music Association's 1982 country radio survey, there are now 147 stations broadcasting country music in Canada, forty-one of them on a full-time basis.[10] In southern Manitoba, the study area for this essay, country music captures about 20 percent of the listening market.

Although southern Manitoba is served by a number of AM radio stations, only two offer total country music programming: CFRY 920 in Portage la Prairie and CKRC 630 in Winnipeg. Both offer twenty-four-hour programming, but although they share a similar signal range (Fig. 21-1) they are oriented toward different sectors of the country music market. CFRY offers mainly a "traditional country" format directed at the rural and small-town market, though a certain amount of "contemporary country" is broadcast as well. In contrast, CKRC is unequivocally "contemporary country," playing little traditional "hard-core" country music but concentrating instead upon "urban country" and "crossover country-pop" material. In the country music field it dominates the urban market of Winnipeg.[11]

Lyrics and Images

The content of the music broadcasts of CKRC and CFRY from June 1981 through April 1982 was randomly sampled. Twenty-four hours of music

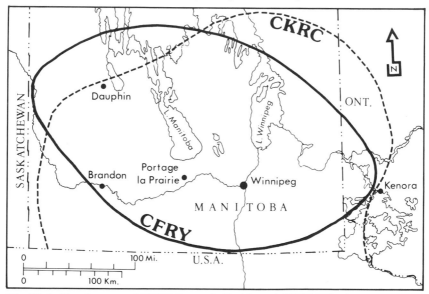

Fig. 21-1. Signal ranges of CFRY Portage la Prairie and CKRC Winnipeg.

broadcast for each station was recorded and coded as to its Canadian content, lyrical content, references to place, and environmental inferences. During the broadcasts sampled, CFRY played 521 records and CKRC 357.

The most immediate and obvious characteristic that emerged from the analysis was the difference in the frequency of references to place in the music of the two stations. The traditional country music favored by CFRY was rich in these references (Fig. 21-2). Settings of events depicted in the lyrics were often explicit, and places were frequently used as a surrogate for an overt expression of values. The country-city dichotomy was readily apparent, and references to the settings and places in the hearth areas of country music abounded. In contrast, references to place were comparatively sparse in the music broadcast by CKRC (Fig. 21-3), reflecting the generally

Fig. 21-2. References to place: CFRY broadcasts.

Fig. 21-3. References to place: CKRC broadcasts.

aspatial settings and abstract themes of much contemporary or "crossover" country music. The standard theme is still "paradise lost" or "love gone bad," overlain by the complications of drinking, cheating, and hurting, but the settings of the events described in the lyrics are less frequently place specific. They deal more in the vague bipolar generalities of "home/away from home" or "home in the country/living in the city" rather than in the place specific terms of "I'm here in Detroit but I wish I were home in Tennessee."[12]

Most of the lyrical imagery from both stations was centered in the United States and notably in the South, reflecting the status of the region as the home territory of the majority of country music entertainers and song writers (Fig. 21-4).[13] References to places in northern industrial states were sporadic, and the images were usually negative; at best they were ambivalent. From the

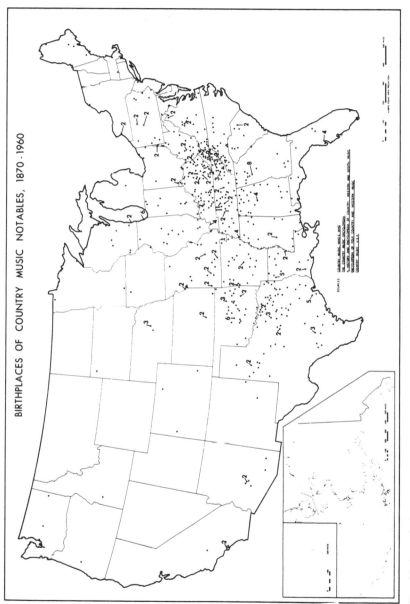

BIRTHPLACES OF COUNTRY MUSIC NOTABLES, 1870 - 1960

Fig. 21-4. Birthplaces of country music notables (1870–1960).

CFRY material came images of home centered in Tennessee, Kentucky, West Virginia, and Louisiana; from both stations came strong images of Texas, promoted as a kind of easygoing, macho utopia. This reflected the mythology created under the combined influence of the Austin country-rock performers and the surge in the popularity of the Texas urban cowboy image, following the popular success of the film of the same name.

Almost 40 percent of all the material surveyed for this study met the CRTC Canadian content criteria, yet the imagery in this "Canadian" material is not less strongly focused upon the American South (Fig. 21-5). This is directly attributable to the structure of the CRTC's rules defining Canadian content. In 1981, for example, a cover version of "When I Die, Just Let Me Go To Texas," written by Ed Bruce, Bobby Borchers, and Patsy Bruce, and initially

Fig. 21-5. References to place in "Canadian context" materials: CFRY and CKRC broadcasts.

recorded by country-rock artist Tanya Tucker, was recorded in Canada by the Canadian country singer Tracy Lynn. It received considerable airplay by CKRC. But, while there may have been economic benefits from recording and playing this song in Canada, the lyrics scarcely contributed to the building of a Canadian self image, and the cause of cultural nationalism was not much furthered:

> *When I die, I may not go to heaven,*
> *I don't know if they let cowboys in.*
> *If they don't, just let me go to Texas,*
> *Texas is as near as I've been.*[14]

Here a mythology of place is being promoted; its promotion is encouraged by the government of Canada through the CRTC Canadian content regulations, yet the results are inimical to both the spirit and the intent of the government's policy.

It is here that Canadians face their strongest challenge. Regional and national identity arises from a feeling for place; such emotions lie deep in the subconscious and are closely bound with the popular mythology of place. These myths, if strong, feed upon themselves and become self-perpetuating when the place itself comes to represent a conglomeration of attitudes, feelings, and values. When a place is used in popular culture as a surrogate for a quality or feeling, the myth is in place or is at least partly fabricated.

Images of Place

The CRTC can encourage Canadian composers and lyricists, but it cannot ensure that they will celebrate Canadian places in their music. The chance of commercial success in the North American market is improved if the lyricist can deal in familiar images and can use place as a surrogate for other values and employ settings identifiable and meaningful to the audience.

Canadian country music labors under a further disadvantage in that it has yet to develop distinctive regional substyles that are readily recognizable to the average listener. In contrast there are seven distinctive substyles of American country music, each with a strong regional association.[15] In American country music, therefore, musical styling may be used as an effective nonverbal reference to place. By including a few bars of western swing, some bluegrass picking, or the strains of a Cajun fiddle—even the Cajun yell—the American musician can imply an unambiguous spatial association that is effective at the conscious and subliminal levels.

Less obvious devices can both complement a direct verbal statement and be effective in their own right. An example of all three mechanisms in a single Canadian song is "Lone Star and Coors":

> *Let's go down to Texas*
> *Leave this cold Canadian winter far behind*
> *I'll buy Lone Star, you buy Coors*
> *You'll drink mine and I'll drink yours.* [16]

The overt reference to Texas is followed by a few bars of western swing, strongly identified with the Texan musician Bob Wills. The imagery is further reinforced by the references to Lone Star and Coors beers, both of which enjoy regional distribution in Texas and the southwestern United States. There is a cost, which may well be financial, which must be borne by the Canadian writer who strives to employ Canadian images of place rather than relying upon the long-familiar aural and verbal images from the United States—images the mass audience can identify, understand, and relate to without effort. In the early 1970s, for example, a Manitoba country musician, Rick Neufeld, composed the song "Moody Manitoba Morning." He was pressed to change the title to "Moody Minnesota Morning," to guarantee easy acceptance in the American market. [17] To his credit he did not do so, but although his song enjoyed Canadian success, it did not become popular south of the border. Neufeld missed the chance to earn thousands of dollars.

For place imagery to be effective in music the image must be believable, even if overstated and owing as much to fiction as to fact. A casual reference to a place or region with an implied value attached is probably more effective than continued references to places that add little to the mood or feeling that the singer strives to convey. Otherwise unremarkable places have achieved worldwide fame from the lyrics of a popular song, places such as Strawberry Fields, in the drab suburbs of Liverpool, as described by John Lennon: "Strawberry Fields is a real place. . . . We would go there and hang out and sell lemonade bottles for a penny. We always had fun at Strawberry Fields. So that's where I got the name. But I used it as an image. Strawberry Fields forever." [18]

Other examples are Penny Lane in Liverpool; the Suwannee River; Chattanooga, Tennessee; and latterly, Luckenbach, Texas; all of which have become *celebrity places*, famous only for being well known. Indeed, Luckenbach, which consists of a post office, a sometime dance hall, and a handful of houses—scarcely a hamlet—has come to epitomize a socioeconomic attitude and regional life style to millions of people and has been the subject of reportage by *Time* magazine:

Let's go to Luckenbach, Texas, with Willie and Waylon and the boys,
This successful life we're living has got us feuding like the Hatfields and
   McCoys . . .
Back in Luckenbach, Texas, ain't nobody feelin' no pain.[19]

Since the late 1960s Canadian songwriters have begun to employ the prairies and Alberta as an image with complex structures similar in some ways to that of Texas or Tennessee in the United States. At the most basic level the West is used as a surrogate for the ideal, in much the same way as California was by the writers of popular music in the mid-1960s.[20] But the image of the Canadian West is more complicated, since it has been used as a place-specific metaphor of the rural-urban dichotomy basic to country music. In part, the image of the West has been molded by the demographic shifts that took place in Canada after the revitalization of the hydrocarbon resource industries in Alberta and Saskatchewan in the early 1970s. Economic growth led to rapid immigration into the urban-industrial centers of Alberta and Saskatchewan and some erosion of the dominance of the national economy by the metropolitan heartland of Ontario. It is therefore easy to understand how Alberta may be used as a surrogate for opportunity, the good life, while the prairies can be used to suggest freedom of movement. Their physical expanse becomes a metaphor for limitless economic or social horizons.

Some of Canada's most successful songwriters have employed the image of the West in this fashion, thus contributing to its entrenchment in the minds of Canadians. Gordon Lightfoot's "Alberta Bound" is one such example, while the work of Ian and Sylvia Tyson has contributed greatly to the emergence of an image of Alberta in Canadian country music. In the early 1960s their "Four Strong Winds" captured the spirit of the prairie West, and its strong nostalgic imagery proved to have a lasting appeal to the Canadian public. More recently, Ian Tyson's country song "Old Alberta Moon" alludes to the migration from Ontario to Alberta, using images of place in a way that demonstrates the emergence of a popular mythology of place in western Canada. In the best traditions of country lyrics, Tyson romanticizes reality and describes a side of Alberta that is experienced by few immigrants, because most immigrants gravitate to the established metropolitan areas or the towns of the northern resource frontier. But the listener is invited to the rural West:

So, gas up your old Chevrolet and head'er way out west,
To the land of golden opportunity,
You'll get a first hand education of how the cowboy rocks and rolls,
With that old Alberta moon thrown in for free.[21]

More telling, however, is the ability of a Canadian songwriter to convey major sociogeographical regional differences with precision and feeling through the use of simple spatial imagery:

> *Toronto may be Rhythm and Blues but if you migrate here,*
> *You'll be howlin' at that old Alberta moon.*[22]

According to a brief presented to the Federal Cultural Policy Review Committee in 1981 by the (Canadian) Academy of Country Music Entertainment, there is no shortage of Canadian-oriented country music being written, performed, and recorded by Canadians.[23] Yet a distinctive Canadian exchange of images, analogies, and metaphors has not yet impressed itself through Canadian broadcasting; market demands do not argue in favor of Canadian performers and writers dealing with their subjects in Canadian terms. Paradoxically, it is easier for a recognized star performer of the United States to legitimize Canadian images than it is for a struggling Canadian performer.[24]

Many rising Canadian songwriters in the country genre are concerned over the neglect of Canada as a setting for country song lyrics. In an oral presentation to the Federal Cultural Policy Review Committee, the Academy of Country Music Entertainment let songwriter and performer Wayne Rostad put their case quite directly:

> We must look in our own backyards; we must not be afraid to name our cities, our towns, our people. We have to stop writing for that American hook, stop prostituting the art form, or the realism. In our own backyard there is a wealth of stories and happenings to tell [of] that will contribute our own unique [identity] to country music.[25]

Conclusion

If the Canadian content regulations established by the CRTC contribute to the enactment of Rostad's philosophy on the part of Canadian country music lyricists and Canadian radio station program managers, they will undoubtedly build toward the creation of a myth of place in the minds of Canadians and so will further one component of regional and national identities. However, if the Canadian country music and broadcasting industry adheres to the letter of the CRTC regulations rather than embracing their spirit and intent, the comment of CRTC chairman John Meisel may prove to be a sad epitaph for Canadian aspirations: "[Canada's] progressively and ultimately annihilating Americanization is in part a consequence of our milquetoastian nationality."[26]

It will be a measure of Canada's maturity and self-confidence as a nation when the material broadcast over the airways of its country music stations (and other stations, for that matter) draws with equal facility from throughout Canada and the United States for evocative images of space and place. If social chatter and formulaic communications numb sensitivity, as Yi-Fu Tuan claims,[27] and if the various governmental agencies charged with the furtherance of cultural life continue to favor the elitist and dilettante audience of high culture, to the detriment of the wider but less sophisticated audience of popular culture, then Canada is more dependent than many may care to admit upon the imagination of perceptive writers in the field of popular culture to evoke the images of places from which a nation fashions the myths by which it lives.

Notes

1. N. Frye, *Division on a Ground: Essays on Canadian Culture* (Toronto: Anansi, 1982), p. 13.

2. Canada, House of Commons, *Debates*, 18 June 1936.

3. *Radio (A.M.) Broadcasting Regulations* (Ottawa: Supply and Services Canada, 1979), pp. 10–11; and *Radio (F.M.) Broadcasting Regulations* (Ottawa: Supply and Services Canada, 1977), pp. 14–17.

4. Press release by Pierre Juneau, chairman, Canadian Radio-Television Commission, 22 May 1970. (Ottawa: CRTC Research Documentation Center, typewritten manuscript, pp. 5–6).

5. A. W. Johnson, "Touchstone for the C.B.C.," *Canadian Broadcasting*, June 1977, pp. 5–6.

6. Personal communication, R. G. Gordon, Canadian Radio-Television and Telecommunications Commission, 29 April 1980.

7. For elaboration of this theme see T. Adler, "The Unplotted Narratives of Tom T. Hall," *Journal of Country Music* 4 (1973), pp. 52–69; B. B. Sims, " 'She's Got to be a Saint, Lord Knows I Ain't': Feminine Masochism in American Country Music," *Journal of Country Music* 5 (1974), pp. 24–30; N. V. Rosenberg, " 'Folk' and 'Country' Music in the Canadian Maritimes: A Regional Model," *Journal of Country Music* 5 (1974), pp. 76–82; and C. F. Gritzner, "Country Music: What's that 'Caterwauling' all about?" in G. O. Carney (ed.), *The Sounds of People and Places: Readings in the Geography of Music*, (Washington D.C.: University Press of America, 1979), pp. 66–81.

8. E. V. Bunkse, "Commoner Attitudes Towards Landscape and Nature," *Annals of the Association of American Geographers* 68 (1978), pp. 551–66.

9. It is debatable whether references to, and images of, places in commercial popular music reflect or create the common attitudes to places and settings: L. R. Ford and F. M. Henderson, "The Image of Place in American Popular Music: 1890–

1970," *Places* 1 (March 1974), pp. 31–37. See also F. M. Henderson, "The Image of New York City in American Popular Music 1890–1970," in Carney, op cit., pp. 270–84.

10. *Winnipeg Free Press*, 17 April 1982, and information from the Canadian Country Music Association, 5 November 1982.

11. Interviews with Peter Grant, president of the Academy of Country Music Entertainment, 1980–81, and station manager, CHMM Winnipeg, 17 June 1982; John Aune, station manager, CFRY Portage la Prairie, 16 April 1982; and John Cook, sales manager, CKRC Winnipeg, 14 April 1982.

12. D. K. Wilgus, "Country-Western Music and the Urban Hillbilly," *Journal of American Folklore* 83 (1970), pp. 157–79.

13. See G. O. Carney, "T for Texas, T for Tennessee; The Origins of American Country Music Notables," *Journal of Geography* 78 (1979), pp. 218–25.

14. "When I Die, Just Let Me Go To Texas," words and music by Ed Bruce, Bobby Borchers, and Patsy Bruce. Copyright © 1977, 1978 Tree Publishing Company, Inc., and Sugarplum Music Company International. Copyright secured. All rights reserved.

15. G. O. Carney, "Country Music and the South: A Cultural Geography Perspective," *Journal of Cultural Geography* 1 (1980), pp. 16–33.

16. "Lone Star and Coors," words and music by Ian Tyson. Copyright © 1978 Speckled Bird Music (CAPAC). Used by permission. All rights reserved.

17. Interview with Peter Grant, note 11.

18. "Playboy Interview: John Lennon and Yoko Ono," *Playboy* (January 1981), p. 107.

19. "Luckenbach Texas (Back to the Basics of Love)," written by Bobby Emmons and Chips Moman. Copyright © 1977 Vogue Music and Baby Chick Music (c/o The Welk Music Group, Santa Monica, Calif. 90401). International copyright secured. All rights reserved. Used by permission.

For an example of the journalistic coverage of Luckenbach, Texas, and its role as a symbol, see *Time*, 19 September 1977 and 18 September 1978.

20. Ford and Henderson, op. cit., pp. 34–35.

21. "Old Alberta Moon," words and music by Ian Tyson. Copyright © 1978 Speckled Bird Music (CAPAC). Used by permission. All rights reserved.

22. Ibid.

23. Academy of Country Music Entertainment, "Submission to the Federal Cultural Policy Review Committee," n.d. Appendix II, pp. 5–6.

24. The disc jockeys on both CKRC and CFRY seemed to welcome records that celebrated Canadian places. Typical of on-air reactions was that of Boris Kozak, CKRC, 5 November 1982, to a release by Johnny Cash, "Ain't Goin' to Hobo No More," a song written by a Canadian mentioning Alberta and Nova Scotia. Kozak commented favorably on "an international star like Johnny Cash singing about our country—making it known internationally."

25. Tape-recorded presentation to accompany the written "Submission to the Federal Cultural Policy Review Committe," Academy of Country Music Entertainment, op. cit.

26. Quoted in I. Anderson, "Plodding Toward a Television Revolution," *Maclean's*, 26 October 1981, p. 51.

27. Yi-Fu Tuan, *Space and Place* (Minneapolis: University of Minnesota Press, 1977), p. 148.

The Image of Place in American Popular Music: 1890–1970

Larry R. Ford and Floyd M. Henderson

During the past decade, geographers and many other social scientists have become increasingly interested in the images that people have of various places. Peter Gould, for example, pioneered work in this area with his 1966 article on mental maps.[1] Interested in the preferences people have for living in various parts of the United States, Gould asked respondents in California, Minnesota, Alabama, and Pennsylvania to rank the forty-eight contiguous states on the basis of perceived mental maps (especially among the view from Alabama versus the other three). There emerged a fair consensus about desirable and undesirable areas in the United States. Since most of the respondents had been to few of the states they were asked to rank, one might wonder how these "state images" were derived. Obviously many possible sources of information could have been utilized by the respondents—geography courses, movies, travelogues, travel, novels, and news—but little is known about the way people utilize these information sources in creating their own place images. Also, little is known about the stability of these images once they are formed. Some areas seem to evoke pleasant images over long periods of time while others may experience drastic reversals in only a decade (witness the decline in the image of New York City, for example). It is the purpose of this paper to explore the place images found in one particular aspect of popular culture—popular music.

People, especially young people, are constantly bombarded by songs

Reprinted by permission from *Places* 1 (1974): 31–37.

describing cities, regions, life styles, ghettos, rivers, and countryside, and it is quite possible that these "music-based" images play an important part in their decision making, especially location decision making both within a city and within the United States as a whole. The perceived qualities of places and types of places may change with their changing appropriateness for popular musical themes. The hypothesis is made that songs both reflect and influence the images people have of places and that these songs and images have changed people's attitudes significantly toward places is one important step toward understanding the "geography of the mind."

Methodology

In order to understand fully the changing images of places in songs over time, an attempt was made to determine all of the big hits since 1890 that included some reference to or description of a place or region. The year 1890 was chosen since it was at about that time that commercial music was beginning to have an impact all over the country through the sale of sheet music. Because "Top 40" charts did not exist during the early decades of the study and since such things as record sales and sheet music sales would be quite incomparable over eighty years, a variety of other sources were used. The best sources were books such as *Variety Music Cavalcade, Popular Music: An Annotated Index of American Popular Songs, Index to Top Hit Tunes (1900–1950),* and *American Popular Songs.*

A master list was created of every "place" song since 1890 (at least every song that was a major hit). These songs were then grouped by decade and mapped. Three different map symbols were necessary. The first, a dot, was used if the place appeared as a point on a map of the United States. This would include cities, streets (Broadway), or very small regions (e.g., the Banks of the Wabash). The second symbol was a circle, designating references to states. The last symbol, an "X," was used for more nebulous regions such as "Dixie" or "Out West." The valence of the song could also be determined since the lyrics were obtainable for most songs. From this it was observed that songs have usually been positive rather than negative image makers.

From the above information, two types of analyses were possible. First, by mapping the places mentioned by decade, it was possible to get some indication of the awareness most people might be expected to have had of various American regions. In addition, it was also possible to identify new musical frontiers as Americans discovered new regions to sing about. As hypothesized, the places mentioned in American music have varied considerably over time, thus giving each generation its own image of America (and quite likely its own consensus mental map of residential preferences). This first type of analysis we can term the regional approach.

The second approach was more concerned with lyrics and resulting valence and was an attempt to gauge changing images of a type of place rather than mere mention or description of specific real places—in this case the city. That attitudes toward cities and urban life in general have changed over the decades is well represented through popular music. Some of these changing regional and city images are described in the following paragraphs.

Changing Regional Images

During the 1890s, when the music industry was just beginning to expand, there were relatively few songs by today's standards, but surprisingly, many of them mentioned place names. However, the number of places referred to were very limited in number. None of the places mentioned in songs in the "Gay Nineties" were west of the Mississippi, and only New York City, Kentucky, and Georgia were mentioned as many as three times. Songs such as "Kentucky Babe," "My New Hampshire Home," "In Good Old New York Town," and "By the Banks of the Wabash Far Away" were typical. While New York City was often the setting for songs, most other American cities were ignored. The "far away" Wabash was as deep into the interior as hit tunes went (Fig. 22-1).

During the decade of 1900–1910 New York continued to dominate the music scene, although references to the Bowery were now being replaced by references to Broadway. While New York was still the place to be, Dixie was beginning to shed its Reconstruction image and become romanticized as (perhaps) an alternative to the bustling industrial north where subways and skyscrapers were drastically changing the urban landscape. The West was still largely ignored during this decade except for one reference to "Ida of Idaho" (probably more of an alliteration than a place) and two references to Texas. Places familiar to New Yorkers were still emphasized including Hackensack, the Hudson, the Mohawk, and Boston. In addition to the increasingly romanticized Dixie, there were football songs ("On Wisconsin") and Indian songs ("Cheyenne") perhaps reinforcing the image of the interior as rural, quaint, and far away (Fig. 22-2).

Between 1910 and 1920 the dominance of New York declined slightly, and many songs now featured a new international awareness of such places as France and Germany due to World War I. Back home, however, Dixie was beginning to reach its peak as a glorious heaven of happy darkies, magnolias, and even shieks. References to Dixie far outnumbered references to any other

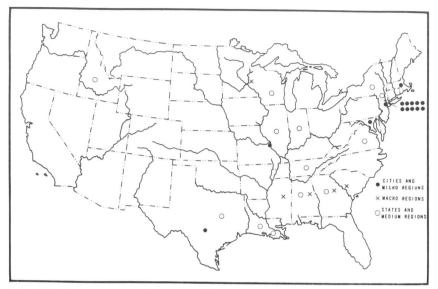

Fig. 22-1. Places mentioned in song: 1890s.

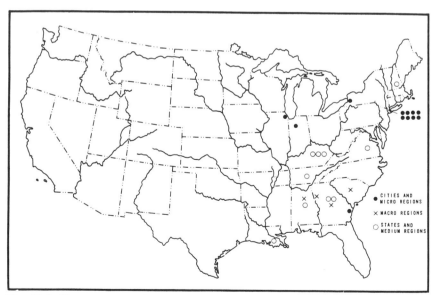

Fig. 22-2. Places mentioned in song: 1900s.

place or region. Perhaps this emphasis on the nostalgic South was a reaction
to the chaos of the war years. More importantly, the desire to preserve the
romantic life style alluded to could have contributed to the Ku Klux Klan
revival of the 1920s. Jazz also came onto the scene during this period and
with it an increasing number of references to such places as New Orleans,
Memphis, and St. Louis. Even as jazz was beginning to bring attention to
the Mississippi river towns, the West was beginning to be mentioned for the
first time in popular songs. So far, however, this remained a rather unfocused
"cowboy" version of the West ("Out Where the West Begins" for example)
although there were definite references to the "Goldfields of Nevada" and
"Sierra Sue." In the city category, San Francisco and Miami both made the
charts for the first time in the late teens, perhaps marking the beginning of
large-scale tourism and recreation in the United States (Fig. 22-3).

During the 1920s, the pattern of the teens was largely repeated with one
exception. As the image of fun in the sun was beginning to seep into the
world of popular music, far more references were made to Florida and
California. Cities were becoming more imageable as Charleston, Savannah,
Mobile, and Louisville together received as much attention as Dixie. While
Kansas City, San Francisco, and Hollywood were sung about, the West was
still largely unfocused in terms of its image. Jazz and musicals such as
Showboat kept attention focused on the Mississippi, and New York (as well as
Broadway and Manhattan) began to make a strong comeback as the epitome

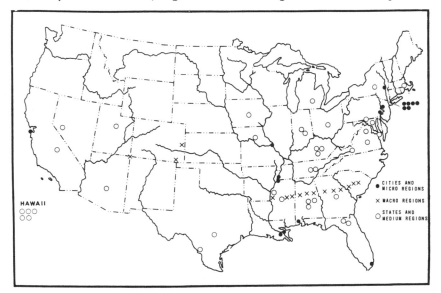

Fig. 22-3. Places mentioned in song: 1910s.

of the Roaring Twenties. Although "Broadway Melody," "Manhattan Serenade," and other New York songs dominated the city category, "Chicago" and a great many other cities in all parts of the country now shared the stage. The interior was no longer perceived as being quaint and rural in the music world. "California Here I Come" coincided with a huge migration into that far western state (Fig. 22-4).

During the Depression years of the 1930s, a fantasy world of New York luxury dominated popular songs. Songs such as "Penthouse Serenade," "Stars Over Broadway," "Slumming on Park Avenue," and "Lullaby of Broadway" helped New York to dominate the music scene even more than it had in previous years. Broadway glitter was the image sought as bread lines grew across the nation. Beyond New York there were few references to specific places (especially cities), a pronounced contrast to the 1920s. These were replaced by rather unfocused, romantic regional songs about the South and West such as "I'm an Old Cowhand," "Carry Me Back to the Lonely Prairie," and "Is It True What They Say About Dixie?" There were few songs in praise of particular cities and towns. Real places no longer represented the euphoria of the 1920s but the problems of the Depression (Fig. 22-5).

The 1940s did not bring a revival of musical interest in Europe (as had occurred in World War I) but rather an extreme interest in Latin America, perhaps perceived as a happy place where people drank rum and Coca-Cola in peace. Back home, cities were making a comeback as soldiers sought

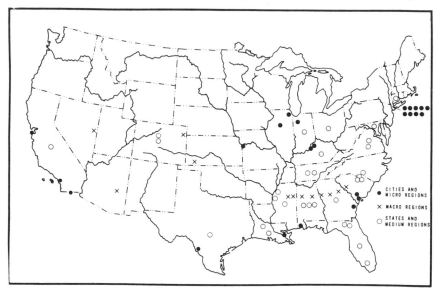

Fig. 22-4. Places mentioned in song: 1920s.

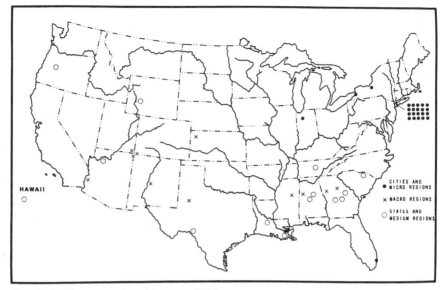

Fig. 22-5. Places mentioned in song: 1930s.

concrete references to home or at least to recognizable "homelike" places with real bus stations and waiting sweethearts. Unfocused regional songs died and New York was almost completely overshadowed by such "home town" places as Chattanooga, Kalamazoo, Sioux City, San Antonio, and even Twenty-nine Palms. *Oklahoma* was the hit musical of the decade (hardly a place to sing about during the Dustbowl of the 1930s). Dixie began to fade as civil rights and Dixiecrats marred the image of the happy Southland (Fig. 22-6).

During the 1950s the back-home realism of the 1940s continued, although there was a noticeable revival of traditional favorites such as New Orleans and San Francisco and to some extent New York (even though the latter was somewhat deromanticized by songs such as those from *West Side Story*). All the regions of the United States were fairly evenly represented in the 1950s as places ranging from "Old Cape Cod" to "Pittsburgh" and from "El Paso" to "Highway 101" were sung about. Tennessee became a very popular place for a while just as Tennessee Ernie Ford was a popular singer. The "cowboy" West suffered the same fate as Dixie and "general region" songs disappeared (Fig. 22-7).

The 1960s brought the biggest barrage of songs about a particular place since New York in the 1930s—perhaps exceeding it. Southern California and its associated life style utterly dominated the popular music scene. Although San Francisco remained a strong image maker (especially during the late

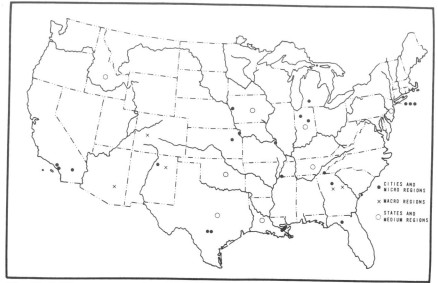

Fig. 22-6. Places mentioned in song: 1940s.

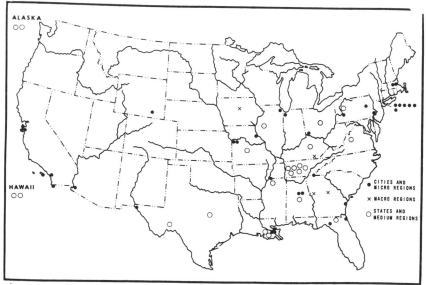

Fig. 22-7. Places mentioned in song: 1950s.

1960s "hippie" era), it was southern California that provided the setting for endless songs about surfers, beaches, hot rods, and little old ladies from Pasadena. In-migration to California reached a peak at about the same time as these songs were popular. Along with southern California, Las Vegas and Fort Lauderdale joined in the "fun in the sun" image of American places. Had the Beatles not interrupted the trend in the mid-1960s, it is suggested that the dominance of southern California might have been even more pronounced.

It is too soon to tell exactly what the 1970s will bring in terms of regional consciousness, but so far it seems clear that both New York and California have lost their magic (as had Dixie before them) and that many of the songs

Another part of the country making a strong showing in the 1960s was the central South from Louisiana to Arizona. New Orleans, Houston, Dallas, Galveston, Tulsa, Abilene, Phoenix, Texarkana, and the Oklahoma hills all made the charts as attention shifted in a southwesterly direction toward the California attraction. Unlike the romantic Dixie of earlier times, songs about the deep South tended to be a bit negative during the 1960s. Even if we ignore the many civil rights songs of the decade, the musical images of such songs as "Ode to Billy Joe" and "Memphis" were of a different genre than "Carolina in the Morning." Nevertheless, a longing for the South could still be found in songs about auto plants in Detroit and Saginaw and the green, green grass of home (Fig. 22-8).

It is too soon to tell exactly what the 1970s will bring in terms of regional consciousness, but so far it seems clear that both New York and California have lost their magic (as had Dixie before them) and that many of the songs

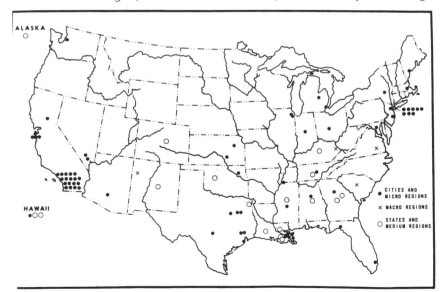

Fig. 22-8. Places mentioned in song: 1960s.

in our present ecology-minded, get-away-from-it-all era are focusing on previously ignored rural retreats like country roads in West Virginia and Colorado Rocky Mountain Highs. If this trend continues, the resulting images could have profound effects on these regions. For example, will the attraction of the Rockies produce an effect on that region similar to that attained when attention was focused on southern California?

The Changing Image of Cities in Song

Just as the images that many people have of various parts of the country may be affected by the region's portrayal in popular music, so, too, may particular types of places such as cities, beaches, forests, or farms. It is the purpose of this section of the paper to explore the image of the city over time, especially with regard to the degree to which those images are positive or negative. The image of the city in songs has ranged from a very positive one that represented the city as the place to be, the center for culture and civilization, a happy place attracting in-migrants from all over; to an image of congestion, problems, and crime. Of significance is, "Which comes first, the general attitude or the image in music?" and "To what extent does one factor influence the other?"

From 1890 through the 1930s, the city was represented in song as a wonderful place. New York, for example, was represented by such songs as "Give My Regards to Broadway," "Take Me Back to New York Town," "The Sidewalks of New York," "Do the New York," "Manhattan," and "Penthouse Serenade." Other cities throughout the country, when they were mentioned at all, were also viewed positively during these decades. "Chicago" was a toddlin' town, and the moon was over Miami. People were set to "Charleston Back to Charleston" and "Shuffle Off to Buffalo" and to make the "San Fernando Valley" their home. Songs of the 1940s were of the smaller, more home-town genre, yet Chattanooga, Sioux City, and Kalamazoo remained great places to live according to the lyrics.

Although "Kansas City" was a big hit in the 1950s, it was during that decade that the image of the city began to change. Not only was there a "Terror of Highway 101" loose in southern California, but juvenile gangs were singing their way through New York in West Side Story. Mass transit problems were brought up in "M.T.A.," which featured poor old Charlie's inability to get off the Boston subway after an "unfair" fare increase. "Naked City Theme," "Tiajuana Jail," "Spanish Harlem," and other songs with mildly antiurban images closed the 1950s along with songs in praise of "Old Cape Cod," "Avalon," and "Alaska." No longer were songs talking about going to New York to find it all but going somewhere to get away from it all. The problems and conflicts in cities began to receive attention, even if it was satirical and often light-hearted.

True, people were still leaving their hearts in San Francisco in the early 1960s, but for the most part the musical image of the city continued to worsen. Lonely nights in Detroit City, lonely brothels in New Orleans, broken families in Memphis, and lonely days in San Francisco were featured in such songs as "Detroit City," "House of the Rising Sun," "Memphis," and "Dock of the Bay." General urban problems were also sung about more pointedly in songs such as "Little Boxes," "Leader of the Pack," "Pollution," "In the Ghetto," "Dead End Street," "Cement Octopus," and "Birmingham Jail." A few prourban songs appeared, such as "Downtown" (sung by a European entertainer), but most of them featured smaller cities such as "Galveston" or Wichita.

It was not until the late 1960s and early 1970s that songs began to reflect a total dislike of cities and city life. Most of these songs do not directly criticize cities, as they did in the 1960s, but rather praise life in the country. "I am Just an Okie from Muskogee" praises a small-town, traditional life style where people do not burn draft cards (as they do in the city). Songs such as "Oklahoma Hills," "Country Road," "Country Comfort," "Woodstock," "Out in the Country," "Arizona," "Alberta Bound," "Aspenglow," and "Rocky Mountain High" provide images of the new idealized settings. Years of cityward migration are reversed in spirit by song combinations such as "Goodbye Columbus" and "West Virginia." The wilderness theme has largely replaced the swinging city as lines such as "hot town, summer in the city" are contrasted to "I know he'd be a poorer man if he never saw an eagle fly" or "Livin' on an L.A. freeway ain't my kind of havin' fun."

Conclusion

It is evident that the regions favored in popular music have changed over time. From a concentration on New York and Dixie in the 1890s, attention has shifted to the South and Dixie in the 1920s, back to New York in the 1930s and to southern California in the 1960s. Today the focus seems to be on rural wilderness areas such as the Rocky Mountains.

Specific cities and attitudes about urban life have also been reflected "through the juke box." From "East Side West Side all around the Town" and "We'll turn Manhattan into an Isle of Joy" the image of the city has evolved into such tinsel-tainted realizations as "In the Ghetto," "The Faucets are Dripping in Old New York City," and "L.A. is a Great Big Freeway."

Certainly, people have had their mental maps of the United States influenced and altered by the discovery of and the ideas conveyed by such songs as "Sioux City Sue," "Wichita Lineman," the "House of the Rising Sun," the "Moon over Miami," and "St. Louis Woman." It appears that people, at least according to song, are now tired of the city where "the streets are brown and gritty" and are instead "Alberta Bound" for a Rocky Mountain sunset. Certainly the hypothesis stated earlier that songs both reflect and influence the image people have of places and that these images and songs have changed over time is substantiated. Most importantly, it is believed that the acceptance of this hypothesis has more serious implications and applications than simply an interesting and somewhat entertaining academic exercise.

It is hoped that this paper will provide a provocative approach to such topics as the diffusion of ideas, perception of environment, migration, and urban versus rural cultural traits. Since it appears that popular songs influence as well as reflect attitudes about cities and regions, it should prove possible to promote musical themes that produce positive images of regions and cities. By emphasizing city pride, we might possibly reverse the increasingly negative attitudes people have of the city, for example, and encourage the middle class to remain there. Although this may sound like shades of Orwell's 1984, music has likely influenced much behavior in the past (patently many moved to California in the early 1960s to be "surfers"), and it may provide a small tool in dealing with our present urban dilemma.

Notes

1. Peter Gould, "On Mental Maps," *Michigan University Community of Mathematical Geographers*, Discussion Paper 9, 1966.

Country Music: A Reflection of
Popular Culture

Charles F. Gritzner

It has been said that North Americans have managed to produce three things that are practically pure corn: tortillas, moonshine whiskey, and country music.[1] Hailed by some critics as America's great musical gift to people the world over, country music has been viewed less enthusiastically by others as being simplistic, unsophisticated, right-wing, boring, bedrock Baptist, redneck, ignorant, and probably racist.[2] No doubt it is all of these and more: a kaleidoscopic self-portrait of a substantial segment of American popular culture set to lyrics and music. If country music is "corny," it may reflect the fact that many of us lead rather corny lives.

The dominant themes of country music tend to satisfy the psychological and entertainment needs of a primarily "blue-collar," working-class audience.[3] It is this class of Americans that has given birth to the art form, established its commercial popularity, and continues to derive the greatest satisfaction from its "down to earth" mode of communication. As one author noted, "mundane themes result from the fact that the modern world is sadly lacking in proletarian heroes."[4] In its own distinct manner, country music communicates in a clear and obviously appealing way to many Americans who identify with "red necks, white sox, and blue collars." Recent innovations in the music can be attributed to the recording industry's awareness of the fact that in a variety of modified forms, country music appeals to an even

Reprinted by permission from the *Journal of Popular Culture* 11 (1978): 857–64.

larger segment of the contemporary popular culture audience, and that its money is green.

Country Music and the American Folk

Country music often has been cited as being the folk music of the working class; it has also been identified as constituting America's only native musical art form.[5] It is understandable that the so-called "common man" may fail to relate to the musical preferences of the supposed "upper crust" of society. For example, I find it rather difficult to imagine Italian opera being understood in an Oregon logging camp, Joan Baez's songs of protest being appreciated by a conservative Montana rancher, the acceptance of Harry Belafonte's rendition of "This Land is our Land" by rural whites in Mississippi, or a truck driver fighting blizzard conditions on I-40 being enraptured by Sibelius's Seventh. There is a marked difference between hearing and listening; country music speaks, and the country audience listens. The sounds they hear are those of their own collective voice.

Scott Turner, country production (A&R) chief of United Artists, provides the following insight into the relationship between country listener and lyric:

> I make my records for the farmer in the Ozarks who's been out there plowing his field all day and who comes in at night and turns on the radio. He doesn't want to think about "The clouded blue haze through the canyons of the memories of your mind." He doesn't want to think about what he's hearing, just feel the kind of direct relationship to a song that will make him say, "Hey, that's me they're talking about!"[6]

The published insights of poets, novelists, essayists, and scholars normally represent a rather limited and biased cross-section of society; one that is well-educated, generally sensitive, and articulate. Folklife studies, by definition, seldom are able to rely on a literary tradition as a source of insight into the individual or collective mind of the folk themselves. The common man's viewpoint is often overlooked or presented in a somewhat romanticized or otherwise distorted form that is seldom prepared for his own edification or consumption.

Because it is important to understand the views and feelings of all sectors of society, it becomes necessary to identify a medium capable of reflecting the true attitudes, while fulfilling the aesthetic needs, of that segment of the population that is not reached by the more "sophisticated" means of communication. In many respects, country music serves this function by providing a penetrating and revealing self-portrait of the blue-collar working class. It is their music: they live it, they write it, they vocalize it, and they listen, understand, appreciate, and relate to it. In this manner, country music serves as a barometer for certain aspects of American popular culture.[7] As the mood of the nation changes, country music adapts to express popular opinion quite accurately—if in its own terms.[8] Assuming a rather loose definition of "folk" in this context, the question can be posed: What better credentials could country music present in support of its claim to the title of America's purest form of folk music?

Just as the United States has drawn strength from a diverse "melting pot" of people, so, too, has country music drawn heavily from a broad array of ethnic, racial, topical, and regional sources. Rather than detracting from its folk status, the claim is enhanced by country music's dynamic ability to keep in tune with changing tastes, technologies, and times. The foregoing can best be illustrated by a cursory analysis of country music lyrics, performers, audiences, and cultural inputs.

Lyrics

Some folklorists are quick to maintain that a true folksong must be of anonymous origin. The assertion should be viewed with skepticism; lyrics are developed by individuals, and so are music and styles of instrumentation. Earlier music became "traditional" only through its "discovery" by urban intellectuals.[9] It is doubtful whether more than a handful of songs we think of as "folk songs" were ever the product of untutored folk; the people have always had their gifted poets, bards, and minstrels. Anonymity does not mean that a poet did not at one time compose a song, though it may later have entered into oral circulation with subsequent modification.[10]

If song is a valid medium of group communication, it stands to reason that much of the lyrical content should be directed toward those matters that are of importance to the prospective listening audience and focus upon those attitudes and feelings that are socially dominant within the particular group.[11] Country music is distinctive in that its lyrics generally overshadow the music. The soul of true country music is found in its rough-hewn lyricism, its directness and simplicity, and its refreshing lack of elegance, aristocratic airs, and pretense.[12]

George O. Carney has provided an excellent summary of the importance of lyrics:

Country music, in particular, has provided a feeling of security by voicing a particular quality of a land and the life of its people. It is a type of music that

. . . deals with universal themes . . . subjects that other forms of music would not touch. The simplicity and commonality of this expression . . . appear to make it understandable to the average person.[13]

Performers

A respected scholar of country music, D. K. Wilgus, has stated, "Unless we are willing to consider the professional [country singer] and his milieu as more than a mere transition or interruption in folk tradition, we shall largely ignore one of the most significant fields for the student of twentieth century American folk music. Here are the performers for the folk, and sometimes of the folk . . . the materials, backgrounds, and experience."[14] The background of many country artists is common knowledge of most country fans. Most performers, it would appear, have "paid their dues." With a few exceptions, the majority of traditional ("hard core," a term that defies definition with unanimity) artists either write their own material or adopt material authored by others within their relatively small, closely knit, professional community. This appears to be an extremely important link in the folk chain; the message emanates from within the tradition itself. When Merle Haggard sings, "Mama Tried," by God, you somehow really believe she did!

Considering the recent trends toward mass-produced, popular appeal, slicked-up "countrypolitan" sounds, and the rather dubious credentials of many recent entrants in the race for top position on the country charts, the uninitiated might justifiably ask, "who is country and who isn't." The answer to that question lies not as much in semantics or ivory-towered polemics as in public acceptance of the artists and their music by the folk themselves. As country performer Tom T. Hall noted succinctly, "Country Is," and the folk readily discern the difference between their music and opportunistic imitations. Professional colleagues with a propensity for measurement and quantification could no doubt identify and manipulate a plethora of surrogate indices in a scientifically acceptable manner to establish "who is" and "who ain't." Whose records do the folk purchase? What type of fans will drive 200 miles to hear what artists and under what kind of conditions? At a particular concert, what is the ratio of pick-up trucks caked with red clay to motorcycles, vans, and VW's? What is the average hair length and style, age, religious affiliation and conviction, voting preference, income, educational attainment, attire, and preferred stimulant of the audience assembled to hear various performers?

Audience

Country music is a derivative of the people to whom it belongs. Its core identity has not changed simply because the fundamental lifestyles of the folk

Uncle Floyd Holland, American folk music performer, sings and picks for the crowd at the Ozark Folk Center in Mountain View, Arkansas (photo by George Carney).

audience have not changed. Country music, other than as a passing fad, is not and cannot be "kiddie noise." It is music for adults who have directly or indirectly accrued the life experience to identify with and relate to its many themes. One might say, "if you ain't lived it, you can't appreciate it!" Merle Haggard expressed this relationship between listener and song by noting that "no one could really know [country music] unless they've been there."[15]

A survey of the "hard-core" country audience has disclosed that it is almost exclusively white, between twenty-five and forty-nine years of age, rural and small town in residence [or background], most likely to have completed grade school only, skilled and semiskilled blue collar in occupation, and of relatively low income.[16] These are the folk who stand up and may become misty-eyed when they hear Vernon Oxford's "Redneck National Anthem." They are also the individuals who long to hear Webb Pierce, Hank Snow, Bill Monroe, Roy Acuff, Porter Wagoner, Jim Reeves, the Carter Family, Merle Haggard, Loretta Lynn, Hank Williams, and a host of other "purists" (the list represents the biased opinion of the author) on their local country-politan, Top Forty station—as often as not, in vain.

Cultural Blending

Final evidence in support of country music's folk character is found in the varied cultural inputs that have given rise to its diversified contemporary forms. It is truly the outgrowth of a blending of styles representing a cross-section of American music. A Saturday night Grand Ole Opry show might include samples of Appalachian bluegrass, Louisiana Cajun music, East Texas honky-tonk, Mexican border melodies, mountain spirituals, western swing, rock and roll, and alas, a touch of pop. Entoned within each style would be a veritable cross-section of themes derived from hard work, hard religion, hard politics, hard drinking, hard lives, and hard times. References may be made in lyrics to whites, blacks, Chicanos, or Native Americans; indeed, the stage performers themselves may represent each of these groups.

A well-tuned musical ear may catch a note of the blues, a fleeting jazz beat, or the high-pitched nasal rubato of a true Anglo-Celtic folk tradition. Musical punctuation may take the form of a Swiss yodel, a Cajun "AAA-HYEEE," or a fervent fundamentalist backwoods stomp-and-holler. Accompaniment will most certainly include hot-licks guitar picking introduced by blacks, the African banjo, the harmonica (introduced to the Opry by DeFord Bailey, a black) or the haunting wail of the Hawaiian-introduced steel guitar. Top it off with a gaudy spangled suit adopted from Mexican mariachis and a cowboy hat, and one begins to grasp the notion that there is a degree of eclectic purity, albeit somewhat homogenized, to the stage performance.[17]

Country music instruments (photo by George Carney).

Youth culture, too, has made an impact on country music, because the young tend to be the ushers of musical innovation and new tastes. Their impact is much in evidence in the recent trends that have taken place within the country music industry. At the moment, country is "in" with the college-age set and the expanded marketing potential has wrought basic changes in the music; former rock and pop artists have flooded the field (e.g., John Denver, Dickey Lee, Billy "Crash" Craddock, Freddy Fender, Charlie Rich, and Conway Twitty). Some artists from the country tradition have altered their style or appearance substantially in order to accommodate the larger youthful audience (e.g., Waylon Jennings, Willie Nelson, Earl Scruggs, Dolly Parton, and Hank Snow), and a host of newcomers, including many with highly "suspect" credentials, have fashioned their sound to gain popularity among the mass audience (e.g., Ronnie Milsap, Olivia Newton-John, Mickey Gilley, and Tanya Tucker).[18] To the country purist, the sounds are strictly pseudo, tailor made for the pseudocountry audience.

Prejudice against Country Music

Commentary on the widespread prejudice against country music could easily begin and end with a quote from "Superbunny" Barbi Benton: "I thought [country music] was for Okies or for people who didn't have enough intelligence to appreciate rock music."[19] For those of the faith, that pretty well sums it up!

Whereas country music, in its contemporary form, is currently enjoying widespread popularity, the great majority of the populace continues to view the sound with contempt and associate it with the plebeian masses (a reality that may help to explain its recent popularity among the young, who see in their identification with country music a chance to further rebel against established social norms). John Greenway has articulated the animosity toward the art form in the following terms, "The prejudice of Americans against their only living folk music is so strong and pervasive that it cannot be explained by standards of scholarship or ethics. It is a matter of social pathology."[20] I identify four factors as being of paramount importance in the general public disavowal of country music.

1. *Psychologically*, people who rail out against the music seem to do so because they are afraid of it; afraid, perhaps, that it will remind them of where they came from, who they may have been, and who they may still be deep inside. In a culture where upward social, occupational, educational, and economic mobility are deemed essential to the fulfillment of the "American dream," backward glances and introspective views have little place. Collectively, we manifest a greater concern for where we are going, rather than where we may have been in the socioeconomic context.

Much of the experience of human cultural evolution has been involved in isolating humans in the temporal and situational present from the memory of the past. This holds true for individuals as well: "I can't bear to think of the past, it's too painful." Considering some of the dominant themes of country music—poverty, excessive drinking, broken homes, broken dreams, lost loves, and economic failure—one can only question whether facing these realities, in fact institutionalizing them in the lyrics of songs, is a sign of weakness or a manifestation of strength and a means of coping with hardship. Only after an individual has "arrived" and has social and economic options is it considered fashionable to rediscover those relics of an earlier lifestyle and integrate them into one's behavioral pattern. The present wave of nostalgia may account, at least in part, for the upsurge in country music's popularity. As Archie Green observed, "out of the long process of American urbanization-industrialization there has evolved a joint pattern of rejection as well as sentimentalization of rural mores. We flee the eroded land with its rotting cabin, at the same time we cover it in rose vines of memory."[21]

2. *Historically*, our forefathers arrived on these shores with established notions of what constituted "good" music. There was, of course, the good music of the peasant class and the classical sounds of the well bred. To this

day, many of us are taught that peasantry was something left behind in our European homeland and that the music of the commoner, along with many other behavioral manifestations, was something to be avoided. The same holds true for those traits identified with contemporary commoners within our society. The process of acculturation, it seems, is tasteful only when the direction of flow is from above to below: "They should adapt to our. . . ." Only recently have we Americans begun to cast off the European cultural yoke and begun to accept with pride our own innovations, be they in art, literature, architecture, food, clothing, or music.

3. *Negative geographical and cultural associations* still persist; country music, regardless of its general acceptance among working-class peoples nationwide, still carries a strong association with the rural South. In the stereotype held by many Americans, the southerner remains "poor, white, uneducated, conservative, hard-shelled religious, Anglo-Saxon, free and untrammelled, whiskey drinking, gun-toting, hookwormed, baby-making, rabbit-hunting, Wallace voting."[22] You wouldn't want your daughter to marry one, and for dammed sure you want no part of their music!

4. *Aesthetically*, the acceptance or rejection of country music is very much a personal matter; one either likes or dislikes it, usually with considerable intensity. The vocal style, which is often quite nasal, is repugnant to many individuals, as is the southern "drawl." At the most fundamental level, musical tastes appear to be divided between those for whom music is a form of escape and those for whom it serves as a realistic link to their own real-world existence. Country music has been described as being "truth set to music." To some reality is frightening; comfort is to be found in fantasy.

Geographical Dimensions

In conclusion, I have attempted to portray country music as being the purest form of American folk music. As such, it is an extremely valuable medium of communication, the understanding of which reflects certain intrinsic ideals and expresses a variety of behavioral patterns that are often associated with the blue-collar, working-class segment of American society. From the perspective of a cultural geographer, country music is a distinct culture trait that has evolved over the decades from the fusion of a broad array of American folk traditions and lifestyles. It is music of, by, and for the folk, and undergoes alterations in style and form as needed to meet the changing tastes of its audience. It is their music, "white man's blues," and constitutes a vital document providing penetrating insights into the way of life of the particular social class that calls country music its own.

Country entertainer Bobby Bare has articulated the cultural and historical overtones conveyed in the music's lyrical themes quite well:

> What [we] are doing reflects our society . . . we are showing what society is right now. In other words, 50 or 100 years from now, if people want to sit down and listen [to my music], they'll get a true picture . . . I think that if you wanted to know how the depression was, all you need to do is get a bunch of Woody Guthrie songs, Jimmy Rodgers songs, and some of that old Leadbelly stuff, and you've got it. That's how it was. It's the only true reflection there is.[23]

Such down-to-earth realism, when associated with elements of place; locational conditions; perceptions; social, environmental, or economic realities; customs and attitudes; the pains of social dislocation; historical events; patriotism; folk traditions; occupations; and so forth, carries a message that is clearly relevant to the geographer who seeks the pulse of human reality from a grass-roots source, rather than the pages of scholarly journals or the computer's print-out sheet.

Notes

1. Don Thomas, "The Great Country," *Music City News* 10 (October, 1972), p. 34.

2. John Grissim, *Country Music: White Man's Blues* (New York: Paperback Library, 1970), p. 13.

3. R. W. Hodge and D. J. Treiman, "Class Identification in the United States," *American Journal of Sociology* 73 (March 1968), pp. 535–47. The authors identify a "working class" that constitutes approximately one-third of the American population.

4. Marc Landy, "Country Music: The Melody of Dislocation," *The New South* 26 (Winter 1971), p. 68.

5. Country Music Association release quoted by Paul Hemphill, *The Nashville Sound: Bright Lights and Country Music* (New York: Simon and Schuster, 1970), p. 55.

6. John Grissim, op. cit., p. 189.

7. D. K. Wilgus, "Country-Western Music and the Urban Hillbilly," *Journal of American Folklore* 83 (April–June 1970), p. 178.

8. Paul DiMaggio, R. A. Peterson, and Jack Esco, Jr., "Country Music: Ballad of the Silent Majority," in R. Serge Denisoff and R. A. Peterson (eds.), *The Sounds of Social Change* (Chicago: Rand McNally & Co., 1972), p. 45.

9. D. K. Wilgus, op. cit., p. 166.

10. Frederick E. Danker, "Country Music," *Yale Review* 63 (Spring 1974), p. 398.

11. Tamara Stephenson and Larry K. Stephenson, "A Prologue to Listening," *Antipode* 5 (March 1973), p. 14.

12. John Grissim, op. cit., p. 58. An analysis of the social and psychological significance of country music lyrics appears in Ann Nietzke, "Doin' Somebody Wrong," *Human Behavior* 28 (November 1975), pp. 64–69.

13. George O. Carney, "Country Music and the Radio: A Historical Geographic Assessment," *The Rocky Mountain Social Science Journal* 2 (April 1974), p. 19.

14. D. K. Wilgus, "An Introduction to the Study of Hillbilly Music," *Journal of American Folklore* 78 (July–September 1965), p. 203.

15. Ellis Nassour, "Hag's Songs Reflect Life," *Music City News* 13 (August 1975), p. 8.

16. DiMaggio, et al., op. cit., pp. 47–50.

17. The most comprehensive history of racial, ethnic, and regional contributions to country music appears in Bill C. Malone, *Country Music U.S.A.* (Austin: University of Texas Press, 1968), pp. 3–32. This volume remains the finest example of scholarly research pertaining to the nature and history of country music.

18. A fair indication of those performers who qualify as "hard core" country artists can be ascertained from the biographical data contained in several encyclopedias: Linnell Gentry, *A History and Encyclopedia of Country, Western, and Gospel Music* (Nashville: Clairmont Corporation, 1969); Melvin Shestack, *The Country Music Encyclopedia* (New York: Thomas Y. Crowell Company, 1974); Irwin Stambler and Grenlun Landon, *Encyclopedia of Folk, Country, and Western Music* (New York: St. Martin's Press, 1969).

19. Quoted in Stephen A. Randall, "Barbi: The Superbunny Bides Her Time," *Country Music* 3 (June, 1975), p. 61.

20. John Greenway, "Country-Western: The Music of America," *The American West*, 5 (November 1968), p. 33.

21. Quoted in Burt Goldblatt and Robert Shelton, *The Country Music Story* (Indianapolis: The Bobbs-Merrill Company, 1966), p. 207.

22. Paul Hemphill, op. cit., p. 116.

23. "Interview," *Music City News* 12 (June 1975), p. B-3.

24

Selected Reading and Listening IV

Chapter 19

Guthrie, Woody. *Bound for Glory*. New York: E. P. Dutton, 1943.

Klein, Joe. *Woody Guthrie*. New York: Alfred A. Knopf, 1980.

Lomax, Alan. *Hard Hitting Songs for Hard Hit People*. New York: Oak Publications, 1967.

Reuss, Richard A. *A Woody Guthrie Bibliography, 1912–1967*. New York: Guthrie Children's Fund, 1968.

———. "Woody Guthrie and His Folk Tradition," *Journal of American Folklore* 83 (1970): 273–304.

Stein, Walter J. *California and the Dust Bowl Migration*. Westport, Conn.: Greenwood Press, 1973.

The Woody Guthrie Song Book. New York: Grosset & Dunlap, 1976.

Bound for Glory (Folkways 2481).

Dust Bowl Ballads (RCA Victor Vintage Series LPV-502).

Original Recordings Made by Woody Guthrie: 1940–1946 (Warner Brothers BS-12999).

The Legendary Woody Guthrie (Everest 2058).

This Land is Your Land (Folkways FTS 31001).

Woody Guthrie: Library of Congress Recordings (Elektra EKL-271/272).

Chapter 20

Boswell, Thomas D., and James R. Curtis. *The Cuban-American Experience: Culture, Images and Perspectives*. Totowa, N.J.: Rowman & Allanheld, 1983.

Carpenter, Alejo. *La Musica en Cuba*. Mexico City: Fondo de Cultura Economica, 1972.

Cruz, Francisco Lopez. *La Musica Folklorics en Cuba*. Sharon, Conn.: Troutman Press, 1967.

Grenet, Emilio. *Popular Cuban Music*. Havana: Ministry of Education, 1939.

Linares, Maria Teresa. *La Musica Popular*. Havana: Instituto del Libro, 1970.

Ortiz, Fernando. *Los Instrumentos de la Musica Afrocubana*. Havana: Ministerio de Educacion, 1954.

Roberts, John Storm. *The Latin Tinge: The Impact of Latin American Music on the United States*. New York: Oxford University Press, 1979.

Alma. *Contigo Si* (Alhambra ALS-165).

Alma. *Sin Limites* (Alhambra AS-152).

Cafe. *Cafe* (Vaya VS 28).

Clouds. *Con Class* (TH-THS/AM-2166).

Clouds. *Illegamos* (Common Cause Records CCLPS 13001).

Friends. *Friends* (Common Cause Records CCLPS 13001).

Miami Sound Machine. *Live Again—Renancer* (TH-TH/AM2185).

Miami Sound Machine. *Imported* (CBS International DML 10306).

Miami Sound Machine. *Miami Sound Machine* (CBS International DHL 10311).

Miami Sound Machine. *Otra Vez* (CBS International DIL 10320).

Chapter 21

Coltman, Robert. "Habitantbilly: French-Canadian Old Time Music," *Old Time Music* 11 (1973/74): 9–12.

Fowke, Edith. "Canadian Folk Music." *The Folk Music Sourcebook*. Edited by Larry Sandberg and Dick Weissman. New York: Da Capo Press, 1989, pp. 59–63, 148–49.

Lehr, John. "As Canadian As Possible . . . Under the Circumstances: Regional Myths, Images of Place and National Identity in Canadian Country Music," *Borderlines* 2 (1985): 16–19.

Narvaez, Peter. "Country Music in Diffusion: Juxtaposition and Syncretism in the Popular Music of Newfoundland," *Journal of Country Music* 2 (1978): 93–101.

Rosenberg, Neil. *Country Music in the Maritimes: Two Studies.* Memorial University of Newfoundland Reprint Series No. 2 (1976).

A Proud Canadian-Stompin' Tom Connors (Capitol S2 80010).

Bud the Spud (Capitol C29274).

Country Roads-Micky and Bunny ("V" Records VC 53103).

Cowboyography-Ian Tyson (Stony Plain SPCD 1102).

Ian and Sylvia Tyson's Greatest Hits (Vanguard CS CVM 73114).

Old Corrals and Sage Brush-Ian Tyson (CBS PCC 80080).

Ray Griff Canada (Boot BOS 7201).

Ray St. Germain (Sunshine SSCT 4014).

Chapter 22

Ewen, David. *All the Years of American Popular Music: A Comprehensive History.* Englewood Cliffs, N.J.: Prentice Hall, 1977.

————. (ed.). *American Popular Songs: From the Revolutionary War to the Present.* New York: Random House, 1966.

Goldberg, Isaac. *Tin Pan Alley: A Chronicle of American Popular Music.* New York: Frederick Ungar, 1961.

Hamm, Charles. *Yesterdays: Popular Song in America.* New York: W. W. Norton, 1979.

Spaeth, Sigmund. *A History of Popular Music in America.* New York: Random House, 1948.

Swaim, Joseph. *The Broadway Musical: A Critical and Musical Survey.* New York: Oxford University Press, 1990.

Whitcomb, Ian. *After the Ball: Pop Music from Rag to Rock.* New York: Simon and Schuster, 1973.

Brother, Can You Spare a Dime: American Song During the Great Depression (New World-270)

Praise the Lord and Pass the Ammunition: Songs of World Wars I and II (New World-222).

Smithsonian Collection of American Popular Song (Seven-LP set with twenty-eight-page introduction).

The Golden Years of Tin Pan Alley: 1920–1929 (New World-279).

The Golden Years of Tin Pan Alley: 1930–1939 (New World-248).

Where Have We Met Before? Forgotten Songs from Broadway, Hollywood and Tin Pan Alley (New World-240).

Chapter 23

Carr, Patrick (ed.). *The Illustrated History of Country Music.* New York: Country Music Magazine Press, 1979.

Dew, Joan. *Singers and Sweethearts: The Women of Country Music.* Garden City, N.Y.: Dolphin Books, 1977.

Green, Archie. "Hillbilly Music: Source and Symbol," *Journal of American Folklore* 78 (1965): 204–28.

Grissim, John. *Country Music: White Man's Blues.* New York: Coronet, 1970.

Hemphill, Paul. *The Nashville Sound: Bright Lights and Country Music.* New York: Simon and Schuster, 1970.

Malone, Bill C. *Country Music, U.S.A.* Austin: University of Texas Press, 1985 (Rev. ed.).

Porterfield, Nolan. *Jimmie Rodgers: The Life and Times of America's Blue Yodeler.* Urbana: University of Illinois Press, 1979.

Wilgus, D. K. "Country-Western Music and the Urban Hillbilly," *Journal of American Folklore* 83 (1970): 157–85.

Williams, Roger M. *Sing a Sad Song: The Life of Hank Williams.* Urbana: University of Illinois Press, 1981.

Bright Lights and Honky Tonk (Starday SLP 239).

Country Classics (RCA Victor 2313).

Diesel Smoke, Dangerous Curves (Starday SLP 250).

Greatest Country and Western Hits (Columbia 1257).

Great Country Favorites (MGM 4211).

Original Greatest Hits of the Great Country and Western Stars (Mercury 20825).

The Country Music Hall of Fame (Starday 164).

The Great Ones (Capitol 1718).

Index

319

About the Contributors

Thomas Arkell holds a B.A. in geography from Oxford University and has worked as a freelance journalist for the Royal Geographical Society. He is currently with a publishing house in Lucca, Italy.

Richard W. Butler is Professor of Geography at the University of Western Ontario. His Ph.D. is from Glasgow University and research specialties include tourism and recreation.

James R. Curtis received his Ph.D. from University of California, Los Angeles. He is currently Associate Professor of Geography at Oklahoma State University where he specializes in urban, cultural, and Latin American geography.

Larry R. Ford is an urban and cultural geographer at San Diego State University. He received his Ph.D. from the University of Oregon.

Jon A. Glasgow is Associate Professor of Geography at State University College in New Paltz, N.Y. He is an economic and political geographer with a Ph.D. from Clark University.

Charles F. Gritzner specializes in cultural geography and geographic education at South Dakota State University where he is Professor of Geography. His Ph.D. is from Louisiana State University.

Floyd M. Henderson is Professor and Associate Dean of the College of Social and Behavioral Sciences at the University of Albany-State University of New York. He holds a Ph.D. from the University of Kansas.

A. D. Horsley is Assistant Professor of Geography at Southern Illinois University-Carbondale where he focuses on environmental issues. His Ph.D. is from SIU-Carbondale.

Robert Kuhlken is a Ph.D. candidate in the Department of Geography and Anthropology at Louisiana State University. His research interests include cultural ecology and social geography.

John Lehr is Professor of Geography at the University of Winnipeg, where he specializes in cultural geography as well as tourism and recreation. He holds a Ph.D. from Manitoba.

Christopher Lornell is Visiting Researcher for the Museum of American History-Smithsonian Institution. He received his Ph.D. in ethnomusicology from Memphis State University.

Richard Rose is Professor of Music at Miami Dade Community College and received his Ph.D. in music from the University of Texas-Austin.

Rocky Sexton is a Ph.D. candidate in the Department of Anthropology at the University of Iowa.

About the Editor

George O. Carney is Professor of Geography at Oklahoma State University where he developed the first geography of music course in North America in 1973. His other teaching interests include introductory cultural geography and the history/philosophy of geography. He holds degrees from Central Missouri State University (B.A. in Geography and M.A. in History) and Oklahoma State University (Ph.D. in American Social History). Dr. Carney has authored more than sixty publications consisting of five books and numerous journal articles, monographs, and book reviews. He has been awarded grants from both public and private agencies including the National Endowment for the Humanities, National Endowment for the Arts, National Park Service, Atlantic-Richfield Foundation, and the Smithsonian Institution Division of Folklife Programs. His honors include awards for both teaching and research: *Journal of Geography* Best Content Article, National Council for Geographic Education Distinguished Teaching Award, American Association for State and Local History Certificate of Commendation, and the George Shirk Memorial Award for Historic Preservation in Oklahoma. His music maps have appeared in such diverse outlets as the *Washington Post* and the Public Broadcasting System (PBS) network. Finally, he hosted a weekly show (*Bluegrass Review*) for ten years on KOSU-FM, the local National Public Radio affiliate.